WITHDRAWN

The middle years curriculum series

Teaching the Eight to Thirteens: Volume 2

Editors Michael Raggett and Malcolm Clarkson

Ward Lock Educational

ISBN 0 7062 3542 8 hardback
       0 7062 3543 6 paperback

First published 1976

Set in 10 on 11½ point Baskerville
by Northumberland Press Limited, Gateshead
and printed by Robert MacLehose and Company Limited, Glasgow
for Ward Lock Educational
116 Baker Street, London W1M 2BB
Made in Great Britain

Contents

Preface

This second book on the curriculum of the middle years is again for teachers and students. It is designed to be useful to all those concerned with the education of children between the ages of 8 and 13. It is not a book specifically about middle schools as we felt such a limitation was wrong. In our view such a restriction would have contributed towards the formation of yet another separate enclave. We believe education is a continuous process. The pupils arrive at five years old and experience education until they leave full-time education. The breaks we make in the process are artificial, created and sustained by Acts of Parliament. They arise from a logic that makes no sense to the majority of pupils who come and go as we decree. It is part of the teacher's task to try to make sense of it for the pupils, and nowhere is that more difficult than for the 8–13 age group.

The change from primary to secondary, from childhood to puberty, is ritualized, as the pupil is initiated into the style of teaching considered more suitable for the older child. Middle schools can be seen as arenas where this and the previously experienced style meet. From this meeting, from the consideration of the forms of organization, content and methods which arise, we get a new view of the curriculum for the top end of the primary school and the lower years of the secondary. It is this new curriculum with which this book is concerned and it not only attempts to describe what certain aspects of this curriculum might be but also gives practical advice for teachers wishing to implement it. Too many books point the way but provide too little practical help. Many books detail the ephemeral minutiae without establishing principles to guide the teacher in planning his own work. We try to steer between these two dangers.

In the first instance, each author was invited to write on their area with, where appropriate, the following three major objectives: to review current literature on the area in question; to identify what were, in their opinion, the major issues involved; and where possible to make practical suggestions as to how the problems may be resolved in the context of schools for children of the middle years. The use of jargon is always a problem in that whilst it has precise meaning for the cogniscenti it is often confusing and counter-productive in serving to drive a wedge between author and reader. For this reason authors have been required to exemplify jargon wherever used. Inevitably there is a degree of overlap between the different articles. However we would see this in practice as being an asset as different authors present their personal perspective of different facets of the central curricular issues.

This second book is divided into four sections and attempts to identify those areas not covered by the first volume. The first section deals with the wider issues of the curriculum. This should be read together with section five of Volume 1 of the series, for together they examine the areas of regional and social studies, modern languages and religious education. The second section includes all those areas that are so often found together under a variety of umbrellas like expressive and performing arts, creative arts or combined arts by practitioners of integrated and interdisciplinary studies. Here we do not attempt to justify any such groupings but leave the teacher to pick and mix for herself. Section three looks at the problems of social learning in the classroom and, finally, section four attempts to view the middle years, the middle school, the child and the teacher from four specialist viewpoints – the philosopher, the psychologist, the sociologist and the curriculum analyst.

The middle years is a challenging area which is at last receiving the attention it deserves. Let us make sure we are asking the right questions and seeking the relevant answers. We hope this book will help you do this – but only you and your pupils will know if it succeeds.

1 The broader curriculum

Howard Ainsley and Colin Brent are fully aware that there is a need to come to terms with the many labels that have sprouted around the study in school of the environment. Without wishing to add to them, but rather seeking a defined structure and rationale in which to place them, they argue that regional studies have a particularly necessary place in the curriculum of the middle years. It avoids the narrower concepts of environmental studies and offers a more representative truly integrated study of the complex relationship between man and the environment, and man and man. It also places the school as a focus for the community and makes children aware of the environment in which they live. This can be achieved without becoming too broad or too diffuse an area to confuse and lose both teacher and taught, for the practical nature of investigations undertaken by the children, the examination and analyses of evidence material and the presentation in a variety of forms suit well the intellectual and physical capabilities of children of this age group.

Brian Gates and Colin Alves examine the problems of living in a multicultural and multiracial society. They point out that the school's role is to further community understanding by preparing children to live in society, thus leaving the child's particular parent religious community to initiate him into their own ideologies. The social understanding which is crucial if prejudice and disharmony are to be avoided can only be achieved by a planned programme of education which places emphasis on a tolerant and caring community and on the establishment of the personal worth of each individual in it. This is a life-long process.

1.1 Regional studies and environmental education in the middle years curriculum

Howard Ainsley and Colin Brent

The term 'regional studies' is not new: its meaning and use as suggested in this paper are, however, different. Perhaps not unnaturally, the response to such a term is one of resignation that yet another label is about to be added to the large number already attached to the subject known usually as 'environmental studies'. A recent *Times Educational Supplement* (13 June 1975) rightly expressed concern over the use of 'such diverse labels as rural studies, environmental studies, rural science, environmental science, social biology, social studies, urban studies, community studies, and outdoor pursuits'. To this list might have been added 'environmental education', 'man and the environment' and a host of subgroupings normally associated with the subject – landscape and land use, population and pollution, rural and urban planning, ecology, conservation, meteorology and climatology, oceanography, soil and earth sciences, solar energy and civil engineering. The apparent absence of a clear conceptual rationale for a study of the environment has been largely responsible for this uncontrolled situation. With the prospect of still further additions to come, a proper rationalization of objectives, structures, organization and resources would seem long overdue.

In any attempt to define 'environmental studies' one is immediately made aware of many conflicting interpretations. To some, it is regarded as the study of the natural environment and of those natural forces which have shaped it and are now part of it. To others, it is the study of the relationship between man and his environment (sometimes interpreted as the 'natural' environment; at other times as the 'man-made' environment). Even this useful interpretation may, in practice, turn out to mean very largely the effect of the landscape upon the economic and social needs of man. Recently, the very considerable public concern for the survival of the world's natural heritage has tended to concentrate the attention of environmentalists upon what man has done to and with his environment, and the 'environment at risk' has become one of the most popular themes of educationalists and of the media. There is justifiable concern over man's careless exploitation of the world's natural resources and a proper indignation over the 'quality of living' within his planned, urban environment.

Vital though these issues are, they have diverted attention away from a major reconsideration of the educational objectives of environmental studies. Consequently, certain assumptions have been allowed to go virtually unchallenged. It is assumed, for instance, that the major contributions to environmental studies will continue to come from two sources – the geographer and the biologist. Whilst no one would deny the necessity for their involvement, it is surely unreasonable to reduce to small supporting roles the contributions from the historian, the sociologist, the industrial archaeologist and the artist. For the geographer and the biologist will be concerned to study very largely the natural environment, its formation and structure, its life support systems, its use and misuse by man who, in the expansion of his settlements and conurbations and by his industrial and technological revolutions, has significantly altered his relationship with the natural environment. Given the opportunity, the historian, sociologist, industrial archaeologist and the artist could sub-stantially fill out this view of man's relationship with the environment. The historian would seek to identify and understand those human forces which had been responsible for shaping the socio-economic and cultural patterns which have emerged – forces which might still be at work. The relationship of man with his fellow men, the social systems and services which he creates, and their attendant problems, are already the concern of the sociologist. Inevitably, when discussing these issues, he will wish to consider the influence of environment, the effects of urbanization and the consequences of unemployment and high population. The industrial archaeologist, in his efforts to record and preserve the remains of man's industrial past, not only provides a salutary reminder of our industrial achievement but also uncovers striking evidence of one form of human relationship with the environment: whilst the artist, in his analysis of rural and urban planning, of building styles and materials, can often add a further dimension to our understanding of this relationship.

One of the consequences for environmental studies of such an approach would be to bring together in a more balanced way the themes of man's relationship with his environment, and also his relationship with his fellow man. In brief, it aims to consider together the themes of environment and community. At a time when we are being urged to see the school as a point of focus for the community, such an overview of environment and community would appear to have much to recommend it, pragmatically as well as conceptually.

At the beginning, we drew attention to the list of titles normally associated with environmental studies – a list which although still only selective, does nevertheless highlight a tendency to fragmentation which is, unfortunately, a feature of environmental studies. Some environmentalists see the environment largely in terms of what it may demonstrate about their own separate discipline in terms of content and technique. Even where a multidisciplinary approach is suggested it often lacks conceptual cohesion and ends in each discipline separately studying the environment. Environmentalists often experience difficulties when deciding upon the environment which they wish to study. For reasons again very largely dictated by the nature of their discipline, some may prefer a rural environment, others an urban environment. But perhaps the most disconcerting feature of these separatist tendencies is the difficulty in agreeing upon a common environment. The study, on a world scale, of population statistics, pollution, exploitation of resources, landscape and land use is very necessary to our proper understanding of their significance, but surely, ultimately, the environment which must be studied – and studied comprehensively – is the environment which is of immediate concern to children – their own. If this is done, then the children will view the essential issues with a better understanding, and they may more readily develop an awareness of their own relationship to the environment.

Two principles would seem to have emerged. The first argues the need for a conceptual overview of environmental studies which aims to relate more closely the themes of environment and community. The second principle argues the case for the study of the environment in which the children live: such a study would need to adopt a multidisciplinary approach. The problem which is apparent immediately is how one determines the appropriate parameters (physical, cultural, historical, geographical, biological, sociological) of the environment which is to be studied. Many excellent school projects involving local studies have been done. They vary in range from the consideration of a single topic (for example, village pond, market, church, castle, school, canal, railway, etc.) to the study of more substantial themes (for example, architecture, amenities, farming, 'our village', 'our town', pollution, conservation, etc.). These projects are, however, usually conducted within the local area: the nature of the scheme suggested in the following pages argues the need for a more substantial area – in fact, a region.

The determination of what constitutes the region which is to be studied is, inevitably, an essential part of the preliminary discussion between the teachers concerned. This discussion, coming as it does before the detailed formulation of the course structure, should be as open-ended as possible. Disagreements within the group will probably arise as each contributor describes, in terms expressed by the historian, the geographer, the biologist, the sociologist and the artist, a different view of the nature and extent of the region. Further refinement might become necessary as a result of arguments advanced by those teachers who, through their interest in ecology and conservation, industrial archaeology, building design, social problems, local folk lore, songs and traditions identify other features of the region. Even so, it is most unlikely that the area eventually chosen will contain evidence to support all the themes suggested by individual members of the group. A study of eastern Sussex, for instance, would not reveal evidence of heavy industrialization, or of remote village communities, or of serious ecological disturbance, or of a substantial immigrant population. It would, however, reveal the distinctive effects of the coastal conurbation, the impact of commuter and tourist communications, the significant proportion of retired and semi-retired people, and the very considerable influence of London. Here, again, the point to emphasize is that the study is not meant to illustrate national phenomena but to allow a proper consideration of the interrelationship of those forces which have helped shape that region and may have given it its distinctive character. Such an approach does not, of course, exclude discussion of those forces which had their origin outside the region; indeed, consideration of them is necessary for a better understanding of the distinctiveness of the region.

Although no single definition of 'region' is perhaps satisfactory for every purpose, certain questions ought to be raised during the preliminary discussion. Does there exist already some notional idea of a region (suggested possibly in the name of a railway company, a bus company, a television area, an electricity or gas board, a business organization, the branch of a union or society, etc?). Is it possible to identify an area of quite distinctive natural characteristics (indicated perhaps by its geological make-up, its soils, its vegetation, its farming or market gardening)? Can one point to a region which shows the particular handiwork of man (possibly an area of heavy industrialization); or one which displays certain sociological phenomena? Has the area retained its characteristics virtually unchanged over a considerable period of time due, possibly, to its isolation or remoteness? Such questions, whilst they clearly do not comprise an exhaustive list, nevertheless give an indication of the range of issues raised in any discussion on regional studies.

The economic and social historian and the historical geographer have tended to partition England into areas each characterized by a distinct human response to the challenge of the local physical environment. This response was often distinctive at the economic, the social and the ideological level, as the brief analysis of the downland, marshland and wealden regions of eastern Sussex, given below, will attempt to demonstrate. As such the region is often neglected by teachers of local history. Much attention is lavished on investigation of the local village or town community, which lies conveniently at hand, but the wider physical context in which that community is set is much more rarely studied. This neglect of a wider regional survey narrows unduly the scope of such community studies, rendering them 'parochial' in the worst sense by divorcing them from a wider context essential for a full understanding of community development.

Thus any village study set in eastern Sussex ought to begin by establishing whether the parish concerned is located in the downland, in the marshland or in the weald, or straddles between them. The regional context is all-important. All the South Down communities, whether centred on the dip-slope or along the scarp-foot bench, were founded, or refounded, during the intense and swift settlement which followed the East Saxon conquest. Around each nucleated community was established an agricultural territory which united sheepwalk on the upper chalk with a lower arable acreage of loam, gravel or upper greensand, intermixed with chalk. This union permitted the adoption of a form of sheep–corn husbandry which was pursued, with modification, into the twentieth century and formed the pivot of the downland economy. Around this husbandry there developed a system of common fields, common pastures and common flocks which, although eroded by enclosure from the late medieval period, survived in some communities into the nineteenth century. Downland settlement, landscape and agriculture long retained this Saxon imprint.

By contrast even partial clearance of the damp heavy clays and often sterile sands of the weald was a piecemeal, painful and uncertain process, responding to the tremors of population change in the medieval and Tudor periods and to later improvements in agricultural techniques. Hamlets and isolated farmsteads were common, substantial nucleated villages rare. The fields, hacked with immense labour from the forest, were small in size, irregular in shape, and bounded by hedge or coppice. Rarely, if ever, were they held in common. The landscape was an intimate and enclosed one. The only common was the uncultivated waste on the more intractable soils which extensively survived into Victoria's reign. At least a fifth of this wealden acreage remained wooded. The bias of wealden agriculture was towards dairying and livestock fattening with occasional surpluses of wheat and oats, which grew larger and more regular from the eighteenth century as techniques of drainage and fertilization improved.

The drainage of the coastal alluvial saltmarshes around Pevensey and Rye was another piecemeal and laborious medieval and Tudor achievement. So rich was the reclaimed soil that it could be made to yield heavy crops of corn or lush, almost inexhaustible pasture, whichever yielded the greater profit. In the medieval period the marshland was under corn, from the Tudor period under grass.

By relating the settlement pattern, the landscape and the agriculture of the parish to these regional patterns a much clearer impression may be gained of the forces which have moulded the parish scene, of the contrasts with communities in other regions, and of the extent to which the parish exhibits characteristics unique to itself. The student is provided with a wider perspective allowing a greater range of analysis. The parish study ceases to be parochial but rather reinforces an appreciation of a far broader environment.

But the regional characteristics to which constituent communities normally conformed usually extended beyond uniformities of settlement, landscape and agriculture. Prior to the industrial revolution much manufacturing was carried on in the countryside. But neither the downland nor the marshland communities had the water-power, the timber or the raw materials to sustain industrial activity. By contrast the weald had ample such resources and supported extensive spinning, weaving, fulling, gloving, tanning, brick- and tile-making, glass-making and iron and ordnance production, activities which were often combined with small-scale dairy or cattle farming.

The economic structures of these regions are clearly very distinctive. But they each underpinned a social structure which was equally distinctive. In the downland region from the late medieval period small family farmers steadily sold out to larger farmers who were better protected from the hazards of marketing and able to profit from the cost benefits which large-scale sheep and corn husbandry brought. By the nineteenth century the region contained landowners, substantial tenant-farmers, large numbers of landless agricultural labourers, together with a few essential craftsmen. Downland society was highly polarized, a deep gulf separating the labourer from the tenant-farmer. Because of the malarial 'agues' which persisted into the nineteenth century landowners avoided residing in marshland communities. Moreover, since from the Tudor period marshland pasture tended to be rented for summer grazing by farmers who lived in the weald, marshland residents tended to be mainly 'lookers' and stockmen who tended the grazing cattle and sheep. By contrast wealden society was more complex and more dynamic. Farms remained generally small into the twentieth century. Many of these family farmers and smallholders were also craftsmen, retailers or carters and exploited their pasture rights on the common waste. Wealden labourers enjoyed a wide range of employment opportunity and often had access to a large garden and an allotment. Society was less polarized, less stratified than in the downland, and less impoverished than in the marshland.

These contrasts in social structure were inevitably accompanied by contrasts in social, political and religious attitudes which were – and are – deeply influenced by social structure. The downland labourer tended to be subservient to the Anglican and Conservative philosophy of the large tenant farmer, the parson and the squire. By the reign of Victoria the tone of downland life was deferential, its form was hierarchical, a fact clearly apparent in *A Song for Every Season* in which Bob Copper (1971) reconstructs a downland community, prior to the Great War, near Brighton. The social climate in the weald was very different. Its many family farmers and smallholders were often sufficiently independent economically to incline towards Nonconformity in religion and towards Liberal/Radicalism in politics.

Nothing reveals these social contrasts better than an intelligent and sensitive autobiography. A. L. Rowse (1962) in *A Cornish Childhood* explored the 'marked difference in social structure and outlook between the people of the rough moorlands of the Cornish interior, themselves rough, independent, free, and the people of the coastal plains and arable lands, brought up under the eye of their local gentry, their tenants or employees, more polite, submissive, apt to be yes-men. The former were Radical in politics, the latter Conservative, or, more precisely "conformists".' In *Lark Rise to Candleford* Flora Thompson (1973) contrasts the small village under the shadow of the rectory and the Tudor farmhouse with the more relaxed and spirited life of her childhood hamlet where social activity centred round the pub and the houses were rented from distant tradesmen in the market town some miles away.

Historically, therefore, the region is a far more significant unit of study than has been generally realized. The agricultural and industrial response to a distinctive physical environment helped to mould social and ideological structures which in many instances survived until the First World War. These regional characteristics will inevitably have permeated the parish communities composing the region. Their study should obviously be an essential preliminary to any parochial or local investigation.

Even the urban communities of eastern Sussex can only be fully appreciated once the regional structure of the county is understood. Until the appearance of its seaside watering-places in the later eighteenth century, its towns were market centres or ports controlling the road and water communications along which flowed the exported agricultural and industrial surplus of the regions and imported consumer goods destined for the regions. The character of the commerce which activated these market centres and ports was dependent on the regional economies which they served, while their industries often processed local products. Several of these towns, especially Lewes, also provided professional, administrative and cultural facilities for the surrounding countryside.

Yet regional studies can be seen as something more than a preliminary to a local parochial or urban investigation, however essential such a preliminary step may be. To the historian and the historical geographer the region has increasingly become a basic unit of analysis and discussion. No modern history of agriculture is any longer complete without a map of the farming regions of England and a discussion of their characteristics. 'Industries in the countryside' are now recognized to have been located in 'wood-pasture' regions, such as the weald, which were well endowed with water, water-power, timber and raw materials. The textbook English parish with its nucleated village, its common fields eroded by enclosure, its squire, parson and deferential labour-force, is now realized to have been typical of regions like the chalk downlands, where the economy centred on sheep–corn husbandry, rather than of wooded regions with a pastural bias, which teemed with family farmers, smallholders, craftsmen and masterless cottagers. No study of Nonconformity, of Chartism, of labour history, is now undertaken without reference to such regional social context.

If the school curriculum is in any way to reflect significant advances in current historical research, then space should be found for some consideration of the development through time of the landscape, economy, social structure and ideology of the local regions and of the urban communities which served them and knit them together. Such a study can give the pupil a deeper appreciation of a wider environment than the local or parochial study which is so often the backbone of 'local history' in the classroom. Regional studies, so conceived, also offer greater opportunity for fruitful integration with environmental studies which often encompass the botany, biology, geology, modern farming, etc. of the local regions.

Again there seems no reason why regional studies, in this form, should forgo the practice of documentary research, fieldwork investigation and the collection of oral reminiscence, which all agree to be valuable ingredients of the local historical study. These techniques would simply be used with reference to a wider canvas offering a greater variety of evidence and a greater depth and range of analysis. The parish study would indeed remain, not as an end in itself, but as exemplifying on a small scale the interplay of regional characteristics, while the urban study would explore the interaction between town and regions by which it was moulded through time.

The consideration of issues of this kind is clearly essential: but once the 'region' has been identified, however loosely, then attention can be given to the possible methods of approach. Teachers may wish to begin with a review of the more obvious characteristics of the region: indeed, certain characteristics may be so dominant that to ignore them until a later stage in the study might only produce an artificial course structure. In a region, for instance, which is very largely rural, the study might open with the formation of the natural environment: the pattern of settlement; the early economy; the social structure of these communities; the emergence of urban units; better forms of communication; the effects of industry and technology; and the possible survival of a distinctive culture or cultures. This approach, which is essentially a developmental one, might be as appropriate for the study of a region which has been heavily industrialized and comprises large urban structures which have resulted in the erosion of earlier communities and environment: in which case, the approach might be to begin with a study of the contemporary situation, identifying the extent of the environmental dislocation; the total effect of industrialization (not only upon the landscape but also upon the community, in terms of housing, amenities, clubs and societies, etc.); the evidence of a pre-industrial environment; and the mixture of traditional and more recent culture.

Given a region with fewer dominant extremes, the first priority for a teacher planning a strategy for regional studies within the history syllabus, or integrated studies syllabus, is to establish the boundaries and salient agrarian characteristics of the farming regions composing his county or whatever other area he chooses to make a coherent field of study. Particularly useful starting points are the surveys of English regions in the sixteenth and seventeenth centuries written by Joan Thirsk (1967) and Eric Kerridge (1967). By the Napoleonic period agricultural commentators, such as Arthur Young and William Marshall, were publishing very detailed accounts of regional husbandry to publicize the achievements of the agrarian revolution. Excellent reviews of regional agricultural development since the eighteenth century are contained in the many volumes of *The Land of Britain*, edited by L. Dudley Stamp, such as that by E. W. H. Briault on 'Sussex (East and West)' in volume VIII, parts 83 and 84 (1942). Sometimes of value, if recently published, are the relevant volumes of *The Victoria History* for the county under review, together with specialist articles in the *Proceedings* or *Collections* of the appropriate archaeological or local history society.

Such sources should yield abundant information on regional patterns of settlement, placenames, field systems, manorial custom, enclosure, husbandry and rural industries. Such information can be put to a variety of uses. Development within a region might be related to national trends, such as changes in demand which alter the farming balance and perhaps encourage clearance and improvement. A comparative study might be made of exactly how these regional patterns diverged from each other and of the factors underpinning these patterns. An investigation might be made of how dependent these regions each were on the specialisms of the others, on the interchange of men, materials and finished goods, and on the pattern of road, navigable rivers, seaports and market towns which sustained this interchange and also linked the regions with a wider external market.

Clearly such an area offers considerable opportunity for documentary study and fieldwork investigation. The range of documents available will no longer be restricted by the need to study only a single parish. Documents can be chosen for their singularly effective illustration of some salient regional characteristics. Many books such as that of Stephens (1972) exist offering the teacher an introduction to the wealth of documentary material either published in transcription or available for production at the local County Record Office and there is little point in traversing familiar ground. Mention might be made, however, of certain crucial documents which between them throw a flood of light on regional characteristics in the early Victorian period. For most parishes a Tithe map exists, normally dating from the 1840s and often on a scale of twenty or more inches to the mile. The map, together with an accompanying schedule, gives the name, the location, the acreage, the occupier and the owner of each house, garden, allotment, pond, field, coppice, etc. Moreover for each parish in 1841, 1851, 1861 and 1871 survive the Enumerators' Books made for the National Census. These list for each resident their relationship to the householder, their age and sex, occupation and parish of birth, although the last is not given in 1841. If the head is an employer, the number of men employed is noted; if a farmer, the number of acres farmed. These two sources yield much information on regional social structure. Was the region dominated by resident landowners and large tenant farmers, or did family farmers, smallholders, and craftsmen abound to sustain a Nonconformist minister and chapel? Was regional society 'closed', well-ordered, hierarchical, deferential, or was it 'open', undisciplined, fluid and assertive?

Many commercially produced teaching kits, containing an edited selection of documentary material relating to a national theme, are now available. But normally more relevant to the teacher concerned with regional studies are 'the archive teaching units' now being issued by many County Record Offices, since they are usually explicitly designed to provide materials for the study of a local topic, to suggest background reading and to indicate fruitful avenues of research. Indeed the County Record Office offers an often underused service to teachers. Its staff are usually willing to advise on the documentary sources relevant to a topic and to arrange for such documents to be photocopied or to be exhibited and worked on by school parties in the Record Office. On the other hand the teacher may prefer to consult the very full catalogues, whether printed or card-indexed, which are housed there. Many large reference libraries are now employing a local history librarian whose expertise should also be used.

Many record offices and some reference libraries also contain back-numbers of the local newspaper. For the Victorian period, when their coverage of the local events became increasingly full and comprehensive, these newspapers provide a very important quarry of information, as they do, of course, for more recent periods. They often contain much data on public institutions, such as workhouses, hospitals and schools, on sporting, cultural and 'society' activities, on crime and punishment, on epidemics, floods and other 'acts of God', and on local personalities prominent in the public eye. They are especially valuable for their commentary, usually highly partisan, on the political conflict between Liberal and Conservative, and on the often no less bitter denominational rivalry between Anglican and Nonconformist, which heavily overlapped the political struggle. Some newspapers also feature articles on the history of the locality, often in the form of gleanings from their files published a hundred years ago.

Another major source of information for the region is one that unfortunately has not been used much in schools despite its remarkable interest value. It is the very large group of names – placenames, field names, personal names and street names. Most are recorded in documentary form; many in addition are to be seen on gravestones, signposts, gateways and shop-fronts. A considerable number, however, are not so recorded and are remembered only in folk song and lore. Children should be encouraged to collect names associated with their region. These will include the names of counties, cities, towns, villages, hamlets; fields, hills, woodland, marsh, waste and common; farms, country houses; cathedrals, churches and chapels; streets, housing estates, blocks of flats, community halls, hospitals, schools; traders, craftsmen, businesses; personal names (including 'christian' and nicknames). The sources for this kind of information are many; indeed some will be known already to the children. Perhaps the most profitable ones are likely to be the Domesday Survey; maps (ordnance survey, tithe, estate maps, surveyors maps etc.); trade directories; auctioneers' lists; advertisements (in the regional press, on regional television, on billposters, on railway and bus stations, in parish and school magazines); county and town guide books; walks publicized by rambler clubs; census returns; school logbooks; parish registers; rate books; gravestones and, especially, the publications of the English Placenames Society.

Once this material has been collected, a valuable, albeit impressionistic, view of the region is immediately possible. From such names, we are able to gain an impression of the terrain which confronted the earlier settlers in the region, to know whether it was mountainous or lowland; forest, heathland or marsh; rugged or undulating. We are also able to surmise about the heavy or light nature of the soils, the clearance of forest, the enclosure of wasteland and common and, consequently, the possible form of husbandry practised. Placenames will also reveal evidence about the animals which lived in that area.

Certain placenames which have distinctive characteristics (for example Saxon and Scandinavian placenames in England) enable us to trace the process of colonization and settlement. Others, with equally dramatic characteristics, indicate the sustained activity of a particular religious movement (for example, seventeenth-century jury lists can point to evidence of local puritan influence through such christian names as 'Stand-fast-on-high' and 'Fight-the-good-fight-of-faith').

The plotting of this evidence onto maps, employing, possibly, colour coding, will provide children with an impression of early settlement patterns and subsequent changes. In this same way, early industrialization and urban growth may be shown. The early iron industry is a particularly rewarding subject, with woods, streams, ponds, fields and footpaths bearing still the names associated with it. The spread of transport and communication systems may also be plotted from a host of names involving canals, turnpikes and railways. Although such evidence provides but an impression of the region, it does, nevertheless, show the imprint of man upon the environment and those forces which have influenced the structure of his society. Children will also have become aware of the survival of some placenames whilst the places themselves have disappeared. They will also have noticed from their study of maps that the isolated nature of churches and farms might hint at the former existence of a village or hamlet. A street name or wall plaque might record a similar mishap. The social composition of a community might be suggested by the existence of a large number of names of foreign origin. The survival of names associated with particular crafts or industries could point to the former prosperity of the area. Impressions of change, development, depopulation and migration are readily conveyed, as, indeed, is the realization that, at times, folk memory may be the only available source for guiding our interpretation of names.

The value of folk memory, songs, speech, customs, proverbs (which might also relate to a particular craft), reminiscence and oral tradition in providing a different perspective of a region is rapidly gaining ground amongst environmentalists and the general public. A point of view which is individual, possibly eccentric, often high personalized and undeniably prejudiced is, nevertheless, a valuable aid to our understanding of the nature of a community. Such evidence constitutes a major source for the expression of views by the labouring class. It can be recorded on tape through the interviewing of local residents and may also be available in written form in memoirs and autobiography. Some authors have presented their evidence in a semi-fictionalized form, although it is only faintly veiled. Although the rural tradition is older, urban communities have also developed their own folk culture, especially the larger cities or those which were early industrialized. Nor is the source restricted only to adults; children's games, songs, rhymes and heroes often display a regional character.

The most tangible evidence of man's labour is probably his building – secular and ecclesiastical; domestic and public; business and industrial: from castle and manor house, country house and large town house, to the buildings of the industrial boom and the mass-produced, functional units of today. A study of buildings leads naturally to a study of the community; to the economy which supported this building programme and to the motives which inspired it. The majestic cathedral and the most functional chapel; the wool merchant's home of the fifteenth century; the Victorian splendour of the municipal railway station and the rows of back-to-back industrial housing – each, in their own way, assist our understanding of the community. The style, possibly, and most certainly the materials of the earlier buildings were of a regional character, determined by what was available from the region in terms of labour and materials. The round, flint tower of a Sussex church is a good example of design influenced by the availability of local resources. One may learn other matters of note. Heavily crenellated churches, houses which face in towards a green – both tell us something of the insecure nature of that community. Extra wide windows on the upper storey of a cottage may denote the home of a weaver, whilst the inevitable blocked-up window will lead to speculative observations about design, symmetry and the window-tax legislation. Building and construction programmes usually involve the use of an itinerant labour force which may raise problems of assimilation of different culture forms. An economic boom may leave scars on the landscape in the shape of quarries, open-cast mining, derelict industrial sites, abandoned machinery, canals and railways – a conservationist's nightmare possibly, but still a profitable source for the industrial archaeologist who will see it as symbolizing a different relationship between man and his environment.

This relationship has, fortunately, not always resulted in the despoliation of the latter. Nevertheless, since man has always sought to control the environment to his own advantage, it is hardly surprising to discover substantial evidence to corroborate this attempt. The very pattern of our landscape, in both rural and urban form, provides ready material in village shapes (for example, village green, street village, 'heap' or crossroad village, 'formless' or scattered hamlet); field patterns (open and enclosed); boundaries (for example, mark stones, hedgerows, streams); roads, footpaths, bridleways, hollow lanes, bostals, drovers' roads, pilgrim ways; fords and bridges; market centres and 'planned' communities (not always urban), as well as those changes associated normally with the industrial and agrarian revolutions. Much of this may be of a regional character as the environment, in its turn, controls the human factor through the continuing availability of materials, the nature of the terrain and the suitability of the soil.

These topographical features are, however, more than just the record of man's attempts to control his environment. From them we gain an impression of the possible size and economic level of the community, its crop yield and variety of diet; the resilience of its inhabitants in contending with a possibly unfavourable natural or man-made environment; the skills available to the community; the relationship between neighbouring communities and their responsiveness to external forces.

Although it has not been possible to do more than suggest the value of regional studies in providing children with a balanced overview of the relationship between man and his environment, sufficient evidence has, hopefully, been presented to show the very considerable range of educational pursuits which may ensue. There is every opportunity for child-oriented learning, for practical work and field enquiry, for the presentation of multipurpose resource units involving the collecting of photographs, illustrations, maps, archives, geological and scientific samples, artifacts and models. Children with different interests are able to develop their own specialism, as are those with a preference for a particular learning or recording method. Different levels of work are possible according to the aptitudes of the children. Collaboration between schools in the region and also between the school and the community should be encouraged in an attempt to arrive at this balanced overview of the human-environmental relationship.

We have found when providing such courses – and, especially, in our discussions with teachers – that regional studies are thought to be particularly necessary for the middle years curriculum, very largely for the reasons already stated. The practical nature of the investigations which may be undertaken by the children; the opportunities for them to handle different types of evidence material and to see the relationship between different sources; the preparation of material in a multivaried form – these aspects of the work suggest that a unit structure approach would probably be most effective. This would enable the course to be programmed to take note of its stated objectives and to facilitate the production of unitary pieces of related work as part of the overall build-up of a regional studies resource centre. The gradual build-up of units into such a centre would appear to be a natural corollary to the nature of the work. Ideally, the centre should be located centrally within the region with its material and facilities available to schools and to other interested bodies. It would, moreover, organize regular exhibitions depicting regional themes. If such is the ideal arrangement, the immediate need is for school-based resource centres which would circulate regular information about the units completed and those either in preparation or planned.

Contact with outside bodies would not only reinforce the environmental overview which should be a distinctive feature of regional studies, but it would almost certainly result in the discovery of much valuable information, perhaps not otherwise available. Family albums and scrapbooks, old newspapers lining cupboards and drawers, postcards, old guide books and maps, parish and school magazines, journals of local societies, field sports publications – these, and many others are very likely to emerge from private households. Far more substantial material will, of course, be found in the local Record Office, the Reference Library and the libraries of educational, technical, business and private institutions. Museums, including 'open-air' museums and those depicting rural and industrial crafts (often in working order), will not only mount exhibitions of a regional character but, through their loan service, will make certain parts of it available to schools. Much useful information and direction as to other likely sources might be obtained from the public relations sections of County Councils and major firms, as well as from the local information and advisory services. Nor ought one to overlook the valuable local knowledge and experience of people involved with the Women's Institute as well as those engaged in extramural teaching at various institutions or with the Workers' Educational Association. Technical advice and facilities for the production of material may also be avilable at Teachers' Centres, the educational technology departments at universities and colleges, or obtained via the local education authority.

Whilst regional studies should not be seen as the panacea for all the ills which seem to have beset the environmental studies at the present time, they are, at least, a genuine attempt to encourage children to view community and environment together. Themes dealing with these matters should not be treated separately. Community and environmental problems within an urban unit are not seen as totally inappropriate to a rural area. Ideas of change, the nature of pre-industrial and industrial societies, the debate over conservation and cultural values – these and many other themes are considered. Evidence obtained from formal records and field analysis is set alongside the oral tradition and less structured sources. With these objectives, approach and techniques it is hoped that regional studies will help children to a better perception of the relationship between people and their environment.

References

BRIAULT, E. W. H. (1942) 'Sussex (East and West)' in L. D. Stamp (Ed) *The Land of Britain* Geographical Publications

COPPER, B. (1971) *A Song for Every Season* Heinemann

KERRIDGE, E. (1967) *The Agricultural Revolution* Allen and Unwin

ROWSE, A. L. (1962) *A Cornish Childhood* Arrow Books

STEPHENS, W. B. (1972) *Sources for English Local History* Manchester University Press

THIRSK, J. (Ed) (1967) *The Agrarian History of England and Wales* IV, Cambridge University Press

THOMPSON, F. (1973) *Lark Rise to Candleford* Penguin

TIMES EDUCATIONAL SUPPLEMENT (1975) *Extra on Environmental Education* 13 June

Useful further reading

COPPER, B. (1971) *A Song for Every Season* Heinemann

EWART EVANS, G. (1970) *Where Beards Wag All: The Relevance of the Oral Tradition* Faber

KERRIDGE, E. (1967) *The Agricultural Revolution* Allen and Unwin

STEPHENS, W. B. (1972) *Sources for English Local History* Manchester University Press

THOMPSON, F. (1973) *Lark Rise to Candleford* Penguin

23

1.2 Religious education

Brian Gates and Colin Alves

Even without living in London, Birmingham or Huddersfield, a child born in England in the second half of the twentieth century is born into a multicultural society. Jews from Eastern Europe, Catholics from Poland, Sikhs and Hindus from India (via Kenya or Uganda), Muslims from Bangla-Desh, Cyprus or Pakistan, are but the latest additions to the social and ethnic mixture that has made the Englishman. A report by Townsend and Brittan (1973) which was jointly sponsored by the Schools Council and the National Foundation for Educational Research attempted to estimate the extent to which English primary and secondary schools are alive to this reality. To the apparent surprise of the authors, religious education is specially mentioned by primary headteachers as an area of the curriculum where at the moment much is being done to prepare children for life in a multicultural society. Similarly, in secondary schools the religious education syllabus is demonstrated to have more direct concern with this than any other single subject, more even than the other humanities grouped together. One can understand the apparent surprise of the authors in coming up with this evidence. It has always been difficult to combat the impression that the 1944 Education Act set up religious education solely as a means of upholding specifically Christian values. Yet the seeds of the present multicultural concerns were present in 1944, even as far back as 1870. The Christian teaching to be given in the old Board schools, and then reflected in the agreed syllabuses which were under-written by the 1944 Act, was intended to be comprehensively Christian in a way which bypassed interdenominational strife.

The English educational system was structured to introduce children to the personal and spiritual values common to the Christian tradition at large, especially as enshrined in the charter documents of the Bible. Churches, teachers' unions and political parties all concurred with this. Actual initiation of a pupil into whichever of the many separate churches was regarded as his parent religious community was seen as a matter lying quite outside the concern of the school. Today the situation has of course developed in a significant way. There are still many churches, but there are also many religions, and many alternative ideologies all represented within the one society. In 1944, by involving the churches in consultations about the substance of the curriculum, acknowledgment was made of the larger community context in which schools operate. Religious education has therefore long been seen as an exercise in community understanding. What is now happening is a development of the principle of consultation so as to include the other religious communities as well as the churches and humanistic alternatives. The first steps towards this have already been taken both at local and national levels. Locally, certain education authorities have taken the initiative of involving representatives of minority religious communities in drawing up new agreed syllabuses suggesting the lines along which religious education might best be approached. For example, Birmingham Education Authority (1975) and Bradford Education Authority (1974) have both been active in this sphere. Nationally, a Religious Education Council, under the chairmanship of Edwin Cox, has been established on which all religious communities and teacher associations with an interest in religious education are represented. It has the task of balancing proper professional educational interests with the confessional aspirations of individual religious loyalties. Both elements are indispensable to an effective religious education for the future.

It is not only the confessional aspirations of the various religious communities as such which have to be taken into account. In a matter so intimate as religious education the parental influence and interest within each individual family cannot be ignored. But if the following three statements are in any way typical, it is a multiculturally grounded religious education which would come closest to satisfying the expectations of many parents today.

Anglican
As a Church of England parent I'd like our Michael to be given a glimpse of the riches of the Christian heritage from its beginnings till now. I'd like him to see how it's helped to make England, and Europe and America; something too about the local churches – their history and things they do now. I suppose he ought to learn about other religions, too. We never got the chance when we were young. He should be able to understand how it is that different people believe different things (and stick up for himself!) It wouldn't be right to expect the school to teach him to say his prayers, or get him ready for Communion. I know we aren't as good at it as we should be ourselves, but that's why we have sent him to Sunday School and confirmation class. But school can show him something about the people who have done good by being true to their faith.

Humanist

As a member of the British Humanist Association, I'd like our Margaret to be given every opportunity to love all that is good and beautiful in man's life and history. I think it is important for her to appreciate how people in different cultures used to believe in God and built great buildings, painted, and told wonderful tales about their beliefs. She should see that some people still think this way. But I'd like her to think through for herself why man has outgrown much of this, what I call, childishness; I don't want anyone trying to persuade her that man hasn't to stand on his own feet, or that he's always in need of supernatural help. Don't offend her conscience by asking her to put her hands together and close her eyes and pray. By all means let her look at some of the social justice that has come from religion, as well as the injustice and oppression. But teach her too that not all good deeds are done by people who are religious.

Sikh

As a Sikh I am happy for my children to be in English school and to learn about the British way of life. My religion teaches me to believe in the brotherhood of all men and I don't like nasty feelings between people. Religion should bring people together and not make them enemies. Our children like to hear about the Bible and Jesus; they were even a bit envious that they hadn't heard of so many miracles by the Gurus. But do you not think that the English children would like to hear something of our religion? I can understand why some of the older men have been talking about the idea of separate schools for Sikhs. At times it is as though you want to keep us separate and apart like the Jews. But I hope this doesn't happen. Maybe our children's children will have an easier time.

In any such parental reckoning religious education is a crucial preparation for life in a multicultural society. It prepares the children by reflecting and acknowledging differences which exist in the community at large, so that the children become knowledgeable about the multicultural aspects of their society. But it also prepares the children for living in such a society by developing attitudes of tolerance towards communities other than their own. The political tradition in this country challenges us to seek a social understanding which is a creative synthesis of distinctive social and cultural strands. It will not allow us to attempt the apparently easier way of imposing a compromise uniformity, nor the equally tempting solution of the ghetto – the coexistence of sharply segregated groupings. In other words the social understanding we must seek is not one which can be established solely (or even mainly) by legal and political processes; it must be fostered and developed by a conscious programme of education.

The social and political health of the community, however, does not depend solely upon the spirit of informed tolerance being well developed in its members. Each individual member needs to establish a sense of his own identity and significance, as well as becoming tolerant of any different grounds for establishing identity which may be held by his neighbour. This second major educational task has been defined as 'affording of opportunity and encouragement to each individual pupil to discover and test out a personal value system and undergirding belief system which can give an adequate sense of purpose to his own life and an adequate sense of significance to life in general'. (This statement comes from an unpublished paper prepared by the Schools Council Religious Education Subject Committee for the Council's Middle Years of Schooling project.) The fulfilment of this aim (as of the first one) need not be restricted to religious education as such. It is equally a concern of moral education, of social studies, of literary studies. But the search for personal identity has been a major characteristic of the overall religious quest, and so it is natural to treat it at least in part as a religious phenomenon, to pursue it in school in the context of the study of religion. The personal identity of the religious believer, as also of the unbeliever, is cumulative and on the move. Any shared matrix of meaning into which a child is born will be tried out from within, and expanded, contracted or transformed by new experiences and encounters. Any focusing that takes place around particular cores of experience and which leads one to say 'I'm a Catholic', or another 'I'm a Muslim', or another 'I'm an atheist', is individually achieved.

From the very earliest years every child is developing a coherent world view at once highly individual and highly complex. Religion figures doubly in this process. Firstly it figures institutionally (explicitly) as a child forms concepts (first or second hand) which represent the ongoing presence of religious practice and belief in the neighbourhood. Secondly, it is found unlabelled (implicitly) in feelings and sensations that are basic to being human; a sense of wonder, of trust, or even of contingency ('a floor is so you won't fall into the hole your house stands on'). In these respects every person – parent, teacher and child alike – is privy to a religious identity that is their own. Given that the formation of religious identity is a lifelong process, its beginning and end are beyond (empirically and theologically speaking) the school. But the school curriculum might still be one means of enabling an individual to come more into his own thoughts and feelings in the realm of religion. Whether he leaves as a believing Congregationalist, devout Parsee, or doubting atheist, what matters is that he is this for himself and not in a blinkered or half-digested sort of way. Can the school perhaps help him become 'religiate', whether or not he would go on to call himself religious?

Of course this personal groundwork is not entirely new to religious education. Harold Loukes (1965) in his review of the effectiveness of the

27

subject in the classroom showed convincingly how secondary school pupils were appreciative of the 'personal dialogue' in the classroom that characterized the subject at its best. This was borne out by his later work *Teenage Morality* (1973), and others such as Madge (1964) and Mogford (1968) have urged that opportunity for such dialogue is no less vital in the primary school. Independent corroboration of this comes also from the as yet unpublished report of the Writing Research Unit at the University of London Institute of Education. Samples of children's writing collected over a number of years from many different schools and from all subject departments have been analysed to see what kind of writing is done right 'across the curriculum'. It was discovered that the only place where personal and expressive writing was to be found to any significant extent, apart from in English work, was in religious education. It is not enough, though, simply to give opportunity for 'personal and expressive writing'. For the exercise to be educational it must involve some challenge to the pupil to establish criteria by which to assess the validity of his own beliefs (as well as of others). This is at least one of the processes involved in becoming 'religiate'. And here we can see how the two aims for religious education which we have already established come together and prove to be mutually supportive. Community tolerance grows through the explicit study of religions, through the increase of informed and sympathetic understanding of the different traditions in our midst. But as the pupils gather information about the various traditions, so they broaden the range of evidence by which they can assess their own beliefs, and they enrich the background against which they pursue their own search for identity. Similarly the growth of a sense of personal significance comes through work in the areas of implicit religion, through aesthetic, symbolic, ethical and social activities. But as the pupils deepen their sensitivity in these areas, and particularly as they thereby deepen their sensitivity to other people, so they increase the possibility of sympathetic understanding of people from backgrounds different from their own, and so contribute to the growth of tolerance.

But if these are the fundamental and mutually supportive aims of that aspect of education most appropriately labelled religious education, how does one actually set about the process? The first point a teacher must bear in mind when trying to answer this question is that a great deal has been learned in recent years about the way in which developmental factors affect a child's thinking about the subject. This is not the place to go into this matter at length. The standard treatment of the subject by Goldman (1964) can be faulted in some of its detail, and in respect of some of its overemphases and even omissions, but its major thesis still remains true. Goldman showed beyond doubt that the main stages in Piaget's developmental schema apply as much to the understanding of religion as to other areas of the curriculum. Early verbal facility in a subject does not in itself indicate real understanding of it, and teachers of younger children need to be cultivating the roots of their pupils' understanding rather than simply instilling into them a vocabulary of words and phrases, the acquisition of which may well be achieved at the cost of inhibiting the development of later understanding. Piaget has long insisted that the 'roots of understanding' are to be found in activity, in actually doing things, not in just talking about them or thinking about them. Most of Piaget's research evidence and illustrative examples come from the areas of scientific and mathematical understanding, but the principle is applicable to other areas as well, including that of religion. But the roots of religious understanding are also to be found internally in the feelings and in the imagination. It is significant that at a time when Goldman was trying to wean religious education teachers away from the 'verbal facility' approach typified by the old catechism, Ninian Smart was castigating his fellow scholars at university level for concentrating too much on 'the doctrinal dimension' in religious studies. The other 'dimensions' he insisted, were of equal importance: the ethical, the social, the experiential, the ritual and the mythological.

The classroom implications of these parallel insights from the fields of psychology and phenomenology are still being worked out. The most systematic application of them so far has been in Michael Grimmitt's book *What Can I Do in Religious Education?* (1973). A less technical presentation of the same basic approach is to be found in Jean Holm's *Teaching Religion in School* (1975). Both books divide religious education into an 'explicit' strand and an 'implicit' strand, and both suggest that the explicit work should start with an exploration of the ritual and mythological dimensions, while contributions to the implicit strand come from stories, from creative work, from general 'topic' work, and from the overall pattern of relationships within the classroom. In actual practice 'explicit', as well as 'implicit', work may also arise from, or form part of, topic-centred work. One striking characteristic of the middle school age range generally (despite considerable changes between eight and thirteen in some respects) is what has been described as 'an insatiable curiosity for accurate factual information'. The child in the middle years of schooling is progressively interested in more and more topics which often overlap so that his enthusiasm for one subject is suddenly superseded by an interest in something completely different. The topic-centred work which has been so characteristic of many junior schools over the past few years is therefore to be welcomed as being able, potentially at least, to harness this driving force of curiosity to some pattern of learning which is sufficiently structured without being inflexible. So much of the factual information relevant to the understanding of religion will fall naturally within, or at least strand out from, the normal pattern of topic work undertaken by the class, and where this happens naturally the opportunity should be welcomed and seized.

But it is unlikely that everything which needs to be covered would come naturally into contexts provided in this way. Even courses which 'strand out' from topics cannot be maintained for too long without becoming completely independent courses, and not 'topic work' at all. All this therefore implies that there is still need for religious education to maintain a quite separate, identifiable existence as a subject in the middle years curriculum alongside the opportunities afforded by topic-centred work. This is *not*, however, the same as saying that there must be a regular, daily, biweekly (or even weekly) dose of the subject. At times this might be appropriate; at other times it might be much more effective to spend, say, three afternoons a week working through part of the course over a month or so, and then drop it altogether for another few weeks. The context which makes such a plan of action particularly easy to adopt is the situation where one teacher has a semispecialist function to perform, in the sense that she is responsible for an *area* of the curriculum, broader than the one-subject specialisms of the more traditional secondary school, but more restricted than the jack-of-all-trades approach of the traditional primary school class teacher. Such 'areas' could be produced from various combinations; religious education, history and geography (where 'geography' is allowed to cover people's ideas as well as their climates or economies) would be the most obvious combination where the major emphasis is to be on 'explicit' studies (while religious education, English and the creative arts would be equally important where the emphasis is on the 'implicit' side, as we shall see later). Items to be covered by such explicit studies would include, as already suggested, ritual practices and festivals (such as Christmas, Diwali, Hannukah) and the sacred places often associated with such ceremonies (sacred buildings such as churches, synagogues and mosques as well as specific sacred sites such as Jerusalem, Mecca, Benares, Red Square). They could also include some of the social activities currently being undertaken by the major religious bodies. ('The Christian Church in Action' is a fairly familiar topic in religious education programmes already, but one needs comparable studies referring to the Jewish community, the Sikh community, the Muslim community, etc.) Wherever possible these explicit aspects of religion should be studied in relation to the family background of actual members of the class, and the fullest possible use should be made of the contribution which these individual pupils can bring to the work from their own immediate experience. For example, if there is a Muslim child in the class, when Ramadan is approaching he could be asked to describe what he will be doing during the fast, and this can then be supplemented by 'research' done by other members of the class. Where the class is from a predominantly Christian background, however, some other point of relevance will have to be found (newspaper or TV reports, for example) in order to tie material concerning 'other faiths' more closely into the world already familiar to the children.

Some 'explicit' material, however, will impinge on the children's lives in quite a different way. Many middle schools already devote some part of their time to the study of early man, and the religious ideas of early man will almost certainly be touched within such a study. The particular benefit of this will *not* be the contrast between early man's 'funny ideas' and our 'more enlightened' scientific ideas today, but the introduction to the realm of mythology which this study can hardly avoid. Work with early myths will form one step on the road towards understanding the uses of religious language.

One can probably place enough confidence in the accuracy of Goldman's description of intellectual development to acknowledge that it would be fruitless to attempt any detailed linguistic analysis during the middle years of schooling. However, towards the upper end of the age range the beginnings of *literary* analysis can profitably be embarked upon (as, for example, has been done in the series of work books *What is the Bible?* published by Rupert Hart Davis) and this in turn can lead on to experiments with actual *use* of language of different types. Technical descriptions of a few minutes' play in a football match can be contrasted with a more colourful description trying to capture the mood of excitement occasioned by those same few minutes. Careful historical accounts of certain events can be deliberately reworked and extended into legendary versions in order to heighten the impact they make on the imagination. Myths can be deliberately created to 'answer' questions on origins, values and purposes. The ability to recognize the different uses of language which comes from actually *using* it in different ways will make easier the later more abstract work connected with sorting out the rules of the different language games. (This particular area would greatly benefit from the work of an 'area specialist' with expertise across the range of religious education, English and science, an unusual but very important combination.)

The function of mythological language is closely allied with the function of stories generally and here we begin to move over into the 'implicit' realm of religion, into the quest for personal identity. A few years ago Huw Wheldon of the BBC was quoted by *The Observer* (19 March 1972) newspaper on this theme. He began:

> Of all the instruments of communication, the story is the most important. It is by stories that people learn to look at themselves and discover what the world is like. It is no accident that religion, and indeed, civilization itself, is based on parable and myth. And a story lies behind every television programme; the news consists of stories, a documentary is a story. There are stories in even the most unstorylike programmes. Take a general election results programme; behind it lies the story of two kings who fought at sunset and all the world knew

that only one of them would live to see the dawn. 'Softly, Softly' is the archetypal story of the pursuer and the pursued. There's no doubt that what we all like best are stories.

Stories from books, stories from television, from daily papers or women's magazines, or even from the hairdresser's or barber's shop, continue even for adults to be a major part of our life world. Somehow in stories and in gossipy conversations which are kin to them, we try out, confirm or transform each other's expectations in life, our views of the world. Story is a vehicle for exploring what it means to be human for children and adults alike. Children are doing this when they produce stories of their own; the books of Britton (1970) and Holbrook (1964) abound with examples. Children are also doing this when they listen to stories and play with them in their minds.

Now as Wheldon (following Cassirer (1953) and Langer (1957) and many others) remarks, it is no accident that religion and civilization are based on stories in the form of parable and myth. What better way then for initiating children into the religious concerns of mankind than by letting them work and play with stories? Admittedly there is some danger of the stories being misunderstood, as Plato and Rousseau were at pains to point out long ago. But adults too can watch or hear the same story and end up with very different understandings. Carefully handled by the storytelling teacher, the story can be a vital vehicle throughout the process of education.

A bigger problem perhaps is the selection of stories in the first place. Once upon a time it was possible to pretend that there was only one set of stories that really mattered. Now we are faced with diverse sets of stories. The broadcaster meets with the same problem, for Wheldon continued:

> You could say that the business of broadcasting is choosing what stories to tell. Now if the audience is united there is no difficulty. *The* story of the nineteenth century was Stanley's meeting with Living-stone; it had everything: Christianity, the empire, exploration. The audience was united. There was no difficulty broadcasting during the last war; the nation was united and everyone wanted to hear the same story. But when the nation is divided as it is now then broadcasting becomes very, very difficult . . . the only thing to do is let all the singers sing. And as we grope our way ahead, we may sometimes tell a story so good that it transcends all division.

Letting all the singers sing in the course of religious education will entail sensitive selection of stories from different religious and cultural traditions. Fortunately, there is no dearth of stories here that can celebrate differences and yet transcend boundaries. If stories are verbal ways of learning to look at ourselves and of discovering what the world is like, ritual action and gestures are ways of physically representing meanings in our lives, both trivial and profound. They too are significant for enabling man to order his world. One thinks, maybe, of an alcoholic friend who finds in tidiness and care for detail an order which is missing elsewhere in his life. In children the Opies (1959) have reminded us of 'Ring a ring of roses' in which all fall down, but all get up again (unlike Humpty Dumpty) and get back to the security of the rhythmic circle; or of the gesture of touching a sailor's collar for luck. A child going to bed may well perform certain ritual actions before settling down – putting Teddy in the right place, looking under the bed, climbing the stairs on one leg, saying prayers. An explicit religious ritual such as this last is not of an entirely different order from the other rituals mentioned. Not all ritual (one thinks of some school assemblies) will necessarily be meaningful; some may be empty and dead. But others gather up deep layers of hidden significance and association and so become a vital vehicle for sensing meaning with our bodies. Erich Fromm (1956) elaborates its importance in the following way:

> What was the function of Greek drama? Fundamental problems of human existence were presented in an artistic and dramatic form, and participating in the dramatic performance, the spectator – though not as a spectator in our modern sense of consumer – was carried away from the sphere of daily routine and brought in touch with himself as a human being, with the roots of his existence. Whether we think of Greek drama, the medieval passion play, or an Indian dance, whether we think of Hindu, Jewish or Christian religious rituals, we are dealing with various forms of dramatization of the fundamental problems of human existence, with an acting out of the very same problems which are thought out in philosophy and theology.

Children as well as adults learn from ritual. By making their own or watching the gestures of others, pupils can be taken into the heart of a religious tradition. The breaking of the bread in Eucharist, the family celebration of Pesach, can disclose in a bodily way much more of what it means to be a Christian or a Jew than much talk. As the Smarts (1967) point out, the level of understanding may be primitive in early years, but a sense of the significance of the occasion will certainly be communicated to be filled out in more elaborated reflection at a later age. Equally, ritual (in the form of ceremonial, or in the more directly 'dramatic' forms of movement and dance) can express in a bodily way much more of what it means to be 'me' or 'us' than much talk. Ritual joins hands with story as a fundamental means for exploring identity and relationship.

The third formal vehicle of human and religious understanding is example. And as we have seen, looking at characteristic activity is an important way of getting at the heart of what a religion is all about. This arises from the fact that imitation is a basic means of learning in life. We all of us, consciously or unconsciously, have models to emulate, and perhaps to avoid too. In school especially there is the opportunity to size ourselves up, and to find out more about who we are or who we would like to be, in relation to the example of others – classmates, teachers, older children, people whose lives we read about in biographies or even novels. The teacher's task here is to remember the power of imitation not only when selecting 'lives' for his pupils to study but in the inevitable presentation of his own life as an 'example' to the children – an 'example', that is, of what it can mean to be human, an example perhaps to be followed, or perhaps to be rejected. He should remember too that many children naturally (if unwittingly) follow the basic principle of Adlerian psychology: watch what they do rather than what they say they do. What a person actually does tells us more about his real identity than any number of things he may claim about himself.

Story, ritual and example, then, are three vehicles that can so conjure with the imagination and thought of the individual at any age that his world is enlarged considerably and the religious experience of mankind can come alive for him. Here is firm ground for the teacher to stand on, ground without which there can be little exploration of identity or education for being. A religious education that is deeply personal and yet world-embracing in its horizons will, as we have seen, have far-reaching curriculum consequences. For instance, it may lay claim to special time of its own in which the distinctive features of religion can be scrutinized, but it will frequently appear as an element in other subject areas. It will also lend itself to attempts at topic-centred integration, and in its dissatisfaction with penultimate answers it will encourage thoroughgoing enquiry methods of work as well as imaginative exploration of ideas. Further, it will be impatient about the traditional act of worship in school, seeking to generate in its place class, year, or whole school rituals that authentically explore and express the human, and (dare it be said) implicitly religious, identity of a community of learning.

References

BIRMINGHAM EDUCATION AUTHORITY (1975) *The Birmingham Syllabus and Handbook* Birmingham Education Department

BRADFORD EDUCATION AUTHORITY (1974) *Guidelines to Religious Education in a Multi-faith Community* Bradford Education Authority

BRITTON, J. (1970) *Language and Learning* Penguin

CASSIRER, E. (1953) *Language and Myth* New York: Dover Publications

FROMM, E. (1956) *The Sane Society* Routledge and Kegan Paul

GOLDMAN, R. J. (1964) *Religious Thinking from Childhood to Adolescence* Routledge and Kegan Paul

GRIMMITT, M. (1973) *What Can I Do in Religious Education?* Mayhew-McCrimmon

HOLBROOK, D. (1964) *The Secret Places* Methuen

HOLM, J. (1975) *Teaching Religion in School* Oxford University Press

LANGER, S. (1957) *Philosophy in a New Key: A Study in the Symbolism of Reason, Rite and Art* Boston: Harvard University Press

LOUKES, H. (1965) *New Ground in Christian Education* SCM Press

LOUKES, H. (1973) *Teenage Morality* SCM Press

MADGE, V. (1964) *Children in Search of Meaning* SCM Press

MOGFORD, B. (1968) Ideas on primary ineducation *Ideas* 6 (March) University of London, Goldsmiths' College

OPIE, I. and P. (1959) *The Lore and Language of School Children* Oxford University Press

SCHOOLS COUNCIL (1975) *The Development of Writing Abilities (11–18)* Macmillan Education

SMART, R. C. and N. (1967) *Children, Development and Relationships* New York: Macmillan

TOWNSEND, H. E. R. and BRITTAN, E. (1973) *Multi-racial education: need and innovation* Evans/Methuen Educational

Useful further reading

COPLEY, T. and EASTON, D. (1974) *What They Never Told You About Religious Education. A Bedside Book for RE Teachers* SCM Press

GRIMMITT, M. (1973) *What Can I Do in Religious Education?* Mayhew-McCrimmon

HULL, J. (1975) *School Worship: an obituary* SCM Press

LORD, E. and BAILEY, C. (1973) *A reader in religious and moral education* SCM Press

SMART, N. and HORDER, D. (1975) *New movements in religious education* Temple Smith

Note: Parts of this chapter have been adapted from an article which appeared originally in *Ideas* 29, (October 1974) published by University of London, Goldsmiths' College.

2 Physical education and the creative arts

Frank Dain and Helen Stubbs suggest that physical mastery gives the child his first sense of identity and personal realization and it is essential for the school to exploit the child's physical capabilities to the full. There would be few physical education specialists who would disagree with this point of view, and fewer still who could be confident that children of primary school age are being given the opportunities to achieve in physical education. The blame would seem to lie in a number of directions. The colleges appear to be failing to give their students sufficient understanding of sound basic programmes of physical activities, preferring rather to present wide-ranging courses; the DES has always appeared ambivalent concerning the place of physical education in the education of young children; and primary schools on the whole are poorly provided with the necessary equipment and specialist help to provide a viable programme of physical activities. There has also been the shift, largely in secondary schools but having its effect lower down, from the educational to the recreational aspects in physical education curricula and it is feared that this has resulted in a loss of quality and depth. But Frank Dain and Helen Stubbs are very clear in their understanding of the basic problem facing a teacher of any practical course at any level, and that is the fundamental need to understand the methods whereby the teacher presents the required skills to children. For this there must be sound training, a clarity of purpose, an understanding of children and an enthusiasm to teach.

Jan McKechnie would agree with the points made in the preceding paragraph when it comes to planning adventure activities for the middle years children – an age group hitherto thought unsuitable for such activities. But she would stress, like Frank Dain and Helen Stubbs, that no amount of teacher's enthusiasm can make up for practical experience in the field. The unexpected is almost the expected in teaching. When it happens in the classroom the teacher has control over most of the variables present in the situation; when the unexpected happens out of doors only experience and sound common sense can stop it becoming a disaster. One of the editors will carry to his grave scars of the experience of an unexpected twenty-four hour blizzard catching him and his small party of twelve-year-olds on a desolate and remote plateau in the middle of a Tasmanian summer. He swears that it was that day his hair started to go grey! If children of this age group are to be introduced to adventure activities which it is hoped will encourage them to continue after leaving school, then the basic groundwork must be thorough, the activities chosen with care, and a well-developed connection be established to allow an easy transition from the school-based activities to those in the adult world outside.

Seymour Jennings, in looking at art in the middle years, avoids the opportunity to present a variety of teachers' tips which appear to typify many books for teachers of art. Instead, he presents a process for curriculum development in the shape of a well-defined planning model for the would-be teacher of art. The process of selection of material to teach and the constraints involved are examined in a rational, novel and stimulating way and present a model which has universal application in the area of curriculum development.

Kate Fleming and John Miller follow up their article in the earlier book by looking at drama again, but this time with specific reference to the development of language. They acknowledge that the one-time innovative nature of drama has become almost institutionalized and what is needed now is another look at the whole area of drama in the school. They develop one aspect of drama and illuminate from their experience with children and students a whole range of possibilities open to the lively and imaginative teacher that require few facilities or space and which are suitable for children of every ability to participate.

Music, David Gray would agree, is for doing and enjoying. But enjoyment comes from doing it well and possessing the basic knowledge and skills to do so. Whilst not all children have a capability in this direction all children should be given the opportunity to try. Music, like the other subjects in this section, appears to suffer from too little time being allocated to it on the school timetable; too narrow a concept of the subject in the school context; too few qualified staff to teach it, and too often being housed in poor accommodation with unsuitable equipment. The clanging instrument trolley has made the music teacher more mobile, often to the disadvantage of those wishing to see the subject fixed in a permanent place in the school and the timetable.

2.1 Physical education in the middle years

Frank Dain and Helen Stubbs

'A child's movement is an integral part of himself; he needs opportunities to utilize, develop and enjoy it.' (DES 1973) Physical education can be judged to be complementary to other aspects of the curriculum in their total endeavour to educate the child. To consider the education of the 'whole child' is to acknowledge the need for mental, physical and social development. Physical education will have a unique contribution to make to the child's development, as distinct from the other aspects of the curriculum. This is not to overlook the fact that physical education is also acknowledged as a rich provider of social and emotional experiences and to have an intellectual content. This 'education through the physical' starts at birth and continues throughout life, as Oberteuffer (1945) observed: 'all living things use movement as an instrument of expression and impression'.

Within the school, the primary years have been regarded as the time and place to focus on the development of a child's resources in movement through giving him the widest possible range of experience, both functional and creative, in such a way that he is free to work within the limits and toward the limit of his own unique capacities. The Plowden Report (DES 1967) aptly characterizes these years:

> With young children, the work will be very general and it will not always be easy to separate different modes of movement and experience. By the time they are ready to leave the primary school, however, the work and teaching will be more closely related to specific ends; gymnastics, games, dance, drama and swimming will be the normal elements of a weekly or seasonal programme.

This indicates a change from general movement learning to more specific skills development, which still have a wide application and interpretation.

Within the secondary age range, this developmental change continues. In the first years the programme is orientated towards consolidating the understanding and efficiency of movement, through the practice of skills and the introduction of traditional adult games activities. Later comes the time for 'choice' to be introduced, which in itself is the forerunner of a diversified 'optional' programme intent on skill, development and satisfying physical endeavour that results in positive attitudes towards participation in post-school recreation.

Method reflects content. At primary level the principles underlying the teaching method are similar to those in other areas of the curriculum. It is child centred, allowing for self-discovery, self-awareness, individualized pacing and interest development. Initially the teacher is very much concerned with creating learning environments which provide opportunities for play, exploration and discovery, experimentation, repetition and modification. Through an understanding of movement and an ability to observe it accurately and sensitively, the teacher can give effective guidance and direction as the child searches for greater skill and quality of performance. To emphasize the child-centred approach, the class teacher is the individual normally responsible for taking physical education lessons. The teacher thus has the unique opportunity of knowing the individual child in all facets of his development.

Once the child reaches secondary school, a radical change in approach is apparent. The specialist teacher, knowledgeable of his subject, but less so of the individual child, becomes involved in a more direct 'skill acquiring' approach. This emphasis on skill requires more objective planning and is characterized by 'direct' rather than 'exploratory' teaching methods. The pressure of the many aspects, in an ever-restricting timetable, leads to a concentrated skill development programme from the outset. In addition to this specialization, the sex of the teacher becomes significant in catering for the now diverging interests of adolescent boys and girls.

In the transition from primary to secondary schools, both method and content are seen to change direction and emphasis dramatically, leaving an unfortunate impression that the child becomes a near-adult in the six weeks summer vacation during his eleventh year. This 'gulf' is an unnatural one, but perhaps enforced and certainly reinforced by social pressures from school and community. The creation of a school for children of the middle years, part primary, part secondary, creates the challenge of satisfying the developmental needs of the child in broadly-based and specific skill development, and eliminating the 'gulf' by fully preparing the child for an easy transition into the senior school and its high-pressure skill demands. The vast range and change in growth and development during this period merely accentuates the complexity of the problem with which the teachers of these children are faced.

The middle years child
Some consideration of the developmental changes in the physical motor and social growth of children is needed, for the content of any programme

should have implicit within it an understanding of these specific changes and how they relate to skill development.

Physically, children vary enormously, in just the same way as does their reading age or IQ. Individual growth rates and a range of maturational development affect the stage of development of such factors as strength, height, weight and speed. Social development is very closely related to physical development and both will have a significant bearing on the programme and character of physical education. While differences in stages of maturity, in physique and innate abilities are present in any class, the relative characteristics of that class will tend to remain the same in the primary years. It is only when the adolescent growth spurt begins to take effect that differences, for the moment, become exaggerated and more extreme.

The average eight year old is reaching the end of a phase of development, when his greatest enjoyment has been the freedom of movement. He still tends to whole body movements, but is becoming increasingly aware of specific functions of various parts of the body in a given movement. Balance and neuromuscular improvement suggest that all forms of locomotion and activities demanding simple hand/eye coordination should be developed. Socially his development is recognized by his enjoyment of group activities and his ability to cooperate within the group, if the size of that group is small – two or three, preferably. It might be noted that even at this age, motor skill is a great asset to the child in winning group acceptance.

During the nine to eleven age group, better body proportions assist good balance, agility and flexibility. While enjoying physically demanding activities, those dependent on strength and stamina do not come easily, and while experienced should not be developed to any great degree. Not until speed, steadiness of movement and accuracy are developed should skills requiring, or dependent on, these factors be introduced into the curriculum. This is the age for developing motor skills. Physically he is developing the capacity, and mentally he is becoming interested in making his actions effective and efficient. Not only should skills be experienced, they must also be taught. Many skills tend to be specific and need to be specifically learnt. It is often much better to approach their development through direct teaching, bearing in mind the child's capabilities and limitations of maturational level. His attention span is short and practices need immediate and short-term objectives. The child is more social in out-look and strong attachments to one another develop. They are intense about rules and fair play. The image of personal success and self-value is very much related to winning. The older children are capable of coping with more complex group formations and codes of rules. However, it is un-wise to expect adult levels of participation whether in terms of skill, team cooperation, periods of play or size of playing area. It is also well to remember that high levels of competition and the resulting stress and anxiety will seriously lower their skilled performance when the more complex skills patterns are in use.

The physical and social maturation of the individual continues to develop during the eleven to thirteen age range. The onset of adolescence, primarily for the girls, sees a very rapid growth change. The accompanying development of sex characteristics and the social expectations of such evidence of maturation makes it desirable that the major games are developed each to its own sex. The development of social relationships and understanding take on a new importance, so the other areas of the curriculum can still be mixed to advantage. The readiness of these children to practise and master skills at this age must be harnessed in order that maximum progress can be made, before the changing attitudes, lethargy and distractions of a questioning confidence can make such basic learning difficult.

Theoretically there is little difference between boys and girls up to the age of eleven. In practice, however, variations do exist. These are considered to be influenced in the main by social rather than physical factors. Differing interests will themselves affect initial abilities. While boys and girls may differ, there will be a far greater range of variation within one sex than will be seen between the sexes. While it may often seem expedient for the teacher to group the children by sex, mixed groupings provide a far more satisfying and profitable learning and competitive situation where relevant. The value-ridden factors of (i) femininity, which encourages sensitivity, grace, poise and flexibility, and (ii) masculinity, which encourages the dynamic qualities of strength and speed, are admirable foils for one another and should be exploited. The provision of mixed activities and groupings will help to ensure that every child will have a far greater opportunity for a balanced and satisfying diet.

The problems associated with differing maturational stages must be minimized if the personality of the child is not to suffer. The span of maturational levels may range by up to four years. For example, the class of ten year olds may contain children with the appearance and physical potential of an eight year old, alongside those who possess developing secondary sex characteristics and whose reaction time, speed, height and stamina – all very significant in terms of skill performance – are near those of a twelve year old. The satisfying of their differing needs are not too difficult in the individualized activities such as dance, gymnastics and swimming. In those activities which are strongly influenced by physical growth factors, more careful grouping is needed in order to neither create overconfidence nor sap confidence. There are dangers that the late maturers, seen as less skilful, are denied adequate fostering of their skills, with a consequent losing of interest in 'catching up'. Early maturation can give a false assessment of 'skill', when its lack can be compensated for by greater comparative strength, speed, height, etc. It must also be remembered that the child who looks mature physically is still a child in attitude, understanding and interests. Significant grouping is most likely to be by physical maturation or skill, when competition is involved, if security and confidence are to be maintained.

To ensure the suitability of the curriculum, therefore, we need to equate it with the growth of the child in all its aspects – physical, social and psychological. To ensure the success of the curriculum we must have clearly defined aims and objectives, which should reflect this understanding of the 'whole' child.

Aims and Objectives
Physical education in the middle years will aim to provide opportunities for (i) sound physical growth and health; (ii) a comprehensive range of basic movement experiences; (iii) an increasingly efficient use of the body through the development of skills; (iv) the development of sensitivity and an awareness of quality; and (v) social development and responsible behaviour.

In order to achieve these aims, it is recommended that the basic programme should have as essential elements gymnastics, dance, games, athletics and swimming. At eight, the child will be experiencing all these elements directly or indirectly at an appropriate level, with enthusiasm and anticipation. Professor Ross (1971) would support the idea of the continuation of this pattern even as the level of skills develop through to thirteen. In other words, specialization is not advisable and no area of the curriculum should be dropped. It is important in the achievement of these aims that the elements are present in such a way that they provide a balanced programme throughout the middle school years. Such a curriculum, requiring the teaching of a wide range of skills and providing such a width of experiences, must never allow quality to be sacrificed for quantity. This will demand careful planning, sound organization and skilful teaching – in other words, purpose and direction.

It is well to remember that the child will get most from the curriculum if he gains enjoyment and satisfaction from achievement and success. More effective learning takes place under these conditions. This is not to say that enjoyment should be the main aim of any lesson, rather that the enjoyment should be considered an essential quality of any learning situation.

Now we must consider in detail each one of the elements of the curriculum.

Curriculum content
GYMNASTICS
Gymnastics is the area of the curriculum which concentrates attention on the body and its own actions in all their diversity, with awareness of their potential and quality. The child, with often gay abandon, loves to run,

jump, roll, climb and swing. The joy of movement must be exploited and channelled into skilful movement. The achievement of this develops a poise, a confidence and an awareness, which in itself heightens the child's sensitivity in other physical activities. The opportunity to experience extremes of suddenness, slowness, extension, thrust into the air and other such qualities, develops understanding and provides a physical experience difficult to substitute.

Aims

The continuing aim of all lessons will be the consistent development of an increasing range of movement, greater control and greater clarity of action and intent, thus ensuring evidence of quality and understanding.

Content

The following stages of progression through the curriculum are possible means by which the teacher can ensure a comprehensive development of gymnastic movement and skill:

Stage 1 – first year

Locomotion – emphasizing moving from place to place, changing directions, and at different levels, by stepping, falling, rocking, sliding, jumping. Development of simple continuous movement phrases.

Stage 2 – second year

Continued development of Stage 1. Curling and stretching (i) in contrast, (ii) using one extreme to recover from the other. Twisting and turning – effecting direction change. Quick and slow. Simple sequence development.

Stage 3 – third year

Flight and landing (i) landing (ii) take off (iii) flight. Swinging and circling. Symmetry and asymmetry. Acceleration and deceleration. Simple partner work – following pathways, copying, as obstacles. Sequence development with emphasis on continuity.

Stage 4 – fourth year

Further development of flight. Balance. Contrasting sudden and very slow. Control of tension – using 'gradually', 'suddenly', 'lightly', 'explosively' as most appropriate for the action. Partner work – matching, taking weight.

The lesson

Within the lesson, learning will progress from a floor situation to the apparatus (or partner work). Work on the floor must always be seen as a preparation and training in a movement idea for its eventual development on the apparatus. While Stage 1 will best be served by dividing the lesson

44

into half floor and half apparatus work, later stages may well be better served as more and more emphasis is placed on quality of movement, for time allotment to be on a sliding scale as the movement idea is developed. For example:

1 floor work only
2 $\frac{3}{4}$ floor: $\frac{1}{4}$ apparatus
3 $\frac{1}{2}$ floor: $\frac{1}{2}$ apparatus
4 $\frac{1}{4}$ floor: $\frac{3}{4}$ apparatus
  (these proportions in terms of time allocation per lesson)

In order to ensure progression and systematic learning, the use of *themes* (which can be compared to a 'topic' in the classroom) is recommended. Each theme may last for half a term. Themes also ensure that learning builds on past experience, and allows for repetition, practice and reinforcement. *Subthemes* used in conjunction with the main theme, ensure a width of development, with often a refreshing change of emphasis as repetition of the main theme takes place. For example, *main theme:* sudden and very slow (sustained); the first lesson would explore and provide for an awareness of these two contrasting qualities. Afterwards, the main theme would be developed in conjunction with subthemes. Possible *subthemes* (one per lesson) include: (a) curling and stretching (linked to the time factor); (b) use of levels; (c) twisting and turning effecting change of direction; (d) partner work; etc.

A progressive development of the work will arise through the teacher setting tasks and teaching within each task, as follows: (a) the task set, creates the particular movement environment desired by the teacher. For example, 'Find different ways of travelling very, very slowly'; and (b) the movements can then be made more diverse and so assist in the extension of movement vocabulary. For example, 'Can you vary the length of the step you take?'; 'Think about using other parts of your body than hands and feet to travel on'; 'Can your movement bring about a change of direction?'.

The teacher may also isolate a skill associated with the theme for more practice, or focus on a particular idea not fully exploited by the class, or perhaps not discovered by them. Only after a full exploration of the possibilities within the theme, and much practice, should linking movements into a phrase or sequence be asked for.

Apparatus, essential for a full gymnastic experience, should be selected to give a wide range of opportunities in weight-bearing, climbing, hanging and flight. There should be sufficient for small groups to operate, so that 'waiting-for-turns' is eliminated. Direct teaching will need to be very specific at times. It cannot be denied that there are recognizable, specific gymnastic 'skills'; for example, forward roll, handstand, cartwheel. When all the class show a readiness and ability to develop such skills, there should be introduced within the lesson specific technique teaching. Not only does this extend the range of movement, but it also helps to develop an awareness of quality. At all times careful and accurate observation by the teacher will be essential if the children's skills are to be developed and their immediate needs satisfied.

DANCE

Dance and gymnastics show the same fundamental principles of movement. In dance, however, the main concern is with expressive movement. Of all physical disciplines, dance makes the greatest contribution to the aesthetic and creative aspects of education. In dance we are developing the natural movements with which the child so freely expresses himself and his reactions to his environment. Dance is a medium rich in sensory experiences, seeing, hearing, touching, feeling and even smelling. Music, sounds, language, speech, colour, textures and sensations are all involved and contribute to the life experiences so vital in a child's total education.

Aims

Through dance the teacher aims to (i) preserve spontaneity of movement; (ii) develop the child's movement skills to enable him to express his ideas and feelings with clarity; (iii) heighten the child's sensitive awareness to movement, sound, shape, texture and rhythm; (iv) provide opportunities for creativity in movement and thought; and (v) highlight relationships, encouraging cooperation and sensitivity.

Content

Dance is a movement discipline no less skilled than gymnastics. To develop this skill of clarity of expression in movement, the following development is suggested:

Stage 1 – first year

The dancing will be of a relatively simple nature with plenty of repetition, activity and elevation. Apart from individual dancing developing phrases of movement, group work will be limited to working in twos or threes developing sequences showing contrasts. Body awareness through a focus on shape, use of body parts to lead movements away from, into, around, and their relationships to one another. Exploring ways of stepping, using different pathways and levels, leaping, running, skipping, moving and stillness. Actions of opening and closing, rising and falling, advancing and retreating. Movement qualities of firmness, lightness, suddenness, slowness. Rhythm development.

Stage 2 – second year

Continued development and clarification of Stage 1 material. This consolidation of previous work will be a feature of all subsequent stages. In addition material will include: successive body action, developed with some attention on the active use of the trunk; symmetry, asymmetry. The exploration of directness/flexibility in relation to time (slow/sudden) and weight (firm/light). Repetition of actions or their combinations, for example, rising, travelling, stillness, sinking; or repetition of qualities, for example, slowly twisting inwards and shooting out like an arrow, develops rhythmic phrases with contrasts to aid clarity. Development of group sensitivity by dancers leading, following, passing, merging; movement conversation.

Stage 3 – third year
Awareness, sensitivity, control and innovation develop. Greater clarity and awareness developed in the use of body in space – its shape, direction, intent, relationships of parts of body to each other and full use of levels to be encouraged. Combining weight/time/space qualities to develop actions of floating, gliding, flicking, dabbing, wringing, pressing, slashing, thrusting introduced. The children can handle larger groups now. Dance sequences should be allowed to emerge from practice and selection, rather than dictation of its pattern. The movement idea will make the dance cohesive, the freedom allowing spontaneity.

Stage 4 – fourth year
In addition to the continuing development of previous material, attention will be given to development of the above effort actions, combining weight/time/space. Contrasting actions when used help understanding, clarity, assist patterned phrasing and add a new dimension to relationships. Relationships between groups are now able to be developed. The form of the group – for example, wedge shape has a piercing quality, circle shape has an encircling protective or menacing quality, scattered, the group becomes weak – should be explored. Work actions such as work rhythms, combat rhythms, machine rhythms encourage the dynamic qualities.

The lesson and use of stimuli
The form of the lesson is basically similar to the gymnastic lesson. After a 'warm up', a movement theme – for example 'flexibility and directness of body action and pathway' – is developed through 'movement training' exploring the movement ideas, leading to the 'climax' or 'dance' where these ideas are used in an individual or group dance. Similar methods of direct and indirect teaching are used; task setting question and answer.

To achieve the essentially expressive character of dance, the use of language in setting and teaching within the tasks is critical; for example, darting, thrusting, swooping, swirling, exploding are different expressions of movement which have the common element of speed. Tasks must be set with care. There is nothing so soul-destroying as trying to 'be like a floating balloon' or 'stand like a tree'. Such dangers can be averted if the teacher remembers that it is the essential *quality* of the action which is wanted. Such imagery can be very helpful for conveying intention, but rather, let us try and experience the lightness of a floating balloon or the firmness and strength of a tree. Other forms of stimuli can be used and the varied ways we can use these will reflect the growing skill and understanding of the children. Voice patterns, sounds, words, percussion of body parts on body parts, on floor, etc. or of musical instruments with their range of tonal quality and pitch; music using records, tapes, piano; textures, colour, moods may be used. To work entirely without such stimuli should not be ignored for it produces a concentration and awareness of the movement itself. The selection of music is not always an easy task, but its clarity and pattern are important at this stage. Complex orchestration is too difficult and should be avoided.

Folk Dance, while unsuitable for the younger children, will be part of *Dance* for the older children. Set patterns of steps and repetitive group patterns may be created by the teacher and by the children as well as dancing simple traditional dances. Such stylized forms of dancing should not dominate the programme.

Dance Drama is an area developing from *Dance* and as such should not be included in this element. It is more appropriate that it should be included in the integrated programme of the classroom. This is discussed more fully later in the article.

GAMES

Games spring from the same movement root as gymnastics – the functional and skilled action of the body in an objective situation, but now associated with manipulating and controlling objects. They have their own parti-cular contribution to make to the balanced programme: (i) development of stamina and (ii) progressive development of general games skills and the particular development of those specific skills related to major games. By the nature of the group/team element in the games, there are opportunities for extensive social learning; for example, knowledge of self and others, cooperation, acceptance of rules, coping with success and failure. We must also make capital out of the child's instinctive and natural interest in play.

A marked development of both physical, social and mental skills between the ages of eight and thirteen is seen. This parallels the change from the child's natural instinct to structure his own games by simple rules when he is eight years old, to his ability and desire to handle the more complex nature of 'the game' which involves a much higher level of skills, team play and tactics.

Content

The BAOLPE Working Party on middle schools (1973) recommends the following pattern of progress which can be identified as stages in the teaching of games during these middle years of schooling:

1 Consolidation and continued improvement of skill attainment through the medium of individual/partner/small group practices, the emphasis being on cooperation rather than competition.
2 The introduction and development of new skills arising from the more complex situations which the children themselves will have naturally discovered in their inventive play.
3 The development of skills and concepts directly related to a variety of 'traditional' games situations through the medium of small group activities directed by the teacher. Competitive situations should be well controlled in order to ensure a degree of success for all participants.
4 A more direct presentation of activities in their adult form with appropriate modifications to rules, equipment and pitch specifications to meet the needs and limitations of the pupils.

The Lesson

The interpretation of such progress could be illustrated by the following allocation of games periods throughout the years:

8 years: 2 single periods (mixed class):
lesson content and organization as indicated in Stage 1 with (i) opening activity, (ii) skills training and (iii) group activity/game.

9–11 years: 1 double period (mixed class):
lesson content and organization as indicated in Stages 2 and 3 with (i) opening activity, (ii) skills training and (iii) group games (6: 3 v 3) – a variety of games would be played with groups rotating.

11–13 years: (a) 1 single period (mixed class):
lesson content – introduction to a variety of minor indoor games such as volleyball, basketball, skittleball, badminton.
(b) 1 double period (single sex, except for some summer activities):

lesson content – the development from 11–12 years to
12–13 years will be seen in the progress in skill level and
the increased numbers playing in each team. 11–12
years – as in Stages 3 and 4 but limiting the development of the game to mini/junior level as recognized by
the national bodies of sport (hockey, soccer, rugby,
netball, cricket).
12–13 years – extending the development of the game to
near adult form. .

The following plan indicates a progression of lesson development,
indicating the apportionment of time. With an improved skill level and
greater experience of the children, stages three and four may have greater
emphasis.

Division of time ────────────────────────────────➤

1	A	B	C	D
2	A	B	C	D
3	A	B	C	D
4	A	C		D
5	A	D		

Key: A   Opening activity
      B   Small group practices without opposition
      C   Small group practices with opposition
      D   Game

      1   Introduction of new technique
   2/3   Changing emphasis as skills improve
      4   Whole of skill training now devoted to practices with
          opposition
      5   Occasionally the lesson may be devoted to the game

School games
For the 11–13 year olds, interschool games become an integral part of the
total games programme. However, it is vitally important that these do not
intrude upon the normal school programme to the detriment of other
children's learning and of team members themselves receiving a liberal
programme. There should be encouragement for interschool *friendly*
rivalry at varying ability levels in a variety of games (minor and major).

This will ensure the stretching of the more able child as well as maintaining the enthusiasm and interest of many, through maximum participation.

ATHLETICS

Athletics provides an avenue for the child's interest in and enthusiasm for the natural movement of running, jumping and throwing. It is primarily an individual activity which is essentially competitive by nature. Such characteristics enable athletics to make its own particular contribution to the curriculum.

Aims

In the middles years of schooling, athletics should aim to (i) provide vigorous activity, thus contributing towards the fitness, health and growth of the body systems; (ii) develop the specific skills of running, jumping and throwing; and (iii) develop such attributes as determination, self discipline, courage and positive attitudes towards competing.

Content

The pattern seen in the development of the other elements within the physical education curriculum is yet again repeated in athletics. During the middle years running, jumping and throwing are transformed from initial vigorous free activity (by a continual process of practice and reinforcement) to ultimately become stylized athletic events.

Stage 1 – 8–10 years

During this period 'athletics' will not be specifically identified. Throughout the physical education programme the three basic athletic activities will be practised and developed where appropriate. Emphasis will be placed on (i) running – the development of speed, which will be helped by encouraging balance, a smooth and controlled action and a strong leg thrust; (ii) jumping – the development of spring, varying the take-off, direction and speed of approach, position in the air; and (iii) throwing – encouraging correct patterns of action, throwing for height, distance, accuracy at targets, on the move and stationary.

Stage 2 – 10–11 years

Athletics will now be identified as an activity in its own right, taking its place alongside the summer games. Emphasis will be placed on developing the basic techniques which will improve the general efficiency of the action. Hurdling will be introduced at this stage. Although recognized as a complicated action, we are able to start at this age, because the flexibility and suppleness of these children enables them to produce and establish the correct actions more easily now than when they get older. Emphasis will be placed on (i) running – emphasis on strong arm and leg actions, smooth easy action running, short 'driving' sprints; (ii) hurdling – the emphasis will be on smooth running over low obstacles and the build-up for a rhythmic stride pattern between them; (iii) jumping – (a) for height, (b) for distance – encouraging single foot take-offs, appropriate speed of approach, upward thrust of legs and arms; and (iv) throwing – standing throw emphasizing forward transference of weight and (b) running throw from behind a line.

Stage 3 – 11–13 years
Athletics should now be approached with the aim of developing and improving the techniques of the individual athletic events.

The Lesson
The lesson should follow the same development of warming up, skill training and group activities as for other forms of physical education, as follows:

Warming up: teacher directed activities designed to get the body warm;

Skill training: basic skills of the various athletic events; introduced as class activities (suggest two areas to be covered);

Group activities: the training is developed into the form of group work following the pattern of organization set out in the games lesson. Preferably the six groups will comprise of running, jumping and throwing practices, each duplicated. This should ensure balance of lesson. Their arrangement and organization will need to be carefully determined to ensure safety for all.

Competition
Competition will appear in varying forms. Starting at the lower age range, where it will arise from teaching situations within the daily lesson; for example 'Who can run to the line and back first?'. Competition will progress through such forms as 'against-oneself', 'against the standards set by the teacher', to more formalized competitive situations; for example, high-jump competitions. It is important that everybody becomes involved and tastes success sometimes, thus ensuring that the majority of children retain their interest in athletic activities during these middle years. Watered-down versions of adult sports days should be avoided.

SWIMMING
Swimming has its own special place in physical education. Working in

such a different medium provides its own experiences, sense of freedom and ways of moving. It is the *ability* to swim that brings its own rewards and satisfactions. This ability provides a tool for survival primarily, but also gives immediate access to a wide range of further swimming and recreative activities. The earlier the child is taught, the easier he will find it to learn to swim.

Aims

There is one fundamental overriding aim for all teachers of swimming. *Every* child must learn to swim. We would define 'swimming' as being no more than 'the ability to move through the water unsupported'. Further aims for this age range would include (i) increasing stroke efficiency through progressive skill development and (ii) developing watermanship – which implies the understanding and ability of how to use the water in a relaxed and confident manner.

Content

Time and swimming bath availability will vary considerably from school to school and will therefore influence the extent of development of all skills. However, such time limitations should not affect the overall presentation of a fully balanced swimming programme, which should include:

1 the development of breast stroke, back crawl and front crawl
2 the opportunity to experiment with hybrid strokes
3 simple water stunts, for example, floating, sculling, somersaulting
4 simple lifesaving and survival techniques
5 foundation practices for diving
6 games activities
7 competitive activities from cork and spoon races to sprint racing.

The problems presented by a wide range of ability within any class can most easily be met by ability grouping, which not only allows for the need of the children to be more easily satisfied, but also ensures the most economical use of bath space. Swimming is unusual in its tendency to produce greater extremes of ability within the age range than found in other activities. The able swimmer must look to the local swimming club rather than the class situation for full satisfaction and development.

Awards

Swimming lends itself to the gaining of a number of awards from a variety of bodies, in distance, speed and survival swimming. The first 10–15 yard certificate is unquestionably the most significant award to the child. Not only is it a measure of his achievement, but it also acts as an incentive and confidence booster to further progress. Whereas succeeding awards in distance or speed may be popular, the 'striving after' of survival and lifesaving awards is likely to be of greater value to this age range.

Integration with other areas of the curriculum

Having dealt with the five distinctive elements of the normal programme, it should be recognized that physical education can also make a valuable contribution to other aspects of the curriculum. There are three possible areas for integration which can be easily identified.

OUTDOOR ACTIVITIES

The countryside should be seen as a laboratory for further learning and the gaining of experience, outside the classroom situation. Environmental studies, with all its attendant disciplines, springs to mind immediately. The scope of such work can be greatly extended if the children have access to a variety of terrain by virtue of their ability to exist and look after themselves in open country. Physical education, which recognizes outdoor activities as part of its content, including within it such skills as camping, walking and route finding, becomes an integral part of outdoor education. Outdoor activities, as an area of physical education taking place out of school time, is dealt with in more detail by Jan McKechnie in the next article.

MOVEMENT/DANCE STUDIES

Within the dance section we have dealt with movement as a means of expression in itself. However, it also can be used as a vehicle of expression in other arts. Joan Russell (1965) suggests that 'movement indeed, can be considered as an integrating factor in all manifestations of the creative impulse'. Apart from the more obvious channels of dance drama as an area of integration, movement itself can be a catalyst, for example, for creative activity in art or poetry. This can also work in reverse. Within a single art form such as music, such aspects as phrasing, rhythm, pitch, instrumental qualities can be further explored and understanding reinforced, by relating them to dance/movement actions. It is the fascination of movement which stimulates and the actions of dance which reinforces learning.

PHYSICAL EDUCATION WITH OTHER DISCIPLINES

Physical education has its own body of knowledge; for example, history, literature, culture and science. To use physical education in one of its many aspects as a central idea for a 'topic' or subject study can take advantage of children's natural interests to stimulate learning.

PE as a central theme for topic work

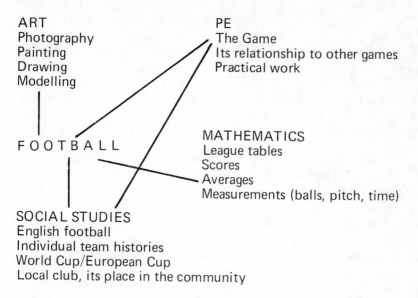

ART
Photography
Painting
Drawing
Modelling

PE
The Game
Its relationship to other games
Practical work

FOOTBALL

MATHEMATICS
League tables
Scores
Averages
Measurements (balls, pitch, time)

SOCIAL STUDIES
English football
Individual team histories
World Cup/European Cup
Local club, its place in the community

PE as a central focus for specific subject studies

English	Excerpts from the classics, for example *Pickwick Papers*, skating; poetry studies – poetry with the central theme of different aspects of sport; newspaper reporting – sports pages; radio/TV commentary.
History	Sport and culture – Greeks, and links with fitness and war; tribal ritual; individual sports and their development.
Mathematics	Measurement of areas, graphs (scores, records, etc.), averages, time (athletics, swimming), setting.
Biology and health	Simple experiments and consideration of the effects of exercise on the body.

All such possible ways of utilizing physical education and extensions of these ways serve to extend the possibilities of experience and understanding within the total education of the child.

Physical education in the context of the middle school
STAFFING
The coming together of the secondary and junior schools brings with them the meeting of the specialist and general class teaching systems. The temptation to use one system or the other, or to compromise on a fifty/fifty

basis is really ignoring the unique qualities and opportunities of these middle years of schooling as a developing community in its own right. The demands of the proposed curriculum in terms of its width and required depth of teaching expertise throughout these years would make it quite impossible for a general class teacher to adequately satisfy all the needs of the children. In fact a single specialist would also have considerable difficulty in adequately meeting these needs. It is clearly evident that there is a need for a man and woman specialist teacher to be on the staff in these schools. Although much of the work will be mixed, the diverging interests of the older boys and girls would be more easily satisfied with this type of staffing.

If one accepts the advantages of class-based teaching for the children, alongside the need for more specialist expertise as the children get older, a pattern emerges of:

1 *8–11 years:*   The class teacher takes the physical education with such help and advice required from the specialist teachers.
2 *11–13 years:* The class-based teaching continues, but with evidence of stranding, so that when needed the specialist teacher takes other classes in addition to his own class commitments.
3 *8–13 years:*   Occasions may arise for the specialist teacher to take some physical education classes where the class teacher is particularly uncommitted to physical education or for some reason unable to teach the subject.

The specialists would be class-based teachers, with some time spent outside their own class teaching physical education. They will also have the overall responsibility of advising on the organizing of physical education throughout the school.

Each school will have its own special conditions and characteristics. The essential requirement is one of fluidity within the total school situation. The main course physical education student, taking an education course for the middle school or junior/secondary age range, should very adequately fit the role of the specialist, yet class-based, teacher.

TIMETABLE

All middle schools should aim for one physical education period per day or its equivalent, allowing a working time of at least thirty minutes. While for the eight year olds, five single periods seem desirable, the remaining classes can more profitably have one double period for games teaching. A suggested allocation of the five elements already proposed to ensure the desired balanced programme would be:

8 years	9 – 11 years		11 – 13 years	
	Winter	*Summer*	*Winter*	*Summer*
Gymnastics	Gymnastics	Gymnastics	Gymnastics	Gymnastics
Dance	Dance	Swimming / Dance	Dance	Athletics
Swimming / Gym	Swimming / Gym		Swimming / Minor games	Swimming / Minor games
Games	Mixed group games	Mixed group games	* Football Rugby Netball Hockey	* Cricket Rounders Stoolball Tennis Padder Ten
Games				

Note: *11–12 years – these games will be played at mini/junior level.

12–13 years – these games will be played in 'near-adult' form.

11–13 years – for these age ranges winter games will be played as single sex games. In the summer all games can be mixed except for cricket.

Swimming/— – indicates the alternative activity if swimming doesn't take place.

It is hoped that these timetable arrangements are sufficiently flexible for a minimum amount of time to be lost when bad weather affects the outdoor programme. It is recognized that the flexibility will be governed to some extent by the availability of the outdoor facilities. Unfortunately, at this moment of time, there are schools which are unable to provide five periods a week for each class. It is hoped that they will not cease in their endeavours to ultimately achieve this ideal. However in the meantime adaptations to the programme must be made. Teachers should ensure that the balance of the programme is maintained and guard against giving more time to their own interests at the expense of others.

FACILITIES

Facilities and equipment will considerably influence the degree to which any programme of physical education can be implemented. These need to be in line with the children's ever growing physical needs.

Indoors: Two separate indoor spaces are required.

1   Gymnasium/sports hall, with the largest floor area possible, fitted with suitable gymnastic and games equipment. This area will have maximum use in a 3/4 form entry school for gymnastics and games activities. For a new purpose-built middle school it is recommended that consideration be given to the provision of dual purpose sports halls as part of a community project.

2   General purpose hall – this will be required for dance and games activities during wet weather.

Changing accommodation: Rooms fitted with showers for both sexes should be sited, so that they can serve both indoor and outdoor facilities. Staff changing rooms will also be required.

Outdoors:

1   Hard-surfaced area. This should be provided so that it will allow rectangular areas of 110′ × 60′ to be accommodated. It is desirable that not only netball and tennis/padder tennis court markings are present, but that there is also a coaching-grid ideally 32 yards × 54 yards (a 36 block grid, 8 yards × 6 yards). The versatility of such a grid in defining playing areas provides for the teaching of skills and minor games. A blank wall would be an additional asset for ball practices.

2   Playing field area. A combination of grass and hard porous surfaces are required with the appropriate pitch markings as required. For athletics, track markings and jumping pits will be necessary.

Conclusion

We end where we began, convinced that physical education is a vital and integral part of education making an essential contribution to the overall development of the child. In terms of physical education, these are critical irreplaceable years, for the child's learning and interest capacities are at their peak. With their insatiable appetites for all forms of physical activity and skill, maximum use must be made of these middle years to ensure that fundamentals are established, otherwise it will become increasingly difficult for the child to make further progress or make up the deficiencies as he grows older.

Balance is our key word. The balance of physical education within the whole curriculum ensures an unbiased development of the 'whole' child. The balance of the elements within the physical education programme itself, ensures the harmonious development of mind and body within this area of the curriculum. This balance is achieved by the teacher deliberately setting out to ensure that skill is acquired, that knowledge is gained and that every effort is made to create positive attitudes towards life. This will best be done by providing a variety of teaching situations and learning experiences which recognize that both direct skill teaching and more open-ended learning situations have their appropriate place.

The teachers are the key to the child's success. Their aims and objectives must be clearly established. Their skill in observation and analysis of each learning situation and their ability to accurately evaluate the programme they present are essential if purposeful learning is to take place. Above all, they must seek to maintain the excitement, enthusiasm and lively interest of the children throughout these years, so that when the time comes to move on, their appetites are not lessened and they look forward to the future with eager anticipation.

References

B.A.O.L.P.E. (1973) Physical Education in the Middle School *Bulletin of Physical Education* 9, 6

DES (1967) *Children and their Primary Schools* (Plowden Report) HMSO

DES (1973) *Physical Education in the Primary School* HMSO

OBERTEUFFER, T. (1945) 'Some contributions of physical education to an educated life' in Paterson and Halberg, *Background Readings for Physical Education* New York: Holt, Rinehart and Winston

ROSS, A. M. (1971) 'The middle years of schooling' in Schools Council Working Paper No. 37 *Physical education 8–13* Evans/Methuen Educational

RUSSELL, J. (1965) *Creative Dance in the Primary School* Macdonald and Evans

Useful further reading

B.A.O.L.P.E. (1975) *The Education and Training of Secondary Physical Education Teachers* B.A.O.L.P.E. Working Party Report

B.A.O.L.P.E. (1975) *Training in Physical Education for Primary Teachers* B.A.O.L.P.E. Working Party Report

KNAPP, (1966) *Skill in Sport* Routledge and Kegan Paul

SCOTTISH EDUCATION DEPARTMENT (1975) *Physical Education in Secondary Schools* Curriculum Paper 12 HMSO

SCHOOLS COUNCIL (1971) Working Paper No. 37 *Physical education 8–13* Evans/Methuen Educational

Athletics

MCNAB, T. (1972) *Modern School Athletics* University of London Press

Dance

MCKITTRICK, D. (1972) *Dance: Schooling in the Middle Years* Macmillan

Games

A.E.N.A. (1968) *An Introduction to Netball in Junior Schools* A.E.N.A. obtainable from A. C. Pearce, 51 Morden Avenue, Mitcham, Surrey

A.E.W.H.A. (1973) *Hockey for junior secondary age group* obtainable from A.E.W.H.A. 45b Doughty Street, London WC1

E.M.B.A. *Mini-Basketball Handbook* E.M.B.A. obtainable from K. G. Charles, Greneway School, Garden Walk, Royston, Hertfordshire SG8 7JF

GARDNER, D. (1971) *Soccer* Jackdaw Publications No. 104

GIBBON, A. and CARTWRIGHT, J. (1972) *Teaching Soccer to Boys* Bell and Sons

KIRBY, G. (1972) the teaching of games in the middle years of schooling *Bulletin of Physical Education* 9, 4

K.T.G. *Batinton* (Know the Game) Wakefield Educational Productions

R.F.U. (1973) *Better Rugby*, Rugby Football Union

WISE, W. M. (1969) *Activity in the Primary School: Games and Sports* Heinemann

Gymnastics

BUCKLAND, D. (1969) *Activity in the Primary School: Gymnastics* Heinemann

MAULDON, L. and LAYSON, J. (1965) *Teaching Gymnastics* Macdonald and Evans

Swimming

A.S.A. (1974) *The Teaching of Swimming* Educational Productions

2.2 Adventure activities for the middle years child: a practical comment

Jan McKechnie

Until recently the stage at which outdoor activities were introduced to children had been firmly fixed at the adolescent level. Educators had seen this stage as a time when patterns of adult behaviour are being established, and the physical and mental development of the average adolescent has reached a stage which enables him to cope with the stresses involved in adventure education. With the raising of the school leaving age particularly, programmes of outdoor activities have appeared in the curriculum, sometimes unfortunately for the wrong reasons, seeming rather to occupy than to teach with a real purpose. Consequently in these circumstances any possible value has been lost.

Presumably the prime objective for introducing outdoor activities within the school curriculum at all is to provide the young person with a competent working knowledge of the basic skills of a particular activity, combined with a sense of enjoyment of the environment in which the activity takes place. One would hope that, armed with enthusiasm and correct basic training, he would want to continue his interests after leaving school. If this is to happen, the following factors need to be present in any programme devised by the school:

1 Enthusiastic, enjoyable and comprehensive introduction by those qualified and experienced in outdoor education;
2 Retention of interest through a full, varied and challenging programme;
3 Provision within the wider community for continuity of activity and enthusiasm.

The first factor should be present in all cases but unfortunately it is not, for too many secondary schools, for example, have assumed that outdoor activities can be conveniently inserted into the curriculum to pad out the extra year at school in order to keep the unwilling out of the classroom. The idea itself does not lack merit, but a seemingly total lack of thought and apparent lack of concern has pressurized inexperienced teachers, sometimes unqualified, into taking pupils canoeing and climbing. This was apparent recently when I was involved in assessing candidates for the British Canoe Union Senior Instructors Award, a qualification recognized by the Department of Education and Science. I was horrified at the unacceptably low standard of performance and attitude of some teachers presenting themselves as prospective instructors. Perhaps it is even more worrying to realize that for a considerable length of time before the examination they must have been introducing the activity to young people. This not only puts the children at very real risk but also, in the event of mishap, the teachers themselves. In Colin Mortlock's (1973) words:

> Adventure education is the presentation of meaningful challenge to individual pupils, within a framework of safety, in order to give them deep personal and social awareness. The situation provided will involve them on mental and emotional, as well as physical, planes, with interdependent balance a necessity for success. Skills are taught appropriate to individual abilities as the tools with which to overcome any problems they encounter.

Assuming, then, that the teacher is qualified, has engendered enthusiasm in his pupils and has secured time for outdoor activities within the school timetable, he needs money for equipment and transport if the programme is to progress. If these are readily available, perhaps most important of all he needs the sympathetic support from his colleagues because invariably some of his erstwhile duties will fall on them while he is out of school. But there still lies the question of continuity within the community. This, at present, is not well developed. Climbing, canoeing and sports clubs are there to be used, but not in every part of the country and not many of them favour the younger age group, most of them preferring a more mature membership. Youth organizations contribute a great deal but the most exciting recent innovation has been the setting up of community sports centres where family participation is encouraged. Taking the problem as a whole, though, there is at present no real link with what is being done in school and what is available within the community. Young people, having experienced fun, enjoyment and adventure at school, generally want to go on participating but too often their interest wanes after one or two rejections from the adult world.

Outdoor activities for the younger pupil: some constraints

I want to argue here that we can begin outdoor activities with children of younger age groups than has been thought practical in the past. Obviously certain activities such as mountaineering are beyond the mental and physical ability of young children but it can never be too early to guide them towards a lasting appreciation of their environment and a positive attitude towards each other and their leisure. For several reasons, there is a danger of attempting to overjustify the inclusion of outdoor activities *within* the school curriculum. Outdoor education in many people's minds means work that some teachers do with children out of school time, in the same way that physical education staff are invariably expected to manage school sports teams after school and at weekends. There seems to be an extraordinary sense of guilt concerned with adventure, freedom and enjoyment in education. Academic considerations are obviously central but they are only half of total education, for education for the whole person means for leisure as well. If, as one hopes, activities will eventually be continued in leisure time, then enjoyment combined with a controlled element of fear must be the pivot on which an adventurous pursuit revolves.

If a school decides to become involved it has to determine its commitment. Once a programme has been introduced its success or failure depends on the degree of involvement by staff. In this case the formal timetabling of an activity should be seen as a logical introduction to facilitate progression. A comprehensive programme requires a combination of the following time usage: school-based in school time (within the formal curriculum); school-based out of school time (weekends, etc.); and school-organized in holiday time (expeditions away from local areas). In this situation a major problem is one of staffing. Because of the demanding nature of outdoor activities, young pupils need more individual attention; also large numbers are not conducive to the peace of the countryside. To ensure safety, continuity and progression, more than one person needs to be involved. However enthusiastic they may be, demands on time and energy are very heavy in this area of education and they must have the practical support of colleagues and, most important, the wholehearted support of the headteacher. In an attempt to overcome this problem, or at least to provide assistance for the individual teacher, a number of local authorities have appointed secondary school-based specialists. Their aim is to coordinate programmes, not only in the school in which they are based, but in neighbouring schools as well so that resources of manpower and materials are pooled and a wide range of activities covered. It would appear timely to have this facility extended to include primary schools.

Another factor is that safety considerations demand that there must be adequate financial backing to any venture. Progression within an activity means that sophisticated equipment is necessary and this is expensive. For example, children should not be taken into mountains unless they all have boots and waterproof outer clothing. Risks through poor or inadequate clothing cannot be taken where children's lives are concerned. There is a need for every local education authority to establish its own equipment and instructional centre, staffed by experienced teachers, to which individual schools have access to both specialist equipment and expertise. This would avoid the apparent necessity for duplicating and jealously hoarding expensive items in separate schools which tends to happen too often at present. Advice and practical assistance, readily available, would greatly advance the attitude with which outdoor education is approached and raise the level.

Whilst the groundwork of outdoor activities must be laid within the school, if it is to be of lasting value, use must be made of established residential centres with specialist staff. Although these centres have evolved from various sources, all have one aim in mind – to promote outdoor education. Those centres most relevant to the eight to thirteen year old age group are those provided by the local authority, and those controlled on a professional basis such as the Youth Hostels Association. If the school staff are sufficiently experienced, then unstaffed adventure centres, often set up by local youth administrators, are an economic proposition. There are several of these in the West Country, for example, which usually provide bunkhouse-type accommodation and cooking facilities.

If the ideal situation attained, every local authority would have enough centres for every child within that authority to experience a residential course in outdoor activities, both at an introductory and a more advanced level of attainment. As it is, in authorities where there is an established centre, each school is allocated one booking per year allowing it to send perhaps only twenty to thirty children from the whole school. However, for those who are fortunate enough to benefit, it is evident that there are certain guidelines which must be followed by teachers in order that the children obtain optimum value from such a course. To begin with, a visit to a centre should be seen as being the culminating experience of work done throughout the school year. This is not always so and in consequence centre staff expertise is often spent on such work as basic map reading which could have been introduced at school. The result is that the surrounding countryside cannot be used to its fullest extent because the children are not equipped with sufficient basic skills to do so. In addition, a concentrated course of perhaps one week's duration excites a great deal of enthusiasm and sense of achievement which very soon wanes if there is nothing to continue with or refer to on return to school. The use of a centre should be complementary to the scheme of things, not the scheme itself.

On a course at a centre the child's whole living structure is changed. Parental restrictions and guidance are exchanged for those concerned with safety and comfortable communal living. For the first time, perhaps, he has to share a bedroom where he learns that if he wants any consideration from others, he must show some towards them. He must look after himself and be prepared to do his share of domestic duties. Very often the enormity of this experience on a young child is overlooked. In addition to this, he is subjected to the excitement and adventures of group experiences in unfamiliar surroundings and with people he doesn't know. The impact of this very often makes the depth of experience greater. On the adventure and activity side, the scope will probably be very much wider than that offered in school. Resident centre staff are not hampered by a school routine or other teaching commitments. They will have accumulated a wealth of local environmental knowledge and their approach will often vary considerably from that of the school-based teacher. Equipment and specialist clothing will be available and of a good standard. All this combined provides both visiting children and staff with admirable opportunities for furthering knowledge, stimulating new interests and thoroughly enjoying themselves.

It is essential that school staff accompany their children to the centre. Within the centre itself, school staff will usually be responsible for supervising any domestic duties that the children are asked to do and generally looking after the children's needs. Young children need a reassuring link with the world they know when everything else is strange. If this important side of a centre's existence is run smoothly by the school staff, far more effort can be put into the instruction side. No instructor at a centre feels very sympathetic towards a group or its staff if they are repeatedly involved in what should be the school staff's duties while the offenders rest in the staffroom. Unfortunately, it is very often said that centre work would be very much easier if school staff did not accompany their children. From my experience I would not subscribe to that point of view. From both the children's and the teacher's point of view, a residential course can be a unique experience. For once, the teacher can stand away from his children and observe without having total re-sponsibility for their welfare. Hidden qualities and abilities very quickly emerge and both children and staff learn a great deal about each other as people over a prolonged, informal length of time. In this respect, one incident will always remain in my mind, involving a very heavy, ungainly lad. Whilst of Billy Bunter proportions, John was timid and withdrawn. His classmates were normal, capable individuals concerned mainly with themselves, as most children are. This day it was pouring with rain and the ground was a quagmire. Having watched John fall down on the pathway and dissolve into tears several times, I was surprised to see the amount of concern and practical assistance given by those around him. Not only that, some of them appointed themselves his guardian for the day with the result that John finally reached the summit of a climb. The look on the lad's face and the resulting change in his whole outlook, defies explanation. He no longer fell, he guided others up 'his climb', and he became a valuable member of the group. How much more knowledge of those children was revealed to the accompanying teacher.

The selection of suitable outdoor activities for young children
There is nothing worse than a rigid instructional approach to children. Very clearly adventure education requires the sympathetic presentation of a flexible programme, taking into consideration two very important factors. First and most important is the children themselves and their capabilities; their age, physical and mental readiness for learning a particular skill and the degree with which they are able to cooperate as group members. Secondly, the school locality must be examined in a realistic manner to ascertain its suitability for adventurous activities. Age, physical and mental development will, to a large extent, dictate the type of activities that can be offered to young children. He certainly cannot cope with the prolonged mental concentration and endurance required in a two-hundred-foot rock climb although physically he may be very capable. I have seen a five-year-old girl still full of energy after the extremely long hike to the top of Scafell and back from the Langdale Valley. Children in a group are in a different situation because they will not have total responsibility taken for them; indeed, it is not desirable that they should if it is to be a learning situation. To children anything new and challenging involves an element of fear and can be termed adventurous; a definition which gives a very wide scope to the teacher.

The basis of all outdoor work is being able to use a map and a compass and this can never begin too early. Making maps and plans of the local environment, following a route while travelling in a vehicle, recognizing map symbols and then actually going out and finding the landmark will soon build up a real working knowledge of maps and their relevance to the land. An excellent and comprehensive book which can greatly aid the teacher in this respect is John Disley's *Map and Compass Way: Orienteering* (1971). It comprises a teacher's book with accompanying children's copies and is readily available. Generally speaking, the adolescent seems to regard map reading as a chore; to children it is adventure in itself. They take great pride in recognizing signs and symbols and very quickly learn to find their way around. A logical progression of this basic school-based work is to venture further afield for lowland walking expeditions using Youth Hostels or unstaffed adventure centres as bases. On a recent expedition along the eighty miles of the South Downs Way with ten children aged eleven to twelve, it was not necessary for me to do any serious map reading. The children insisted on doing it themselves, having undergone a comprehensive and obviously enjoyable introduction at school.

Camping deserves a special mention. Training for this at an early age can be quite adventurous enough in itself. A large amount of basic work can be covered in schools, for example, lighting stoves, cooking, the art of sleeping and living in a tent and general camp organization. At eight or nine years of age, if the experience is new, camping should be taken as an activity in itself combined with the main emphasis being placed on environmental appreciation. We are asking the child to cope with too much if camping is used as a means of taking part in another taxing activity too soon in his career. When and if he finally does come to use camping to facilitate canoeing or climbing in remote areas, sound training will have been given to him. If, on the other hand, he goes no further, we will at least have introduced him to the enjoyment of sharing the environment and giving him the experience in the skills with which to do so.

Schools should beware of introducing activities which are more suitable for older children; for example canoeing and archery require heavy financial outlay and the equipment is rather restricted in its use in that it must be child-sized. Even if children can use adult equipment, they may soon become bored and exhausted. Interest is not easily maintained if no degree of skill is attained. If the individual child is really enthusiastic about this kind of activity at this age, he can be guided towards reputable activity clubs or youth organizations who will help him. A recent development in several local education authorities is to combine parties from all middle schools in their area to take part in skiing trips abroad. Parents are being persuaded to part with large sums of money in order to send their offspring to Austria and Switzerland to experience a new sport. There is no denying that such a trip can be a valuable experience for a young child but taking into consideration the expense involved and the lack of continuity available in this country, it is not a realistic proposition. If an artificial ski slope is available then the situation is slightly different. However, I would prefer to see children guided towards using their own environment in a creative way rather than being introduced to expensive and exotic sports largely out of their reach.

I think that rock climbing is a possibility in the middle years. A short time ago, being firmly convinced that it wasn't, I undertook to teach elementary rock climbing techniques to several small groups of nine and ten year olds. They proved themselves thoroughly capable and enthusiastic, able to take pride in correct rope handling and technique, provided that they were receiving almost individual attention. The staffing ratio here needs to be one adult to a maximum of two children if any degree of success is to be achieved. Older children have a greater degree of self reliance and fewer adults are necessary.

If the scope of activities seems somewhat limited for this age group it is worth looking at adventure material provided by the local environment. With careful planning in the use of relevant skills, technique practice can be achieved at a micro-level which will prove a real asset in preparation for later stages. For example, a rocky seashore can be used for artificial courses involving crossing boulders and rocks systematically; wooded areas for finding the way by map and compass, simple orienteering courses; and tree climbing using rock and rope techniques; streams for crossing and traversing without getting wet, and using a stick as a probe; and night walks to give the child the experience of familiar territory at an unfamiliar time of day. Almost every area provides opportunities for imaginative use. If it doesn't, then it is possible to create them artificially. Assault courses can be constructed consisting of ropes and man-made objects such as old tables, gymnastic equipment, etc. It is not *what* is used that matters but *how* it is used. But it must be remembered that because only a tree is being climbed it is just as painful to fall or potentially as dangerous as climbing a rockface. Safety must be a keynote at all times.

Perhaps the most exciting realization concerning outdoor activities is that individuals are not competing on an academic or even a physical basis. In fact, they are not competing at all. A bright child may grasp the fundamental requirements of a skill more quickly but there is no guarantee that his eventual level of achievement will be any greater than that of his slower classmate. Physically the most uncoordinated child, having suffered agonies in the school gym, suddenly finds that it is not a matter of comparison with others any more. With guidance, through adventure, he comes to accept his own limitations, very often overcoming them altogether. Children with handicaps such as severe hearing deficiencies need not be excluded. They often make superb pupils. Undisturbed by noise their technical level of achievement, in rock climbing for example, goes far beyond their physically more fortunate companions. Concentration and real determination to overcome their disability makes the activity an invaluable medium. Teaching certain activities to partially hearing children does have its special problems, such as remembering to give all instructions facing the group to facilitate lip reading. Facing the challenge of an unfamiliar outdoor activity can be a great leveller where children from a variety of backgrounds and conditions can start to learn the lifelong process of coming to terms with themselves in the company of their peers and under the guidance of caring adults.

Some implications for the teacher

Teachers should never undertake to teach an adventure activity unless they hold the relevant teaching awards and/or have sufficient experience. Although it is common for teachers to learn new skills on the job so to speak, to do so in the adventure field is potentially dangerous for them and the children. Any amount of enthusiasm cannot take the place of sound practical knowledge. In any adventure activity there are certain prerequisites for safety and correct instruction. These cannot be learnt solely from books or secondhand experience. Teachers must beware of being pressurized by the children or the school to undertake an activity for which they are not qualified. In the event of a fatal accident, it is they who will have to stand in front of the coroner and justify themselves and it is they who will suffer both for the death/injury of the child and their own revealed incompetence. After all the publicity concerning the accidents that have happened in mountain areas, I found it incredible recently in North Wales to count 360 young children accompanied by ten adults in one group. Apart from the fact that they were dressed inadequately, this is just not a safe number. In another instance, while on Hellvellyn in a thunderstorm, we unavoidably became involved with a mountain rescue operation because the leaders of a group were attempting to drag an unconscious boy suffering from exposure to the foot of the mountain. If we had not intervened, he would very likely have been dead on arrival; as it was, he was in a coma for three days. There is no excuse for this type of irresponsibility. Accidents obviously do happen to the most highly qualified, but their training and experience give an even chance of avoiding more serious consequences because they should be able to cope with the situation.

To gain qualifications costs well-spent time and money. All the recognized outdoor activities have their own training schemes and awards. The DES recognizes a large number of these as satisfactory evidence of experience. The Sports Council holds courses in all activities at their centres. Many local education authorities run their own inservice training schemes and are often prepared to give financial assistance. If teachers are unqualified, then their main sphere of interest must be in the very valuable groundwork of map and compass work and the introduction of children to the use of the countryside. If they wish to extend their range of activity beyond their capabilities, it is possible to enlist the help of the area representative for a particular activity. The British Canoe Union, for example, appoints Area Coaching Organizers, who will make it their responsibility to contact a suitable instructor to help. Enquiries among parents often produces surprising results. There are many resources available if teachers have the time to look for them. Below is a table of some activities most suitable for the 8–13 year old child, the necessary equipment and some indication of the level of proficiency necessary for those in charge of the activities.

Map and compass work

Equipment:	1/50,000 Ordnance Survey maps. At least enough for one to two children. Silva compass, ideally one each.
Group size:	Immaterial; the smaller the better.
Knowledge:	How to use a map and compass; familiarity with local countryside.
Essential qualifications:	None.

Lowland walking

Equipment:	Maps and compasses, comfortable shoes, warm clothing and waterproof outer clothing. First-aid box.
Group size:	One adult to maximum of twelve children, preferably smaller.
Knowledge:	How to use map and compass; familiarity with country code; familiarity with area. Safety training.
Essential qualifications:	None.

Outcrop rock climbing

Equipment:	Ropes – one rope per three children; karabiners and slings, enough for the number of climbs set up; training shoes, plimsolls or rockboots. First-aid box. Climbing belts.
Group size:	For young children, one adult to maximum of three; ideally 1:2.
Knowledge:	Working knowledge and proficiency in rope handling and safety techniques. Knowledge of particular outcrop being used. Climbing experience and ability.
Essential qualifications:	None as yet.

Hill walking

Equipment:	Map and compass each, rucksack each, boots, warm clothing, gloves and hat, windproof and waterproof outer clothing, food, polythene bag; the leader must also carry rope, emergency food and clothing, flares, whistle, sleeping bag, stove and brew kit. First-aid box.
Group size:	One adult to maximum of six, preferably less.
Knowledge:	Mountain leadership training and experience.
Essential qualifications:	Mountain Leadership Certificate.

Canoeing

Equipment:	Canoe and paddle each; lifejacket each; spray deck, wetsuit tops, windproof anoraks, plimsolls. The leader must carry polythene bag, sleeping bag, spare food, means of making hot drink. First-aid box.
Group size:	One adult to maximum of eight. Preferably two adults to each canoe group.
Knowledge:	Proficiency training of British Canoe Union.

Essential qualifications: Senior Instructor Award of British Canoe
                          Union.

The field of outdoor activities and education for young children of eight
to thirteen is still in its embryonic stage. For a number of years,
environmental studies have been seen as the only appropriate type of
outdoor work for younger children. One enquiry at a youth hostel recently
produced the information that over five thousand children of this age had
used the hostel as a base for this form of work in 1973. The pattern was
repeated in other centres. Scout and Guide organizations, for a long time,
have been involved with adventure activities. In the next few years it is
hoped that more middle schools will also begin to see themselves as
important innovators; that teachers will see the necessity of gaining
adventure qualifications and that more children will benefit as a result.

Appendix 1

A check list of equipment for a group of 11/12 year old children on a seven
day expedition along the South Downs Way.

Expedition: Walking the South Downs Way (eighty miles) from
                  Buriton to Beachy Head.
Time available: Seven days.
Group: Five boys and five girls from top year of a middle school
                  accompanied by one member of staff and one female
                  instructor from an Outdoor Pursuits Centre.
Accommodation: Youth hostels
Kit list: Rucksack, canvas and nylon anorak provided by
                  Outdoor Pursuits Centre; sheet sleeping bag, night-
                  wear; changes of underwear, toilet requisites; towel;
                  indoor shoes; change of clothes for the evening; two
                  shirts or blouses; two pairs of trousers; three jumpers
                  (two thin, one thick); four pairs wool socks; hat and
                  gloves; strong, comfortable boots or shoes; one pint
                  water bottle; drinking mug; tin of plasters; small
                  amount of pocket money.
                  The rucksacks, when packed, should not weigh more
                  than twenty to twenty-five pounds.
                  Leader also carried: Stove and brew kit; sleeping bag;
                  large comprehensive first-aid kit; polythene bag and
                  spare food.
Planning: 1 At least three months beforehand, work out the cost
                     and add on one pound for additional expenses. (It is
                     very easy to return excess money after an expe-
                     dition but virtually impossible to ask for more.)

2 Select children.
3 Send out consent forms to parents with full details of the proposed expedition, including qualifications of those in charge. Forms should be returned at a set date with the money at least two months beforehand.
4 Plan exact route and book accommodation.
5 Send out itineraries to parents; better still, hold parents' .meeting.
6 At least one month beforehand, start familiarizing children with the equipment they will be using and do some practice walks.
7 On the trip itself, a list of the children's names, addresses and telephone numbers should be carried in the event of illness.
8 On return, check all equipment and write letters of thanks to hostel wardens and others who have given help.
9 Follow up children's enthusiasm.

Appendix 2: Training organizations and qualifications available for teachers

Mountaineering
Mountain Leadership Certificate (Summer)
Mountain Leadership Certificate (Winter)
Mountaineering Instructor's Certificate
Mountaineering Instructor's Advanced Certificate
Full details from The Secretary, Mountain Leadership Training Board, The Sports Council, 70 Brompton Road, London sw3 1ex

Canoeing

Proficiency Awards:	Inland Kayak
	Inland Canadian
	Sea Kayak
Advanced Proficiency:	Inland Kayak
	Sea Kayak
	Canadian
Coaching Awards:	Senior Instructor
	Coach

Details from The General Secretary, British Canoe Union, 70 Brompton Road, London sw3 1ex

Sailing
rya National Elementary Day Boat Certificate

RYA National Intermediate Day Boat Certificate
RYA National Advanced Day Boat Certificate
Coaching Awards: Instructor
                    Senior Instructor
                    Coach/Examiner
Details from Royal Yachting Association, 5 Buckingham Gate, London
SW1E 65T

Appendix 3: Some adventure organizations

Canoeing
British Canoe Union, 70 Brompton Road, London SW3 1EX

Mountaincraft
British Mountaineering Council, Crawford House, Precinct Centre,
    Manchester University, Booth Street East, Manchester M13 9RZ
Mountain Leadership Training Board, Scottish Sports Council, 4 Queens-
    ferry Road, Edinburgh EH2 4PB
Ramblers Association, 14 Crawford Mews, London W1

Orienteering
British Orienteering Federation, 3 Glenfinlas Street, Edinburgh

Sailing
National Schools Sailing Association, Education Officer, County Hall,
    Chichester, Sussex
National Sailing Centre, Arctic Road, Cowes, Isle of Wight
Sail Training Association, Ferndown, Hill Brow, Liss, Hampshire

Skiing
National Ski Federation of Great Britain, 118 Eaton Square, London SW1

General
Camping Club of Great Britain, 11 Lower Grosvenor Place, London SW1
Youth Camping Association of Great Britain and Ireland, 25 Longmoor,
    Cheshunt, Hertfordshire

References
DISLEY, J. (1971) *Map and Compass Way: Orienteering* Blond Educational
MORTLOCK, C. (1973) *Adventure Education and Outdoor Pursuits* Five Arches
    Press

Useful further reading
There is a vast amount of literature on different aspects of adventure

activities. This varies from the autobiographies of eminent 'adventurers' to books of a technical nature. The different training organizations and the local authorities could best guide teachers to the most suitable literature available for their own situations. The books listed below are those of a more general nature.

MORTLOCK, C. (1973) *Adventure Education and Outdoor Pursuits* Five Arches Press

DES (1972) *Safety in Outdoor Pursuits* HMSO

DES (1971) *Education Pamphlet No 58: Camping* HMSO

SCHOOLS COUNCIL (1972) *Out and about: a teacher's guide to safety on educational visits* Evans/Methuen Educational

2.3 Art in the middle years: a curriculum planning model

Seymour Jennings

This article is an attempt to clarify the reasons for teaching art, and to present methods whereby the content of the subject can best be revealed and organized within the school curriculum. The central thesis of the article is that art, frequently perceived as a bewildering mixture of unrelated and contradictory theories and practices, can be organized within identifiably different and rationalizing conceptual categories for the purposes of curriculum development. The categories suggested are those forged by the mental effort of aestheticians, educators and philosophers interested in the visual arts. Many other subjects have long-standing precedents and traditions in which underlying logical structures have greatly facilitated the rational planning of teaching and learning experiences. Art as a curriculum subject has developed in no such way. Frequently it has been presented as a ragged and piecemeal collection of odd and conceptually unrelated activities: teaching and learning strategies adopted for its engagement are a logician's delight, full of the most entrancing ambiguities and inconsistencies.

The present approach, in no way novel within subjects built on a more rational platform, is a new and challenging departure within art education. The view is explicitly expressed that art, like many other subjects, is susceptible to rational discussion and development: if it contains conceptual uncertainties (which it most certainly does) these are neither greater nor smaller than the uncertainties met in all subject areas. In order to expand this view, the present article is divided into six main headings, each of which contributes to the total approach being formulated. The first two of the six headings introduce the value of art as an adult cultural experience, and its corresponding value within the experience of children. The remaining four headings develop the curriculum planning model. For those who wish to research issues raised within the text in greater depth, a final section is included that suggests further reading. The main headings are:

1 Art in the adult world

Art in the adult world

Art is an area of concern in its own right, where theories and skills specific to the subject operate, and also an aspect of the general cultural climate. Works of art, and the theories of art, draw sustenance and intellectual impetus from their relations with other cultural activities, and also contribute to those activities. To understand the concepts embodied in art is to understand the cultural heritage, and therefore better to comprehend the attitudes European man has adopted towards his perceptions of the world, the values he has placed on his environment, and on his peers. Art in the general environment, as opposed to the environment of the school, is represented by the numerous activities of making works of art, the theories associated with their meaning, the works themselves, the history of the works, and the techniques adopted for their manufacture. These functions interweave and overlap to form the complex of activities subsumed under the misleadingly short and simple global term 'art'. These diverse but related activities can be presented more succinctly by the division of 'art' into the pictorial principles of art, the practice of art and the theories of art.

· Pictorial principles of art are generally rules of pictorial layout which help the artist to achieve a desired result. Examples would be principles of ornamentation and principles of perspective. Principles are applied to give coherence to a work and to guide its production, but not precisely to define the form the work shall have. Principles similarly exist in disciplines other than art, and have in common the capacity to guide the subject's elements through a rich but related set of possible permutations. Examples from other subjects would be principles guiding the playing of games, principles guiding the use of grammar, or the principles guiding mathematical operations. Certain doctrinaire stances have emerged in recent years that question the value of recognizing the existence of such principles, and have directed that such principles should not consciously be used in image making.

The practice of art represents the stage of manufacture in which principles and theory meet, and where skill is exercised in the making of material objects. A craftsman may undertake this stage in that he may

76

work to a prepared formula without understanding the theories that generated the plan on which he works. An artist is usually one who has mastered both theory and practice and displays invention in relating the two.

Theories of art are generally theories that dictate the ends towards which the pictorial principles of art shall be directed, and hence the types of images that are made and the meanings which are to be conferred upon these images when completed. Theories of art have varied from those of the widest compass, that have attempted to establish works of art as concrete representations of universal values, to the more narrowly conceived contemporary speculations that avoid metaphysical flights and embrace the comparative security of psychological, sociological, or linguistic explanations. Theories of art may motivate the form of the work, and hence exist anterior to the production of the work, or may endeavour to define the meaning of the work retrospectively. Theories of art are as numerous as theories in other fields, and, like theories from other fields, have become displaced by other theories that provide apparently wider and deeper insights into the nature of the problems they seek to confront.

The value of art within the curriculum

The potential value of art within the curriculum closely parallels the value of art within the wider setting of adult society, and these values are examined within the writings of authors that have investigated the foundations of the subject. The diversity of theories reflects the range of attitudes that may be brought to bear on the meaning, scope and limits of the activity. The misplaced desire to formulate one central, absolute, or 'essential' theory of art on which to base the school curriculum has, regrettably, diverted attention from the recognition that accumulated insights afforded by differing viewpoints offer to the curriculum planner a wide range of rich and varied philosophical approaches. It is unfortunate that concerted attempts to utilize theoretical concepts have centred around strictly limited sets of choices.

The traditional and current value placed on art within the curriculum is found reflected in the choice of subject matter placed before the children for development. The subject matter is gleaned, in turn, from images executed by artists working with concepts related to a theory of art. Where the theory of art engages concepts that are paralleled within an accepted theory of education, the aims and beliefs in one field are seen to be implicit within the other. Activities examined and pronounced of value in the study of art are therefore, if felt to be of value for other reasons within a generally accepted theory of education, almost certain to receive serious consideration as possible curriculum material. The introduction of such material is finally affected by conscious appraisal and understanding, or, more frequently, by the corporate and passive acceptance of longstanding and unexamined precedents. Art within school has become accepted by educators as an activity that possesses significance transcending its importance as an academic subject. The educator's view of art may be almost totally divergent from the concept of the activity held by the adult artist, critic or historian. This regrettable schism is caused by art in education being attributed to a limited spectrum of values exclusively associated with the concept of psychological maturation. The complacent acceptance of limiting theories of psychology and self-expression has hindered the recognition of the need for further development. A long overdue critical reappraisal of the scope and limits of the psychological and aesthetic theories that have generated the now traditional concepts of child art might serve to liberate teaching from the strict and limiting confines of the popular ideological and doctrinaire view. A revival of interest in theories that do not over-emphasize self-expression would greatly encourage the development of new and experimental curricula. Where aesthetic theories explore ideas that have parallel concepts within the theories of science, mathematics and other arts, stances are revealed that could be valuably utilized to enrich the teachings of art in new and productive directions. Regrettably, the value of such congruences has only been explored by a limited number of well-read and mentally alert visual artists. Experimental curricula, based on the system explained within this article, could well reveal the form that such new and productive schemes would have and the contents they would encompass.

The curriculum planning model: filters A, B, C, D, E – the selection of curriculum experiences
The selection of curriculum experiences is achieved by filtering a pool of material constituting the total scope of the subject for those aspects of the subject suitable for introduction into an education programme. The filters designed to achieve this end are placed to screen out certain suggestions as impractical, and to allow passage to others that may be successfully developed. As the filtering process proceeds, an increasingly large body of knowledge is rejected. The material remaining is then introduced into the next major filtering phase, designated 'The presentation of curriculum experiences'. At this stage in the planning, material constituting the final material for curriculum development is isolated, and strategies for its presentation are actively considered. In the major phase designated 'The selection of curriculum experiences' five major filters operate. These five filters sift material sequentially from the initial pool constituting the scope of the subject. The filters are:

The pool: The pool of material constituting the scope of the subject.

Filter A: Theories of art dictating the grouping and categorization of elements drawn from the pool.
Filter B: The selection of activities where art is to be presented and developed as a subject in its own right.
Filter C: The selection of activities where art is to be presented and developed as a core subject within interdisciplinary studies.
Filter D: The selection of activities with the learner as main factor.
Filter E: The selection of activities with the resources of the school as main factor.

The following describes the filters in greater detail:

THE POOL: THE POOL OF MATERIAL CONSTITUTING THE SCOPE OF THE SUBJECT
The pool consists of the theories of art, the practice of art and the pictorial rules of art. The pool is organized into rational groupings by the application of the different theories of art that are, in themselves, members of the pool. These theories of art are represented diagrammatically on page 92 as a set of filters at A.

FILTER A: THEORIES OF ART DICTATING THE GROUPING AND THE CATEGORIZATION OF ELEMENTS DRAWN FROM THE POOL
Categorization and organization of material drawn from the pool is effected by examining the pool material for congruences with certain theories of art. Where such congruences occur, material is withdrawn from the pool and added to the collection of material that is logically subsumed by the theory of art under review. Understanding of these theories of art is critical in the logical selection of material from the pool. Regrettably, these categories represent the area of knowledge most lacking on the part of curriculum planners at all levels of the education services. The theories of art marshalled in order to categorize the material available within the pool are as follows:

Art as communication
Art is conceptualized as a means of communicating through the unique symbolism of the image, hence art is posited as a communication system fundamentally different from communication systems based on speech or the written word. It is asserted that visual descriptions of the world are able to describe aspects of the world that cannot be described by other means. It follows that visual communication has a unique and irreplaceable role in our culture, and that inability to utilize this means of recording and describing, or to understand the ways in which it is used by others, severely hampers both the passive and the active aspects of intellectual life. A curriculum developed from this basic set of assertions would be concerned to teach art as a form of language.

Art as imitation
Art is conceptualized as a means of undertaking a searching examination into certain properties of objects, and of recording the results of such a search in terms of images. Through the act of imitation, a careful and prolonged examination of the object under scrutiny is involved. Such an act will involve the viewing and handling of the object to be imitated. Careful viewing and handling will ultimately result in an understanding of, and a sensitivity towards, the object that could not be stimulated by a rapid and cursory examination. The making of images, undertaken as an ongoing corollary to the handling of objects, will involve the endless re-assessment of initial impressions. The qualities sought when imitation of an object is undertaken are usually those of surface, and include the colour, form, texture and pattern.

Art as self-expression
Art is conceptualized as a means of externalizing mental states through the act of image making. A similar conceptual framework existing within the dramatic arts asserts that mental states can be externalized through the use of movement and voice. Art as self-expression emphasizes the unique communication a person can make by forming images freely and without professional training. The belief in the possibility of self-expression has become associated with the belief that the results of such self-expression will bear resemblance to the visual work of primitive peoples, and will become structured in design through the operation of an instinctive capacity for creative organization. This particular theory, having no one specific exponent, nor being treated in one definitive treatise, is entwined in both educational and aesthetic beliefs that can be traced back to the writings on 'natural man' expounded by Rousseau, and further promoted in the writings of numerous authors since. Self-expression is also linked to the concept of 'empathy' that asserts that if self-expression is practised with honesty, the sensations that promoted such activity will naturally be understood by others. The self-expressive artist is therefore said to be able to establish contact and communicate his inner state to others.

Although self-expression is the dominant theory of art to have common educational currency, its basic tenets have been much attacked in recent years. It is questioned why an untutored person can produce images of charm and value when working in the visual arts, but can only produce vulgar and excruciating sounds when practising self-expression in music. The concept of self-expression probably provides certain valuable insights into the early stages of the creative process, but fails to account for the ways in which these initial stages become subsumed within the cultural themes of the society in which the artist matures. It may also be a philosophical stance based on truths pertaining to other branches of the arts, such as drama, that has been erroneously extended into the visual arts in order to account for phenomena beyond its realms of concern.

Art as craft

The products of art, rather than the conceptual theories underpinning the making of art objects, are immediately obtrusive, and are therefore taken as evidence that art is a manufacturing, rather than a conceptual activity. Interest is therefore directed to the techniques of art rather than to its subject matter. The fact that early visual education in this country was particularly intended to raise the standard of design and manufacture, rather than promote a knowledge of the fine arts, both generated and entrenched this view. The concepts of education as a means of providing skilled artisans still pervades (perhaps rightly) the educational climate. The craft element in education has followed a chequered career, aspects of it being pursued in their own right as metalwork and woodwork, whilst experience in other materials, such as stone or clay have been pursued for no logical reason in art studies. These demarcations have recently become more fluid. Time is allowed during art activities for experiment with all materials, but emphasis is placed on making 'art objects'. In the traditional woodwork and metalwork areas both wood and metal continue to be used mainly to make 'craft objects'. The enumeration of the endless redrawing of the boundaries between the two subjects of art and craft is a study in its own right, and beyond the scope of the present article.

'Art as design' is perhaps the lastest restatement of the 'art as craft' theory, and is often the fall-back position of educators and curriculum planners who are unaware of other conceptual frameworks, and who therefore classify art as a technical, rather than a conceptual, activity. It is perhaps the case that a new area of concern, named perhaps 'manual dexterity' or 'tool handling' could emphasize and develop the teaching of craft techniques. Such a radical departure might perhaps serve to confront educators with the need to classify the relation between manual and conceptual skills. A curriculum developed from the concept of art as craft would be concerned with teaching art as a set of manufacturing techniques.

Art as cultural history

Art is conceptualized as an activity, the history and practice of which alerts the students to the role of art in cultural affairs. As a distinct subject, the study must incorporate a study of the traditional branches of the visual arts, the main trends and sequences to develop, the main schools, the main exponents, the main practitioners, the techniques current in different periods and the ideas that have been expressed.

As a study in its own right, art reveals the manner in which the arts have affected the concepts and the actions of men, and the ways in which the subject has cumulatively influenced the visual appearance and attitudes manifest in the times in which we live. Studied as a distinct subject, art requires to clarify its role as an activity affecting both the general environment and the current attitudes of individuals to the meanings placed on that environment. In an interdisciplinary role, art becomes studied as an aspect of cultural history, and the interpenetration, influence on, and influence from, other intellectual disciplines and activities current within a specified cultural setting are examined. A curriculum developed from the concept of art as cultural history would be concerned to teach art as an aspect of the cultural climate, and to study the influence of art on, and within, the cultural setting.

Art as imagination
Art is conceptualized as the making of images that represent imagined states of affairs. Images are put together that represent situations that might, but do not, exist, or are made to represent bizarre and impossible situations. Most imaginative art falls into the latter category. Through the exercise of the imagination, objects and situations are presented in new and unexpected configurations. Imagination in the visual arts is often exampled in works of visual fictions, where creatures and architecture unseen in the waking state are represented, or where spiritual and moral values are represented as tangible beings. Imaginative art is often related to imaginative writing, and the richest and strangest examples of imaginative art have often been produced as an adjunct to works of literature. The illustration of imaginative ideas derived from religious texts furnish some of the most spectacular examples of imaginative painting, and sculpture.

The relationship between word and image, and the mutual reinforcement one by the other is obscurely recognized in the injunction that children should base paintings on written descriptions. It should be noted that imaginative art utilizes images seen within normal experience, and, therefore, if a fund of images is not possessed by the artist, the artist cannot mix these images in the unexpected configurations typical of imaginative art. A curriculum developed from the concept of art as imagination would be concerned to present art as a means of producing images that suggested new and unusual worlds to the viewer.

Division of the theories into component parts
Six theories of art have been proposed from which to select. The list may legitimately be lengthened, but for the purposes of this brief article the number has been consciously restricted. The use of theories of art illustrates one possible set of categories that may be used to guide the intelligent selection of material from the pool. Other categories of a less theoretical

nature could equally well be used, such as the lives of individual artists. In this instance the writings on the artist, the writings by the artist, the works of the artist, the pictorial principles found in the artist's work, the techniques and processes used by the artist, and the skills necessary for the personal exploration of the visual interests of the artist, would all be appropriate areas of research. The same procedure would apply if a particular school of painting, or attitudes towards art in a specified historical period, were researched.

After selection of a specific theory of art, it is necessary to isolate those aspects of the subject that may be developed within the compass of the chosen theory. The practice of art, and the theory of art that dictates the practice, are both to be included. Material that is congruent with the chosen theory is set aside for possible inclusion in a developed curriculum. Material that is not related to the ideas proposed within the theory is rejected. Such a sorting process leads to the selection of materials specific to the particular theory chosen by the curriculum planner. The selection of experiences from the pool can best be achieved by grouping the material under headings. A suggested set of headings to guide the selection of material from the chosen theory is as follows:

Writers: Isolate and list the main writers that are associated with the theory.

Writings: Isolate and list the main artists that have exploited the main tenets of the theory, or whose works have contributed to the emergence of the theory.

Works: Isolate and list the main works of art that are illustrative of the theory.

Pictorial principles: Isolate and list the main pictorial principles used by the artists associated with the theory. Such principles may be methods of achieving feelings of distance, lighting effects, patterning methods, use of colour, organization of elements within the picture and so forth.

Processes and techniques in existing works: Isolate and list the main processes and techniques used in the works existing.

Processes and techniques to be mastered: Isolate and list the processes and techniques that must be mastered if the ideas explored by artists working within the compass of the theory are to be explored in similar ways as part of the planned curriculum experiences.

Such an analysis of the material from the pool may take many weeks of patient work on the part of a team of planners and, when completed, will represent a body of related and coherent knowledge. This body of knowledge will then require further sorting in the light of other constraints before finally emerging as material for inclusion in the planned curriculum. The process is shown schematically in the appendix to this article, but for clarity only instruction on how to amass material is given. The material accruing from implementing the instructions is necessarily omitted.

FILTER B: THE SELECTION OF POSSIBLE CURRICULUM EXPERIENCES IF ART IS TO BE PRESENTED AS A SUBJECT IN ITS OWN RIGHT

If the subject is to be developed as a subject in its own right, the material collected under the divisions of the theory given previously becomes the material that is forwarded for further development. Material amassed within this filter is then passed directly to filter D for processing, missing filter C.

FILTER C: THE SELECTION OF POSSIBLE CURRICULUM EXPERIENCES IF ART IS TO BE PRESENTED AND DEVELOPED AS A CORE SUBJECT WITHIN INTERDISCIPLINARY STUDIES

If the subject is to be developed in an interdisciplinary setting, the aspects of the subject that intersect other subject areas must be discovered. The total possible content, revealed in filter A, must be sorted to display intersections with the other subjects to be studied. Such a sorting represents a research programme of considerable magnitude. In order to make the sorting exhaustive, cooperation would be necessary between subject experts. The results of the sorting would not represent the final curriculum, but would, in turn, be subjected to further processing by passing through further appropriate selection filters.

Filter C is best conceived as a collection of related filters, ranged one behind the other. Each of the filters making the group is a subject filter, and may be labelled mathematical studies, geographical studies, historical studies, and so forth. Material selected from the pool, and organized by the application of the selected theory of art, is then passed through the subject filters. If, for example, the study of pottery is listed as a technique or process that is related to the theory of art selected, then aspects of pottery that can be examined by scientific means (the chemical constituents of clay, the physical changes affected by firing) are listed as a technique or process that is related to the subject filter of scientific studies. The study of art would therefore intersect with the subject areas of science, and at that nexus material suitable for introduction into an interdisciplinary examination of the area would be revealed. The process is shown schematically in the diagram on pages 92–98. The limited space available within the diagram restricts entries within the filter to instructions on how material is to be amassed, rather than displaying the content of the amassed material itself.

FILTER D: THE SELECTION OF POSSIBLE CURRICULUM EXPERIENCES FOR DEVELOPMENT AND PRESENTATION: THE LEARNER AS FACTOR

The proposed content, established as a result of earlier selection procedures, must be further examined in order to establish its suitability for presentation to the learner. A number of factors guide such an examination, and these factors cumulatively seek to reveal a satisfactory congruence between the practical and conceptual accomplishments of the learner, and the demands made by the study of the proposed material. Crudely, the work should be neither too easy nor too difficult, but must, ideally, exist in that difficult-to-define hinterland where skills are developed, but stress is not imposed. In the study of the creative arts both conceptual and practical skills are required. Decisions as to whether children are able to understand and respond to certain conceptual and practical demands may be answered empirically – that is, by knowing through experience what constitutes a reasonable expectation of performance within a particular school. Theoretical expectations, on the other hand, must be based on psychological theories and research findings that give general guidance in performance and attainment for learners within specific age or maturity groupings.

Broadly, the learner's conceptual understanding of the material to be studied rests on comprehension of text, spoken word, or demonstration, used either singly or in combination. Evidence of understanding rests on the learner's ability to translate such forms of communication from one mode to another, and to use these forms in interpersonal contacts. Manual skill is necessary for the transformation of the studied theoretical concepts into images. Skill in many diverse practical processes may be required, but the ability to handle materials with delicacy and firmness will be fundamental within all techniques. Such skill is only developed slowly, and a carefully devised programme will have concentrated on developing knowledge of materials and techniques over many years. Regrettably, in art education, such a carefully structured approach is the rare exception rather than the common rule.

FILTER E: THE SELECTION OF POSSIBLE CURRICULUM EXPERIENCES FOR DEVELOPMENT AND PRESENTATION: THE RESOURCES OF THE SCHOOL AS FACTOR

Each area of content that remains a contender for inclusion in the completed curriculum is brought forward from the previous filter. These areas selected for potential inclusion must now be considered against the resources of the school. These corporate resources can be selected more easily if broken down into a number of discrete divisions. Where the resources of the school can match the academic and practical requirements of the area of study, material for study can go forward for further development. In some instances, where the resources of the school cannot meet the exact needs of the planner, it will be necessary to consider a hierarchy of possible resources that are sufficient to establish some of the main points that the teacher will be attempting to convey. The resources of the school can be divided into the school organization; the school staff; studio, workshop, and teaching spaces, and media resources. Where necessary, these basic divisions can be further refined and subdivided. School organization affects the way in which the staff in the school make contact with the children. School organization may be flexible, placing the teachers in command of the time allocated to activities; or rigid, thereby dictating the pace at which various subjects are studied. School organization will also dictate whether or not children will work with one member of staff, or several, and whether the children's studies will be subject centred, or interdisciplinary.

School staff will possess a number of different skills, and may be able to work productively within one particular subject area, whilst feeling unhappy in others, or may have skills within a number of subjects. In the middle school a number of staff may be subject specialists, whilst another group may have experience in teaching in a wider range of subjects. Information on the range of skills and interests represented on the staff is of vital importance to the curriculum planner, and is of even greater value within an educational system in which staff change their appointments frequently. Without the ongoing collection of such information, continuity within educational programmes becomes difficult or impossible to maintain.

The availability of studio, workshop and teaching spaces will dictate the extent to which children may pursue the practical implications of their areas of study. Media facilities will affect the range of teaching techniques that may be adopted. The environment will furnish children with the opportunity of seeing original examples of the many images that have been the object of their studies, and of studying images that can, in turn, enrich their personal work. In the study of art and the techniques of art, it is essential that children are exposed to the most skilful examples within their particular field of concern. Visits may be arranged to see artists or craftsmen working on the production of various types of images, and to see such works in their intended settings, and original forms. The film or the coloured photograph can only be a substitute for personal contact with works of art, or the techniques adopted for their manufacture.

The curriculum planning model: filter F – the presentation of curriculum experiences

Material passed by the previous filters is material that is both suitable for the intellectual maturity and manual skill of the learner, and is capable of presentation and development within the structure and organization of the school. Techniques adopted for the final presentation of this material to the learner must again be suitable for the level of intellectual and manual attainment reached. Broadly, curriculum experiences will be presented by utilizing the various basic symbol systems that have evolved and have been developed in our society, and that have subsequently been interrelated in a bewildering set of permutations to record and communicate our acts. Such systems can broadly be divided into visual systems, verbal systems and written systems. Clearly, no system is of use in the presentation of curriculum material if the learner is unversed in its use and is unable to understand how ideas are articulated within its domain.

Visual symbol systems are exampled by the act of demonstration, the use of moving films, photographic slides, drawings, maps, paintings, diagrams and so forth. Verbal systems are exampled by speech – either from a living speaker, or from recording devices. Written systems utilize the well-known alphabetical notation, and are exampled by books, articles and so on. Selection of the most appropriate system will be dependent on the particular teaching point that is to be made. Technical processes are perhaps best shown by exemplification, where the teacher demonstrates the processes using real materials and real equipment. Below this ideal exists a hierarchy of other choices, starting with the colour film with recorded commentary, down to diagrams on the chalkboard. Concepts are often best examined verbally, through the mutual discussion of ideas expressed in a shared test. However, every act of presentation confronts the designer of the curriculum with special problems and difficulties that can only be resolved through working experience within the categories of communication listed. The designer of the creative arts curriculum should make special note of the need to expose children to works of art, as reproductions of any art form never reveal the sensitive qualities of craftsmanship seen in the original. Special provision should be made for visits to the studios of practising artists, to museums, galleries and so forth.

The curriculum planning model: filter G – the guidance of the learner within the planned curriculum experiences

Guidance is effected by assisting the learner in the ongoing comprehension of the presented material, and showing how it is possible to translate the concepts discovered into visual images. Comprehension is a complex of various mental activities, and the list of such activities furnished by Bloom (1956) in the *Taxonomy of Educational Objectives* suffices if slight amendments are made to the standard use of the categories given. Translation involves the restatement of the comprehended material in different symbolic modes. Such translation within the visual arts leads to the creation of images to mirror the conceptual ideas posited in other symbolic languages. Translation can also entail the restatement, in different visual terms, of concepts already presented within a visual language.

Comprehension
The guidance the learner receives during the experience of the planned curriculum will be dependent upon the learning objectives of that

curriculum. The original divisions of the field of enquiry into the writers, artists and techniques applicable within the field of the chosen theory of art can only prove partly satisfactory. It is further necessary to establish, within the context of these categories, which aspects of knowledge are to be sought from the texts examined, the images viewed and the techniques attempted. The division of knowledge given by Bloom will unexpectedly furnish the curriculum planner in the creative arts area with objectives that can be sought to good effect by the learner. The use of such objectives will invite much criticism from various quarters that can neither be anticipated in detail, nor met with in the scope of this article.

The analysis of the presented material will involve the discovery and recording of the terminology, conventions, trends and sequences, classification and categories, criteria, methodology, principles, theories and processes met with in the writings, works and techniques of the theory chosen for analysis and development. Comprehension over this wide spectrum of categories is established by involving the learner in an analysis of the material in the light of the listed categories. If, for example, the learner has read a selected text in order to discover the specific facts pertaining to a technique of painting, the complete text has to be analysed by the learner in order to extract from it the particular aspect of information that it contains. Other material presented within the text must be purposely neglected or ignored as irrelevant to the needs of the learner at this particular juncture. It is also vital for the curriculum planner to recognize that the visual image is as susceptible to analytical examination as the printed text.

Translation
Material that has been studied can only be shown to have been comprehended by the learner communicating such understanding to the teacher. In normal circumstances such communication will generally involve some degree of translation. If, for instance, the material has been studied in the form of a written text, it may be translated into speech in response to the requirements of the assignment given. The learner exhibits understanding through the re-presentation of issues in a symbol system different from that used to articulate the studied area.

In the visual arts programme the concept of translation from verbal systems into visual systems is central. Guidance in the qualities such visual images should display is dependent upon the particular reasons given for the making of the images. The learner may be investigating means of showing movement in painting, the effect of colour juxtaposition, patterning, or any one of the tremendous number of such possibilities. Clear guidance in the translation of verbal statements into visual images can only be given by a teacher fully aware of the scope and limits of the creative arts as a subject. Traditional art lessons have often been typified by children being presented with amorphous and ill-defined objectives that cannot lead to a conceptual grasp of the issues of the subject.

The emphasis placed in the visual arts programme on the translation of verbal or written statements into images should not mislead the planner into believing that there is no room for the reciprocal translation of ideas expressed in visual work to statements made in the more general modes of writing and speech. Written work, calculated discussion and directed reading are all innovations that are long overdue and of central relevance in improving the quality of practical work. Success in the arts requires that the practitioners be versed in both manual skill and conceptual understanding. The translation into writing or words of conceptual ideas originally existing in visual terms only will encourage general understanding of the aims of personal art work, and will enrich the attitudes which the learner reveals and explores.

The curriculum planning model: filter H – amendments to the programme in the light of experience

A programme in the visual arts, however well planned, will inevitably reveal both strengths and weaknesses when put into operation. It is necessary to record these strengths and weaknesses during the running of a programme, and to amend the teaching of that programme in order that the successful aspects of the course can be maximized and the unsuccessful rejected or redesigned. Particular difficulties face the curriculum planner. The limitations placed on the study of the visual arts by a restrictive pedagogical philosophy has meant that most children (and, as a corollary, most adults) have little idea of the scope and limits of the subject. Within the school, the subject has traditionally been taught as a series of unrelated experiences that may, or may not, make an intelligible pattern to the learner. The absence of shared aims, standards, terminology and knowledge has generated a situation in which it cannot be assumed that age can be any guide to the knowledge the learner possesses. The need to design and test rational programmes to cover the entire spectrum of the learner's career in school is clear. The emergence of such programmes would stimulate much-needed research and development designed to meet certain educational situations and, as a corollary to such activity, would clarify the aims of the subject, the content of teaching programmes and the assessment of results.

Useful further reading

Theories of art discussed within this article are treated in greater detail by:

GOMBRICH, E. H. (1966) *The Story of Art* Phaidon
COLLINGWOOD, R. G. (1938) *The Principles of Art* Oxford University Press
OSBORNE, H. (1968) *Aesthetics and Art Theory* Longman
GOODMAN, N. *Languages of Art* Oxford University Press

Pedagogical theories linked to theories of art are treated in detail by:

MACDONALD, S. (1970) *The History and Philosophy of Art Education* University of London Press

Artists central to the development of the visual arts, and their primary writings are listed by:

GOMBRICH, E. H. (1966) *The Story of Art* Phaidon

Pictorial principles, and their influence on the appearance of images, are examined by:

GOMBRICH, E. H. (1966) *The Story of Art* Phaidon
GOMBRICH, E. H. (1960) *Art and Illusion* Phaidon
WHITE, J. (1957) *The Birth and Rebirth of Pictorial Space* Faber

Techniques and processes are examined adequately by a very large number of authors. The following are authoritative works:

Drawing
RUSKIN, J. (1857) *The Elements of Drawing and Perspective* Dent

Painting
HILER, H. (1937) *The Painter's Pocket Book of Methods and Materials* Faber

Sculpting
MILLS, J. W. (1965) *The Techniques of Sculpture* Batsford
MEILACK, D. and SEIDEN, D. (1966) *Direct Metal Sculpture* Allen and Unwin

Ceramic work
RHODES, D. (1958) *Clay and Glazes for the Potter* Pitman
RHODES, D. (1968) *Kilns, Design, Construction, Operation* Pitman

Printmaking
DANIELS, H. (1971) *Printmaking* Hamlyn

Photography
HORDER, A. (1971) *The Manual of Photography* Focal Press

General reference on the visual arts and a first rate bibliography is given in the invaluable:

OSBORNE, H. (ed.) (1970) *Oxford Companion to Art* Oxford University Press

Coherent approaches to art education are given in:

LOWENFELD, V. (1970) (Art as self-expression) *Creative and Mental Growth* Collier-Macmillan

ROWLAND, K. (1964) (Art as design) *Looking and Seeing* Ginn

JENNINGS, S. (1973) (Art as imitation) *Art in the Primary School* Heinemann

References
BLOOM, B. S. *et al* (1956) *Taxonomy of Educational Objectives: Handbook I The Cognitive Domain* Longman

Appendix: The curriculum planning model

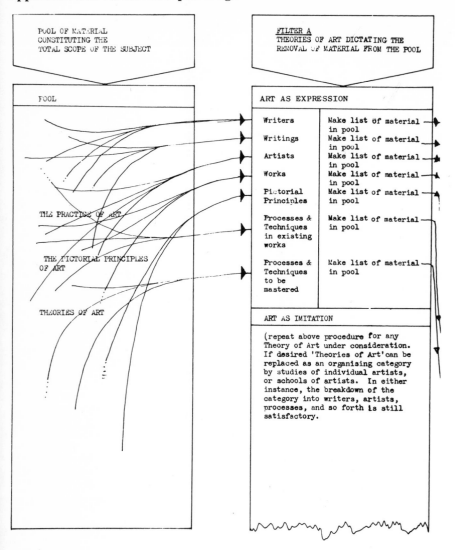

POOL OF MATERIAL
CONSTITUTING THE
TOTAL SCOPE OF THE SUBJECT

FILTER A
THEORIES OF ART DICTATING THE
REMOVAL OF MATERIAL FROM THE POOL

POOL

THE PRACTISE OF ART

THE PICTORIAL PRINCIPLES
OF ART

THEORIES OF ART

ART AS EXPRESSION

Writers	Make list of material in pool
Writings	Make list of material in pool
Artists	Make list of material in pool
Works	Make list of material in pool
Pictorial Principles	Make list of material in pool
Processes & Techniques in existing works	Make list of material in pool
Processes & Techniques to be mastered	Make list of material in pool

ART AS IMITATION

(repeat above procedure for any
Theory of Art under consideration.
If desired 'Theories of Art' can be
replaced as an organising category
by studies of individual artists,
or schools of artists. In either
instance, the breakdown of the
category into writers, artists,
processes, and so forth is still
satisfactory.

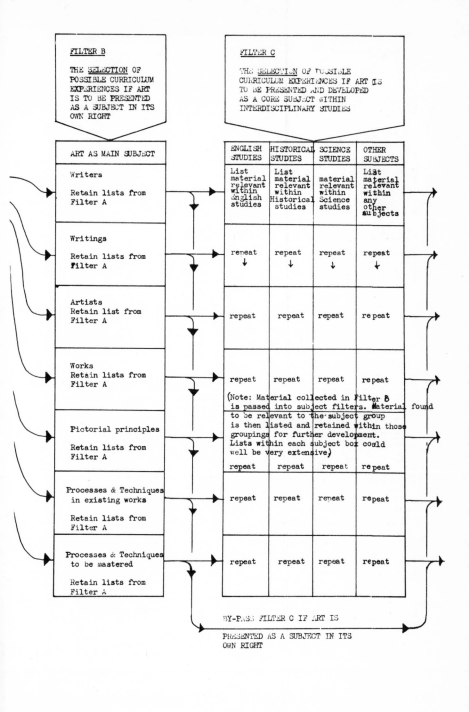

FILTER B

THE SELECTION OF POSSIBLE CURRICULUM EXPERIENCES IF ART IS TO BE PRESENTED AS A SUBJECT IN ITS OWN RIGHT

FILTER C

THE SELECTION OF POSSIBLE CURRICULUM EXPERIENCES IF ART IS TO BE PRESENTED AND DEVELOPED AS A CORE SUBJECT WITHIN INTERDISCIPLINARY STUDIES

ART AS MAIN SUBJECT	ENGLISH STUDIES	HISTORICAL STUDIES	SCIENCE STUDIES	OTHER SUBJECTS
Writers — Retain lists from Filter A	List material relevant within English studies	List material relevant within Historical studies	material relevant within Science studies	List material relevant within any other subjects
Writings — Retain lists from Filter A	repeat ↓	repeat ↓	repeat ↓	repeat ↓
Artists — Retain list from Filter A	repeat	repeat	repeat	repeat
Works — Retain lists from Filter A	repeat	repeat	repeat	repeat
Pictorial principles — Retain lists from Filter A	repeat	repeat	repeat	repeat
Processes & Techniques in existing works — Retain lists from Filter A	repeat	repeat	repeat	repeat
Processes & Techniques to be mastered — Retain lists from Filter A	repeat	repeat	repeat	repeat

(Note: Material collected in Filter B is passed into subject filters. Material found to be relevant to the subject group is then listed and retained within those groupings for further development. Lists within each subject box could well be very extensive)

BY-PASS FILTER C IF ART IS PRESENTED AS A SUBJECT IN ITS OWN RIGHT

COMPREHENSION OF CONCEPTS	THE POSSESSION OF MANUAL SKILLS
Can the learner be expected to understand the concepts dealt with by the writer chosen? If yes, list.	
Can the learner be expected to comprehend the concepts expressed within the texts? If yes, list	Can the learner be expected to translate the concepts expressed in the texts into personally produced art-works? If yes, list
Can the learner be expected to understand the concepts expressed by the artists chosen as representative of the theory of art under examination? If yes, list.	
Can the learner by expected to comprehend the textual or verbal explanations necessary to interprete the meanings within the artists works? If yes, list.	Can the learner be expected to comprehend the textual or verbal explanations of the concepts underlying the artists work in order to use these concepts in personally produced art-works? If yes, list.
Can the learner be expected to comprehend the textual or verbal explanations necessary to explain the pictorial principles used in the making of the artists works? If yes, list.	Can the learner be expected to translate the pictorial principles within the artists works to serve as principles to guide personally produced art-works? If yes, list.
Can the learner be expected to comprehend the demonstrations, textual, or verbal explanations necessary to describe the processes and techniques used in the manufacture of the works? If yes, list.	Can the learner be expected to master the processes and techniques used in the manufacture of the artist's works and to use those processes to serve the needs of personally produced on a similar theme? If yes, list.
Can the learner be expected to comprehend the demonstrations, textual, or verbal explanations necessary in the descriptions of processes and techniques used in the re-exploration of the theory?	Can the learner be expected to master the processes of manufacture seen in the artist's works, and to use such procedures in the production of personal works based on the artist's themes? If yes, list.

THE SELECTION OF POSSIBLE CURRICULUM EXPERIENCES:
THE SCHOOL RESOURCES AS FACTOR

SCHOOL ORGANISATION	SCHOOL STAFF	STUDIO, WORKSHOP & TEACHING SPACES	MEDIA FACILITIES
List timetable arrangements necessary to implement programme	List school staff that are able and available to implement programme	List the studio, workshop, and teaching spaces necessary to implement programme	List the media facilities necessary to implement programme
Repeat procedure for all categories listed	Repeat procedure for all categories listed	Repeat procedure for all categories listed	Repeat procedure for all categories listed
(Note: Can the school organization support the timetabling of the material for presentation? If yes, list needs. If no, reject the material.)	(Note: are the necessary skills and interests represented on the school staff to implement the programme? If yes, list staff. If no, reject material)	(Note: Do the necessary equipment and the necessary teaching spaces exist to implement the programme? If yes, list needs. If no, reject material.)	(Note: Do the necessary media facilities exist for the presentation of material? Are the necessary books available? If yes, list. If no, reject material.)
repeat procedure	repeat procedure	repeat procedure	repeat procedure
repeat procedure	repeat procedure	repeat procedure	repeat procedure
repeat procedure	repeat procedure	repeat procedure	repeat procedure

FILTER F		
THE PRESENTATION OF CURRICULUM EXPERIENCES: METHODS OF COMMUNICATION AS FACTOR		

VISUAL PRESENTATION	VERBAL PRESENTATION	TEXTUAL PRESENTATION
List appropriate means of presentation:- Available films, slides, videotape recordings, television presentations, demonstrations, visits, etc	List appropriate means of presentation:- Prepared talks, seminars, group discussions, recordings, reading, etc.	List appropriate means of presentation:- Books, selected extracts, articles, prepared work-cards, periodicals, etc.
repeat procedure	repeat procedure	repeat procedure
repeat procedure	repeat procedure	repeat procedure
repeat procedure	repeat procedure	repeat procedure
repeat procedure	repeat procedure	repeat procedure
repeat procedure	repeat procedure	repeat procedure
repeat procedure	repeat procedure	repeat procedure

FILTER G

GUIDANCE OF THE LEARNER WITHIN THE PLANNED CURRICULUM EXPERIENCES

COMPREHENSION	TRANSLATION
List the main learning objectives seen as the desirable outcome of the learner's analysis of the presented material: is the learner intended to achieve:-	List the main ways in which the learner is to show understanding of the presented material through its translation into a form that allows its communication to others: is the learner intended to:
Knowledge of Terminology: Example: the names of components within a pottery glaze, the names of processes, the names of tools, and so forth.	Show, during discussion, that the elements of knowledge studied have been understood, and can be translated into a form that allows their verbal communication.
Knowledge of Specific Facts: Example: dates, events, persons, places, related to a study of the arts.	
Knowledge of Conventions: Example: familiarity with the visual conventions adopted to convey informations and attitudes.	Show, by the submission of written scripts, that the elements of knowledge studied have been understood, and have been translated into a form that allows their written communication.
Knowledge of Trends and Sequences: Example: understanding of the history of the development of a particular theme in the visual arts.	Show, by the production of visual images, that the elements of knowledge have been understood, and have been translated into a form that allows their visual communication.
Knowledge of Classifications and Categories: Example: ability to place the work of an artist within an accepted style, school, or period.	Show, by the submission of material that utilises skills in all the previously listed translational categories, that the elements of knowledge studied have been understood, and have been translated in a form that allows their communication.
Knowledge of Criteria: Example: ability to state criteria by which an artist is said to fall within a particular style or school.	
Knowledge of Methodology: Example: knowledge of the techniques involved in printmaking.	
Knowledge of Theories and Structures: Example: knowledge of the various Theories of Art that exist.	

FILTER H

AMENDMENTS TO THE PROGRAMME IN
THE LIGHT OF EXPERIENCE

AMENDMENTS

Isolate the strengths and weaknesses
of the material in the light of
experience. Amend the selection and
presentation of material accumulated
from filters A to F. Amend the
teaching strategies of filter G.

repeat

repeat

repeat

repeat

repeat

repeat

2.4 Aspects of drama in the middle years curriculum
(with special reference to language activities through drama)

Kate Fleming and John Miller

The place of drama in schools has too often had an unfortunate ring. It has been synonymous with 'playing about in the hall in the lunch hour', children being allowed to run wild, wet Friday afternoon activities, and, 'What on earth am I going to do with them after play? I know, I'll do a bit of drama, they like that!' It has been either the domain of the specialist, or a fill-in lesson where the children make up plays, a rest period, or chaos as the case may be, dependent on the interest and skills of the teacher and the children. Alternatively, drama has been seen as suitable largely for the less able child for it appears to possess the staff of life for the remedial classes, in both its therapeutic qualities and non-examination subject status. This may be the case, but the fallacy that drama in education is merely for children of low ability has existed for too long, and as one of the most forceful and exciting teaching media available in the school curriculum, it should be considered more carefully for all abilities, not only by the specialist, but by every teacher. Opportunity is so often lost, for the use of instinctive skills are sadly restricted in the normal process of education, and it is vital that these natural abilities are rediscovered in the development of the child's school experience.

Every child needs the opportunity to use the differing qualities of information and experience that he acquires consciously and sub-consciously, from school, home and environment, through a controlled, directed method. He must use his imagination in a practical, definite way, as he must his body, his voice and his intellect. He needs constant guidance in the ways in which he can expand his concentration, his senses must be kept alive by use, and his ability to work with others in controlled situations can't be expected just to happen, in a haphazard way; it has to grow and develop through this careful direction. The depth of involvement required in this work cannot be demanded on a wet Friday afternoon when there seems nothing 'better' to do. It has to be planned for.

If we consider drama to be one of the methods of teaching which extends the whole range of personal development – physical, emotional, social, imaginative and intellectual; and if we consider the past development of the child, his growth through play, his powers of discovery and exploration, we should be able to use both to advantage in our teaching. Many of the problems and frustrations that we encounter in teaching stem from the artificial attitudes we adopt and the skills and abilities of the children which we choose to ignore. We tend to impose on children an adult concept of learning and expect them to respond. If we recognized the worth of the child and his opinions, and the need for us to explore his way of learning and his individual perspective of the world, and communicated our recognition of the value of his individuality to him, then our task as teachers would not be much easier, but it would manifest itself in more meaningful relationships, reducing wastage of effort from both staff and children. Education for the complex society in which we live demands the need to discover ways in which teachers can simulate situations which will encourage children to stretch out and use themselves to the best advantage. This is not simply a receiving process, a tendency which many schools are inclined to instil, but more a continuous sequence of investigating experience and forms of communication. Language in this respect is possibly one of the most neglected areas in the middle years, and this need to develop articulate powers of expression has become increasingly pressing, and it is this aspect of drama teaching we wish to concentrate on in this article.

The most commonly used classroom teaching technique of question and answer can limit the development of language in many children – and fail to provide situations in which they can experiment with newly acquired knowledge through language. Unless opportunities for active oral expression can be investigated at all levels, language tends to be restricted to the written word, which can hamper understanding and obviate the efforts of teachers who try to develop oral skills. The use of drama as a teaching medium provides varied opportunities for children to use language in an exciting and experimental way, thus increasing vocabulary and developing an interest in oral communication otherwise scarcely touched in normal everyday teaching. This is not to underestimate the value of open discussion with groups or classes of children, but it must have been the frustration of all of us at some time to realize that after such a session many children had not made an active contribution. In fact they might have become bored and recalcitrant while the session followed the familiar pattern of the lead being taken by the usual bright six. We are fully aware of the value of listening and that some children benefit from being passive in discussion, but it should not end here. More should be done to ensure that all children do have the opportunity to expand their techniques of talking in a practical and valid way, for the language children use in writing is vastly different from the language they use in their areas of spoken communication.

Much has been written about linguistic deprivation and restricted language codes, very little about rectification. We tend to accept the recognition of problems as answers in themselves, often failing to incorporate possible solutions in our methods of teaching. Oral skills, for the majority of children in our care, have become at least equal in importance to written skills, but it only needs objective listening to realize that many of us use an extremely limited vocabulary. Is this because we have emphasized the written word, and allotted such a small amount of time to the how, why, when and if we use words? There is a need for experimentation into the basis of words. To provide opportunities for children to experiment with the sheer mechanics of speech in all its many forms can lead to a greater confidence and excitement in this special human attribute. The importance of the physical activity and the sensory memory involved in experimental language situations, albeit simulated, can have lasting effects on the acquisition of vocabulary and the increasing complexities of style.

The use and recognition of specific language for specialized purposes can need as much investigation as the teaching of a foreign language. This becomes apparent when children are trying to communicate their enthusiasms for a spontaneous interest, also when we try to generate debate in our day-to-day teaching. If we are to develop language activities from organized discussion, then the guidance must be extremely clear. The discussion itself must have a definite sequence. Take, for example, *Death on a live wire*, by Michael Baldwin (1973). What is the most basic point from which to start? Not, we hope, the 'What-do-you-think-of-that-poem?' approach, but a series of questions carefully structured to ensure an individualistic response from every child, gradually extending beyond their immediate experience towards personal and philosophical thinking. This can start by examining electricity itself. How is it that when we switch the electric light on the room is illuminated? What is electricity, and how is it controlled and utilized, for good and evil? What are our needs and in what ways are they satisfied by electricity? How was it discovered; will it be replaced? And so on. Who is this man in the poem? Why is he climbing up the pylon? Is he climbing up the pylon? Where has he come from? Who was he with? What was the scene just prior to the incident which brought about this situation? Who is watching? Is he an onlooker? Is he connected with the main character? Is he trying to make contact? How does it feel to be helpless in a case like this? What kind of analogous incidents can you talk about or imagine? What time of day would you say it was? How different would dawn be from midday, twilight? How does the atmosphere of nature vary, and what kind of dramatic feeling do you get from times of day, different weather conditions, and seasons? How does the pain of watching compare with the actual experience? How much value has life, and what kind of responsibilities does this entail? Who would be involved with this man's death – onlooker, doctor, policeman, man from the Electricity Board, reporter from the local newspaper, next of kin, close friends? From this discussion the children could be split into groups of six, each taking on the role of one of those involved, and encouraged to consider how these people would react. They could then be interviewed by the reporter as a preliminary exercise to establish their patterns of speech. Each group could then develop a scene in which some form of post-examination is taking place, and either record it on tape or enact it live. The writing task which follows could then cater for the ability of every child in the group, each one having had a chance to play with the language of his character, so that he can feel that he has a wealth of ideas to use. Useful literary stimuli which can be broken down in this way are plentiful. Two of which we have found particularly successful are: *Phone Call Night Time* from a play *Backbone* by Michael Rosen, published in the BBC pamphlet *Speak*, 1969–70; and an extract from *Snake Man* by Alan Wykes (1960).

An extension of this form of language stimulation can also be investigated from another starting point. We asked the children to draw, or cut out from newspaper, profiles of different kinds of people. These were placed in pairs on an overhead projector, and the children were asked to formulate a discussion based on the two images. The use of a microphone opened up the possibilities of variation in both quality, volume and atmosphere. As the profiles alternated, so the different types of speech changed. The tendency to exaggerate and pick up the cartoon-like speech alongside the comic-cuts profiles was justified by the enjoyment of the children and the recognition of an area of vocal exercise hitherto unknown. A more detailed visual stimulus can be created by building up a collage of faces cut from newsprint or magazines, which is then projected by an epidiascope. These collages can increase in complexity requiring parallel complications in speech patterns. Large life-size, faceless, cut-outs of people, reminiscent of those available in photographers' kiosks at popular seaside resorts, also provide interesting variations in the use of specific language. Each child can develop his own character and with the use of make-up and hook-on paper costumes, the permutations of conversation are endless.

After two years of constant chaos 'doing drama' at a local boys' approved school, we felt that the time had come to rethink our approach. We had used all the recognized drama teaching methods, freedom of movement leading to freedom of speech, the script, mime, dance drama, and nothing had really worked. Each Tuesday evening the session ended up with the boys fighting on the floor and generally looking like the inevitable brawl in the closing sequence of Charlie Chaplin films. We decided that we should try, as a last resort, to place the whole emphasis on words. The boys were not articulate, they seemed to find their expression through physical contact only, and it appeared that this could not be channelled. We thought that if we could provide them with the experience of discovering new forms of language, they might be able to balance physical communication with the spoken. Perhaps freedom of speech would lead to freedom of movement. We thought that the commodity nearest to their hearts was money, so that was the theme for the first 'words' experiment. The evening began by asking the boys to think of any sum of money that came to mind, and to try and visualize this in imaginative terms. From here we went through a series of very quick verbal improvisations in which they bought, sold, made, stole, gambled, won and lost, borrowed, lent and found money in many different situations, most of them well within their actual or imaginative experience. They responded well, playing out scenes with the bank manager, the bookmaker, the rich friend and the car salesman, plus many others until it was time to move them into two groups. One group took up the part of the sellers in a street market, the others as buyers, each group requiring a different type of language. Carefully we moved on asking them to form a queue waiting to go into a bingo hall. Immediately they became old age pensioners using what they considered to be the appropriate language, and playing out an imaginary bingo game with all its excitement, disappointments and triumphs, the special jargon of the bingo caller being the main feature. What would happen, we wondered, if we now placed them in a totally unknown situation requiring a highly specialized form of language, namely that of the casino. The scene began rather roughly, sounding more like a greyhound racetrack. They needed some guidance. Did it really sound like that in a smart casino in Cannes? That question was all that was needed, the scene changed to the smoky, sophisticated atmosphere of roulette, chemin de fer and baccarat; the boys had begun to use language which was completely outside their normal conversation and experience. The evening ended with an interesting sequence based on affluence and poverty, which was both moving and meaningful.

At the end of the session we realized to our amazement that the boys had worked with enjoyment and concentration for two and half hours; there had been no fighting, no aggression, and, instead of just wandering off at the end, they stayed and talked about what they had done. For the rest of that term we followed similar patterns, using various themes, food, mass media, travel, sport, advertising, illness, safety and danger, and, finally, adventure. It was in the last session that the movement that we had tried so hard to develop began to emerge easily and naturally. Previous problems did not arise, and two sequences, one on mountaineering and one on a safari expedition, were completed satisfactorily.

We continued our research into specific forms of language with college of education students who were taking part in a combined course in learning. We were part of a team, which was looking into the whole concept of the growth of language. Using verbal improvisation as the main working method, we asked the students to simulate situations in which different types of language had to be used. The imparting and receiving of information took the students into scenes at the Labour Exchange, the college grants office, the Department of Social Security, the bus depot, the Citizens Advice Bureau, a travel agency, public library and the police station. The language of persuasion as used in the techniques of buying and selling, journalism and oratory was followed by improvisation, where a controlled form of language was necessary, as in the situation where dissatisfied customers are dealt with, telephonists sort out garbled messages of emergency, and an organizer controls an unruly crowd. Parents and children in various situations investigated reprimand, and the building of a garden shed posed the problem of sorting out and solving complicated instructions. The language of rejection and enthusiasm provided talk about the acquisition of new homes, cars and pets of status. We then created scenes associated with job applications which led easily into work on situations requiring pity and concern – such as the homeless, the old, and the deprived child. In small groups the students explored sarcasm, cunning, deception and honesty; a forthcoming social event was the setting for this sequence, and afterwards they analysed the nature of their behaviour and the resulting use of language. In some of these improvisations we found that the students needed definite information as in the exercises set in the Citizens Advice Bureau, for example. To cater for this we provided cards on which were printed all the basic facts which would be needed. These the students assimilated by short periods of concentrated reading, and used as reference during the scenes. In school this information could be found out by the children themselves using a project method.

Researching for information and compiling it is not confined, however, to the purely factual. We have found that much useful language work can be done using a programme building method which combines fact, fiction and the children's own writing. One such piece of work we did used the story *The Silver Sword*, by Ian Serraillier (1968), as the starting point. The activity which followed the reading of the story to the children was the creation of a class poem which was to form the narration for our programme, which concentrated on chapter 9, 'Winter and Summer Homes'. The children suggested words which to them created the many different moods and incidents portrayed in this section. Here are a few of the contributions: survival, invention, cunning, memory, improvisation, isolation, anxiety and frustration. These were then shaped into a piece of blank verse into which we inserted dialogue, readings and sound effects, documentary evidence and music. The children selected a number of major incidents to explore in various ways. The first one was a verbal improvisation set in the Polish Council for Protection, and dealt with the frustrations experienced by the children in the story in trying to discover the whereabouts of their mother. The second insertion was designed to indicate the passing of time by using documentary evidence of the period, dovetailed with the appropriate section of the narration, which was repeated and used in different ways to sustain the personal feeling alongside the factual evidence. We gleaned a lot of information for this section from the Schools Council Humanities Curriculum Project on *War and society*. Ruth's school (the third section) was depicted by the children's own writing and extracts from well-loved stories from childhood; the obvious one to use was the Old Testament story of Daniel in the lion's den, but snippets from others were also incorporated. The fourth section put into sound memories of the days of peace, and here we used music and the children's personal recollections of security and happiness. The last section dealt with the problem of survival, including Edek's encounters with authority, his escape and subsequent disappearance, and the contents of the smuggled copies of *Biedronka*. The final presentation was taped or played alive as appropriate, and bore the qualities of both radio programme and ballad.

The importance of this activity lies in the total involvement of all members of the class, and their use of diverse forms of language, and the strong sense of identification felt by the children with the characters. We followed this up with a programme similar in pattern, but dealing with children in a factual but completely unfamiliar situation. Our starting point was an account of a mining disaster in 1833, in which five boys were trapped underground for six days and nights entirely without food. Apart from using all the techniques used in the previous programme, we also experimented with kinds of effects the voice can create alone, and with the aid of recording devices. Special vocal effects of being underground, hallucinations, physical weakness and dreams, the use of folk songs of the period and poetry were also included.

Our research into language activities with children of this age group continued with college students who were investigating not only the activities of the spoken word, but the means whereby these projects can be drawn together for final presentation. We were trying to get away from the eternal wall display and the folder, and to use a form of visual presentation which was directly linked with the sequence of language. Two experiments would appear to be worth mentioning at this stage. In the first one a student made a frame for the overhead projector depicting a child's face. She used a series of different coloured overlays which changed the atmosphere of the situation and the mood of the face. Each time the change took place a piece of literature was read aloud, and the end of each change was indicated by the shape of a hand entirely blocking out the face. All the readings were taken from novels by Charles Dickens dealing with boys: *Nicholas Nickleby*, *David Copperfield*, *Great Expectations*, *Oliver Twist* and

Christmas Carol; these were interspersed with personal writing and music. Although this was primarily developed by the student as an English teaching aid, it did demonstrate the possibilities of children presenting their own topic in this way. In the other experiments two other students were working on the theme of imprisonment, and their overhead projective image was traced on to acetate from an actual photograph of the inside of a prison. Their overlays were made up of increasingly intensive colours, and cut-outs of heads, faces and mouths, gradually built up to form a composite three-dimensional setting. This was used in conjunction with a tape of sound effects and voices bringing out the desperate feelings of isolation and claustrophobia that they imagined were such an integral part of the visual.

So far we have been concerned with language activities through drama in the classroom situation: we would now like to move beyond these confines to greater use of space and the need for children to experience the actual physical sensation of emitting sounds which do not follow the recognized pattern of communication and integrating these sounds with a movement of the body. Preliminary exercises for this activity can be seen quite clearly in the way in which we work from this extract from *The God Beneath The Sea* by Leon Garfield and Edward Blishen (1970). It is made up from isolated pieces from the chapter 'The Creatures of Prometheus':

> Prometheus shaped the clay into images of the immortal gods. His fingers grew more and more skilful as his great mind wrestled with the mysterious quest for form. His memory and imagination seemed to body forth shapes in the air, and swiftly he enclosed them in the curious clay. . . . The clay was swelling, growing. Channels were being formed within it down which the burst seeds sent crimson tears to course, nourishing, colouring and warming into life. Eyelids grew thin as gauze, flicked open to reveal strange little pools of wonderment. Lips reddened, parted on white teeth . . . and tongues began to stir under the force of mounting breath. And still they grew till their proportions were all but god-like. Everywhere in the vast room limbs were stretching, bodies twisting and hair stirring in the night breeze. At last they grew no more. The seeds had spent themselves; their task was done.

Assuming that the children have gone through a period of relaxation and concentration in preparation for this activity, they are then asked to become shapeless lumps of clay. Gradually the human form is moulded in physical form, and then imaginatively the details of features are added. Concentration is now directed on to the face, the eyes opening and seeing for the first time, then to the breathing apparatus, and the rhythmic inhaling and exhaling of breath, the mouth opens, '. . . and tongues began to stir under the force of mounting breath'. No recognizable words can be heard, even though the human form is now complete. Their next task is to stand, considering all the problems of balance and control, expressing at the same time their fears and pleasures through their ability to make sound. From a safe standing position they begin to move for the first time, as humans, discovering all forms of locomotion. Alongside this movement speech is making corresponding progress and taking on the task of describing each move in detail, until speech and movement are totally synchronized. From this kind of preliminary exercise we go on to the use of sounds and words which are directly related to movement and vice versa. That is the quality of movement associated with the onomatopoeic quality and the literal meaning of the word. For example, one group used the words 'gas tap' to accompany their movement sequence on suicide, another used the words 'circle' and 'line' in their exploration of the movement quality of those shapes.

We developed this further with a class of 8–11 year olds working on the theme of the jungle. The children used the actual words associated with their movement as a controllable sound sequence. For example, smooth, slide, slither, squirm, writhe, wriggle, wrap. They began to experiment with shortening and lengthening the words as they wished and as their movement required. The introduction of witch-doctors and explorers demanded the use of other forms of speech, that of magic for the former and emotion for the latter. The children now broke off to create the environment of the jungle in visual terms with lights, slides, costumes and masks, and all was ready for the development of the story. Story building, commonly associated with the first-school child, has a vital role to play in language activities through drama at this stage of development. It is an active sharing of imaginative ideas, which also imposes the need to use language thoughtfully, to listen critically and to select, as a group, the right word at the right moment. Our story evolved as conflict between humans and animals with the dominating influence of witch-doctor magic. The first section was the changing of the humans into animals, who then gathered at the water-hole. The arrival of the witch-doctors and the disappearance of the water-hole led to the effect of magic in the animal world. This imbalance of nature enabled the animals to utilize their human qualities, and reverse the power of evil to good. In this piece of work specific language had been integrated with the imaginative and experimental use of sounds and words. These two extracts from the follow-up writing show some evidence of the movement and vocal exploration covered in the sessions:

Twine, creep and tangle – that's the way the plants in the jungle grow.
There are things fat, high and low,
The animals which live there, walk run and creep.
Birds screech, scream and weep.

107

A gloomy endless tangle
Plants twining, curling, twisting
Turning round dead tree trunks
Creeping through the treetops . .

Having used the story-building technique and realized its enormous potential, it seemed a natural progression to take another regularly used writing task in schools, namely, poetry. We wanted to see if this device could also provide an opportunity to span the whole area of language development. This would require a definite precision in the selection of words which so far had not been necessary, so we decided to restrict the children to the use of one word only. This word – gladiolo – would have to be made to cater for the wide variety of situations into which we put them. They could treat the word in any way they chose, changing speed, shortening vowels, juxtaposing syllables, using dialect, chanting, singing, or simply making the word sound like a normal conversation. They could also use the word to create a greater onomatopoeic quality, or for any sound effect they needed. Out of the fifty different situations created, the most memorable were army recruits being taught bayonet charges by a tyrannical RSM; a marriage ceremony, followed by the reception; a local jumble sale, and an all-star professional wrestling event at the 'Roxy'. The next stage allowed the children the use of two words in some way connected, or in total contrast in meaning and sound. This exercise extended to a maximum of six words for each child to be used as appropriate to the situation in which he found himself. The formation of the groups for the next stage of development provided the children with the opportunity to select their own words, and share in the creation of a sound montage where their imaginative and vocal contribution fused into a group whole. The first attempts were untidy, but, as the children listened to their efforts on tape, the process of selection and refinement became more subtle. Movement and visual effects contributed to the rhythm of the now established poems. Finally, we placed our emphasis on individual interpretation and, using a similar formula, the children went through drama improvisation of a highly personal nature. They had to find the words which really held feeling and meaning of their imaginative situations, and then they organized them into whatever poetry form they felt appropriate. None of the children wanted to commit their oral work to paper in school, though, we understand, they did at home. Through regular experiments of this nature, however, their writing became far less rigid and showed greater skill.

Mrs Martha Gunn's Seaside Treasure Hunt is the title of a new opera for children, composed by David Gray and directed by Kate Fleming, which was performed for the first time at the Brighton Festival in 1974. It was developed during a week's workshop with children from a Brighton middle school and gave the opportunity to bring to performance level the type of experimental language work we have covered in the last section of this article. Two outstanding examples of this approach formed links between solo points in the music. In the first link, the children devised a sequence of vocal and body sounds depicting the various sounds of a large Regency kitchen, then the movements of winding, stirring, kneading, tasting and chopping were introduced in a stylized form. A zany doctor's surgery provided the scene for the second link, where the children used a series of sayings so well known in doctors' surgeries, like 'Sorry can't help you', 'Too bad, old chap', and 'Stick to the mauve pills', which they wove into a rhythmic pattern, the basic beat being endorsed by percussion instruments. It formed an integral part of the simultaneous improvisation of the doctors and patients. In these two examples, the children were being allowed to experiment with vastly differing speech activities, and it is the provision of this opportunity which leads to greater flexibility in the use of language.

To make substantial progress in this field, playing with words in unknown shape and form must take place, so that children can return to normal methods of communication with an increased sense of awareness and excitement about their language.

References

BALDWIN, M. (1973) *Death on a live wire* in *Buried God: Selected Poetry* Hodder and Stoughton

GARFIELD, L. and BLISHEN, E. (1970) *The God Beneath the Sea* Longman

ROSEN, M. (1969) 'Backbone' in *Speak* 1969–70 BBC Publications

SCHOOLS COUNCIL (1970) 'War and Society' *Humanities Curriculum Project (14–16+)* Heinemann Educational

SERRAILLIER, I. (1968) *The Silver Sword* Penguin

WYKES, A. (1960) *Snake Man: The Story of C. J. P. Ionides* Hamish Hamilton

2.5 Music in the middle years

David Gray

Music literacy

Music is perhaps the most difficult area in which to assess progress in a child's education unless he happens to be learning an instrument and taking grade examinations of the Associated Board. The inability to assess this progress leads to the frustration and failure of many teachers of class music. Several generalities must come into play here. The first, and most important, is for all teachers of this age group to realize that there is a definite swing of the pendulum away from the 'all-creative' notion of music for children. The learning of music is not basically creative but *re*creative. This is not to say that improvisation and imagination do not play a very large role in exploring music. However, it must be emphasized that the dilute application of the elementary stages of Carl Orff Schulwerk in this country has led to many teachers believing that a child's musical potential is fully realized by improvising tunes on a pentatonic scale. The most serious factor of this attitude is that too many teachers are satisfied that this is so, which leads us back to the opening of this section – progression in education. If a child of twelve is still doing nothing more than exploratory work with the pentatonic scale on a xylophone, which should more fittingly be the musical activity of a six year old, then no progress can be said to have been achieved. Many teachers have not achieved progress through creative music, and it is now quite a serious fact that many children at the top end of the middle years of schooling are not able to read music, are not able to listen to music, and are not able to use their voices properly. Secondary school music teachers are often faced with a remedial situation with most of their first-year pupils.

If there has been a swing away from the Carl Orff activities, there is now beginning to be a swing towards more serious use of the voice as evinced by such movements as 'Sing for Pleasure', whose excellent repertoire books are available from the Oxford University Press. Singing should be a natural phenomenon, which activity was traditionally first started in a child's education in his mother's arms. The modern mother no longer appears to know the wealth of nursery songs, finger plays and lullabies, and so the child no longer hears this introduction to simple melody, which he should learn to imitate. Many teachers do not seem to have a repertoire of such songs either, nor seem aware of a suitable graded repertoire for the developing child. Carl Orff's idea was that the voice and classroom instruments should be combined in the learning of music, and it is worth adding that all children have to *learn* to use their voices in the same way as we expect them to *learn* to use their limbs, fingers and brains. The most obvious way to give practice in the use of the voice is to teach children a large number of songs of all types (many of which can be accompanied by classroom instruments). Teachers may justifiably claim that they cannot afford to buy expensive collections of repertoire. The cheapest way is to start to collect all the past BBC radio and television pamphlets.

It is through the use of the voice and instruments that music literacy can best be achieved. It would be unthinkable that teachers should shirk the teaching of reading or the understanding of numeracy, and yet it is accepted in many schools that the same children should not learn how to read music; therefore it is no wonder that progress in music is slow or sometimes stationary. It is much easier to learn music-notation reading than language reading, whilst the secret of success in both is *graded work* and constant repetition. The teaching of music literacy can be done individually, in small or large groups or with a whole class and gives much scope for imaginative work.

The opportunities for teachers to use their skills are limitless. It is worth remembering always that much of learning is to do with visual impact and although music is an aural art, it is important to provide plenty of visual stimulus. It is easy to make charts showing notes, rhythms, melodic fragments and even isolated pitched notes. Apparatus should be big and well labelled. Here are some examples:

Example 1

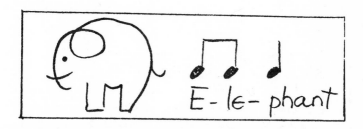

Example 2

Example 3

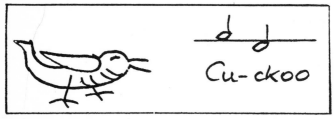

NB: Beginnings of pitch notation. Notice the whole stave is not at first necessary.

Examples 1, 2 and 3 show the sort of visual aid designed for the early stages of notation learning. These visual aids should become progressively more difficult and gradually introduce all common note values and rests. The stave should be extended until the full five lines are shown. Last of all, clefs and time signatures and dynamic markings should be introduced, always ensuring that the children perform frequently from the cards. It is good practice to refer back to earlier, easier ones already learned – even the most accomplished musicians go on practising seemingly simple music which they may have learned years ago. Familiarity in this case breeds confidence not contempt.

Example 4

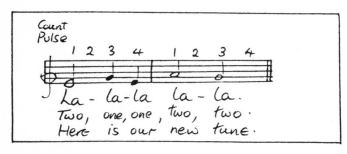

Example 4 is more sophisticated, being suitable for 8–9 year olds, assuming they have previous experience of the more straightforward work. All examples should be played on instruments and also sung. It is well to remember each card can provide further reading exercises by retrogression (backwards) and inversion (upside-down). All early work should be centred round the *doh me soh* chord and stepwise progression introduced.

Teachers who have achieved good results in the teaching of literacy have probably followed an adapted form of either the Ward or the Kodaly method. Both of these ideas based on sol-fah are worth investigation and have been specially adapted for use in English schools. Both methods stress the importance of learning through performance and both stress the use of the voice. The real strength of both systems is the graded approach. Children are usually capable of more concentration than they are credited with and they actually prefer to have some definite goal than an aimless, butterfly approach. Repeated work is of great value in the teaching of music. Too much new material can be confusing and constant practice in all aspects is essential if progress is to be achieved.

Perhaps it is worth indicating as a guide what might be expected from a twelve year old, with regard to music notation. Although there are no strict rules, in my opinion all children of this age group should be able to understand the following music notation and be able to perform it. It *is* possible.

1 The sol-fah names of all the notes of the diatonic scale;
2 Which notes make the tonic, dominant and subdominant chords;
3 Note (and equivalent rest) values of

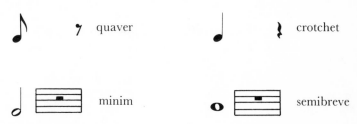

4 The dotted note;
5 The difference between pulse and rhythm;
6 time signatures $\frac{4}{4}$ $\frac{2}{4}$ $\frac{3}{4}$ and $\frac{6}{8}$
7 dynamic vocabulary: *f* (loud), *p* (quiet), *crescendo* (get louder), *diminuendo* (get quieter), *ritenuto* (get slower).

The high fliers will know much more than this, including chords on other degrees of the scales, the beginning of harmony, more advanced time signatures and rhythms, clefs and a more extended dynamic language. The only way to assess whether a child understands all this is whether he can perform from the symbols. The slow learners will, of course, find this the most difficult part of the process, and endless patience is required from the teacher and the child. All this assumes that the teacher has all these skills herself and also practices often her own pitch and rhythm awareness. It is expected that all teachers are literate and numerate; there is no reason why music literacy should not be expected of all teachers too – as it is in Hungary, the birthplace of the Kodaly method. If she fails her children in this aspect of musical education, then she will deny them a great slice of life's possible enjoyment and fulfilment.

Singing
Until recently there has been a sad decline in the popularity of singing in primary schools. However it is now the opinion of most music education-alists that there is again an upsurge in children singing. Nearly everyone can sing, and it is only if singing is made unattractive at school that children will pretend that they cannot sing and that they have no interest in singing. It is very important that boys should sing as well as girls: there is something wrong if boys grow up regarding music in schools as an activity fit only for girls. If there exists the attitude that the boys should be on the games field while the girls are in choir practice, then music will never flourish properly in that school. Boys enjoy music just as much as girls and are equally talented in arts subjects. The fact that they can easily be put off is perhaps a sign that they are more deeply sensitive to their developing sex-role and teachers' attitudes at this age than girls. Unfortunately, much of the material traditionally associated with singing in schools seems to have been chosen by well-meaning adults having little understanding of the sensitivities of children. If you want to kill off singing once and for all, then give your classes a diet of accepted English folk songs and composed children's songs. However natural and beautiful the melodies of these folk songs, and however clever the artifice of the composed songs, the words usually have little or no relevance to a child's experience. When choosing songs, it is essential to pay as much attention to the quality of the words as to the quality of the music. It seems to me that much of the appeal of such music as *Joseph and the Amazing Technicolour Dreamcoat* (Rice and Lloyd Webber, Novello) is in the excellence of the words.

Children have to learn to use their voices for singing and should learn to do so correctly from the early stages. Attention should be paid to posture, vowel and consonant sounds and quality of sound produced; in fact, all the oldfashioned points of the 'singing lesson'. However, these aspects should not be overemphasized but should be related to the activity of singing songs. One factor of utmost importance in the training of musical development, which many teachers fail to effect, is to help children to 'hear in their heads' both music they are to learn by rote and, more important, music which it is hoped they are reading from notation. All this depends on silence as well as sound, and any teacher of music must be able to establish absolute silence with groups and classes at any time. Many teachers find this especially difficult, but it must be established in the first lesson to guarantee success. One big help with the 'hearing in the head' problem is to introduce chord and part singing from the very beginning. Rounds are of a great help here and the singing of simple intervals and chords by groups of children and whole classes, in addition to giving a great deal of aesthetic pleasure, is the best way of all to encourage children to hear inwardly and to want to sing and engage in all other aspects of music. There is now such a great wealth of suitable graded material for singing that to give a list of recommended books and songs here would be inappropriate. Most publishers are very happy to arrange exhibitions and have staff who stage and demonstrate music in different parts of the country. Teachers should try to arrange such a demonstration in their area at least once a year. If at all possible teachers should try to visit one of the general music showrooms, such as the London Music Shop, which carry an inexhaustive supply of material.

Finally, it is well to remember that all music is meant to be performed, and teachers should aim at frequent performance of all music learned. This need not always be the end-of-term parents' concert or the carol service. Classes should perform to each other, give performances in school assembly, and, where possible, visit other schools for a half or full day of music-making with other children. On these occasions the 'growlers' should take part – they can and do improve, especially if they are not always put in the back row!

Listening to music

Listening to music is perhaps one of the most vexed areas in music teaching. The old 'music appreciation' lessons which figured in most school timetables have largely disappeared; music teachers are left to provide for the children the type of listening experience they feel able to give alongside all the other musical activities. The ability to listen to music is an all important part of musical education. Everything depends on it, and teachers must try every ruse to inculcate the development of both the outer and the inner ear.

Listening must be directed. In the first stages children should be trained to listen to what they themselves do. They must explore sound in every dimension, from everyday noises, through the noises of nature and man's artifice, to the noises they make themselves when singing and playing instruments, and, finally, to the sounds that *other* people make when they are performing music. There can be no doubt that the best way to train the ear is to perform music vocally and instrumentally. The listening must be directed in the sense that the teacher must constantly make the pupils aware of what sounds they are making. Thus the children, when performing simple exercises in notation, must be able to hear an example of the correct solution, and then hear themselves giving a correct interpretation. If this is done, then learning to read music becomes easy and the ear is being trained all the time, particularly the ability to hear 'within the mind'.

When it comes to listening to live or recorded music, it is therefore obviously an advantage if the children have some activity rather than merely passively listen to recorded music, which on its own in the classroom can be unproductive. 'Appreciation of music' is one of the slowest maturing areas of development, many people do not get round to it until well after school age, and some never make it. With the right sort of approach, many more could have the natural process hastened and learn to get pleasure and spiritual satisfaction from listening to music at an age when it would be a great help to them. A vital part to remember is that the span of attention for real listening is very short at first. It will vary from thirty seconds to two minutes on average, which is far less than the shortest record. Therefore one must present music for these short time spans and this is most satisfactorily done by recording suitable extracts from records and radio programmes onto tape. The children should always have done some preparatory associated work, and the same piece of music should be heard many times at suitable points during the lesson.

There is a lot more the teacher can do by way of preparing the children than merely asking the class to listen for the flute or the triangle. Consider the following suggestions which are only a few of many activities which could precede listening:

1 *Melody*   (a)   The class learns and sings the melody it is to hear.

           (b)   Class listens to the teacher play it on two different instruments; for example, piano and glockenspiel.

           (c)   Some children can learn to play the melody on whatever instruments are available.

           (d)   Provide notation for the melody. Observe shape; where is it high, where low. Discuss rhythmic shape. Discuss time signature.

2 *Rhythm*   (a)   Class sees notation, learns and performs rhythm on a monotone with voices, or rhythmically with non-pitched percussion instruments or both together and antiphonally.

           (b)   Discuss length of rhythmic phrases.

           (c)   Perform it backwards, upside down. Discuss how it sounds played these ways.

		(d) Half the class performs rhythm, half class performs pulse (beat). Combine, switch activity.
3	*Harmony*	If the children know about simple chords, recognize and discuss a simple chord they might know (for example, the tonic). Add it to a performance of the melody.
4	*Colour*	If orchestral, discuss different 'colours' the various instruments or groups and families of instruments make.
5	*Texture*	Is the texture thick or thin; jagged or smooth; low, medium or high, etc.
6	*Dynamics*	Discuss various possibilities; perform with different dynamics.
7	*Setting*	If the piece is a song or choral discuss the words and how the composer has chosen his melody and rhythm to fit them.

There are many more ways of involving the children, both before and after listening to the chosen extract. When the children have come to like the music they will want to hear it again and again. This fact is what the whole industry of pop music is founded on. If we hear a thing too many times then we tire of it and want something new, so the pop industry is constantly churning out new material to take the place of the exhausted material. When training children in listening care must be taken not to overdo any one particular piece of music. It is a skilful teacher who can judge the exact time to move on to the next activity and the next piece.

The choice of music to play to children always seems to be a problem. The answer is really very simple. Children will happily listen to any possible type of music. The way they listen will depend entirely on presentation. I believe the enterprising teacher should feed as mixed a diet a possible, always trying to choose music which she already knows fairly well and has already found attractive or interesting. A good diet should range from early medieval music through all the various styles of polyphonic, classical, romantic, operatic and more modern styles, and include modern composers working in unconventional media as well as folk music of many lands, light music, jazz, pop music and the music traditions of other cultures (for example, Indian, Balinese, African and others). The aim of all listening should be threefold: (i) to make the ear and mind aware of what is going on – listening as opposed to hearing; (ii) to give awareness of the entire scope of musical style; (iii) to provide aural and emotional stimulus and enjoyment. These points are not given in order of importance, for factors will assume a greater role at any particular time.

Classroom organization
Nothing is more likely to blight the teacher/pupil interaction more effectively than rows of desks looking at the back of an upright piano. The teacher should try to arrange the room informally 'in the round'. Music

flourishes best in an atmosphere which is informal, but at the same time in which all the hardware required is carefully organized beforehand. It is worthwhile making an effort to see that furniture, instruments, stands, etc. are where they are needed before the lesson begins. This is common sense but it will pay large dividends in the long run, since it is time consuming. A more difficult aspect of classroom organization in many ways is the allocation of time within each lesson. The children must never feel that the time is being 'chopped-up' but better and more lasting results will be achieved if thought is given beforehand to the length of each activity within each lesson. At the end of lessons the good teacher will assess whether she has achieved what she set out to do. It is very easy to get sidetracked, and for this reason alone organization of equipment, lesson content and time is of prime importance.

Integrated studies
Music can, and should, play a part in such courses currently and fashionably labelled 'integrated studies', 'creative arts', 'combined arts', etc. The most obvious, and perhaps the most successful, way is to develop links with drama, dance and visual arts – a marriage of disciplines which has been successful, one suspects, for thousands of years. It is in this area of work that children can best make use of 'creative music' activity. I have long contended that the term creative music is a gross misnomer used in an educational context, but nevertheless do not wish to give the impression that this work, which properly should be called something like 'exploratory music', is not valuable. In music, it is a prerequisite to have a fair degree of technique before any real creative work can be achieved. Exploratory work will go some way to consolidate a child's technical ability especially if the teacher is able to give wise direction. Unfortunately, the majority of children seem to be let loose on a veritable battery of instruments, and in this situation, without adequate direction, can soon become lost, without aim and eventually bored. Nothing could be worse for the development of musical interest.

A very important part of this area of work is to devise some way in which created music can be noted, so that further performances can take place without relying on memory alone. The best way to do this is to have ensured that the children are in the process of becoming musically literate; but there are other ways which could be explored, apart from traditional notation, particularly for the more modern approaches; and occasionally, there is a place for music of a purely aleatoric nature. Although it is good to start this exploratory work with a restricted use of notes, such as the falling minor third leading up to the pentatonic scale, there will be no real progression if the teacher does not investigate and make use of other scales and modes and also introduce harmony. Quite a number of note groupings not belonging to the western culture are of use and can lend a real air of authenticity if one is preparing music for a story with, say, Oriental or African content.

In my experience, music often gets a raw deal in integrated courses, eventually being pushed to the background in time allotment. In working with drama and visual arts it is wise to remember that both of these areas have a readier and more instant appeal for the children. Impressive results can be obtained very quickly, and the children soon become aware that similar results cannot be obtained so quickly in music. Preparation for music must by nature be slower, more methodical and less given to spontaneous inspiration. This is reflected in adult life also, for it takes a composer far longer to create a piece of music lasting perhaps fifteen minutes than for a playwright to write a three-act play lasting two and a half hours. For these reasons, the teacher in charge of the music section of such courses must ensure that enough time is allotted and that the work given is both demanding and rewarding. The teacher should try to avoid being coerced into merely providing relatively meaningless background music for other activities, and try to devise something with definite content, for example a dance sequence or a song.

The obvious link between music and other curriculum subjects should also be investigated. Music for listening can often be most effectively linked with literature, geography, history, even science and mathematics, in addition to the traditional areas of dance, drama, movement and visual arts.

Visiting instrumental teachers

The growth of the LEA's work in the provision of instrumental teaching in schools is perhaps the most successful innovation in music education in recent years. This is evinced by the numerous youth orchestras now abounding in all parts of the country. A particularly successful feature of this work is that many LEAs now provide not just an orchestra for the most advanced players, but carefully graded groups at all levels and for different combinations of instruments. This means that quite early on a child has the opportunity of making music with others of the same standard on a bigger and more satisfying level than can be achieved within the usual individual school framework, where the small numbers of children learning some-times make an ill-assorted group where it is necessary to have all levels of attainment performing together. This of course is possible and desirable, but it is also necessary to provide the stimulus of larger groups of the same standard.

Teachers responsible for music in the middle years will increasingly find that they have to deal with young string, wind and brass players, and accordingly should make themselves familiar with suitable repertoire and be able to direct group work. A working knowledge of the technique of the instruments is desirable, and an ability to arrange simple music for them essential. The visiting instrumental teachers will usually help the resident teacher in this field and can be asked to do some directing of these groups. It is the responsibility of the resident musician, however, to arrange the timetable of the visiting teacher to aim at the best possible time. Peripatetic teachers are often asked to teach in unsuitable areas – they should be given the best accommodation available. The school-based teacher will usually have to do a lot of liaison work with other staff and should see to it that the pupils know when their lesson is and that they turn up for it. If the work is on a considerable scale, probably the best arrangement is to make a rota timetable so that the children miss different lesson each week, thus causing other teachers less disruption. I have found, however, that as long as the instrumental pupils know that they have to catch up on missed work, no harm is done at all to progress in other subjects.

The resident music teacher should see to it that there is a good stock of strings, bridges, pegs, reeds, mouthpieces, cleaning fluid and other accessories and make herself familiar with the general maintenance of all instruments which belong to the school. Running repairs are often very simple. Professional repair work is difficult to find, expensive and takes a long time to effect. A little regular maintenance will often save much expense and wasted time. The children's instruments should be inspected fairly frequently. The children should be taught how to clean and care for their instruments early on in their lessons. This is not always done by the visiting teacher, who usually uses most of his time in teaching technique. A good teacher will always ensure that the pupil is taught how to care for the instrument and constantly check the instrument for developing faults. A teacher should *never* try to mend an instrument which she does not understand – irreparable damage may be done.

Children who want to learn an instrument should always be given some kind of testing. There are tests designed to show potential musicianship; for example, the Bentley Tests. It is usually agreed that some children who are not over-gifted musically should still be encouraged to learn if time, instruments and money allow. The first year of lessons should generally be regarded as diagnostic. It usually becomes apparent after this time which children will make a go of it – and teachers should be prepared for some surprises, for the best singer may turn out to have no talent instrumentally, and a child who has shown no marked musical ability may suddenly blossom. There will always be some who do not seem to make very rapid progress but who nevertheless still are dedicated to their lessons. They should be allowed to continue if at all possible. As soon as pupils have acquired enough technique they should start to play together in groups. This is very important and will sustain the interest of many who would otherwise fall by the wayside. The point of learning music is to share musical experience with others.

Concerts

It is desirable that children should hear live music as much as possible. Although the possibility of this is beyond the scope of the classroom, many authorities now arrange concerts and recitals which take place in schools and which are usually shared by groups of schools. If the authority does not arrange such recitals, teachers should, through their headteachers, make requests for them to the advisory service of the local education office. The ideal arrangement is to engage perhaps three to six players, either brass, woodwind, strings, old instruments, recorder groups (and don't forget singers!) who are willing to explain the workings of their instruments, a little of their history and to give an informal recital of varied, short pieces. Many orchestral players specialize in these recitals and, if schools can share the cost, certainly provide value for money.

Occasionally it is a very good idea to organize groups of children to visit orchestral concerts, theatrical musical events and the like, assuming that distance and availability of transport allow. In this case it is usually advisable to prepare the children in some way, although I find that many teachers underestimate the impact visits of this nature will have on the children. The visual aspect is very helpful in directing aural attention, especially if the children know the names of the instruments or can recognize their differing timbres. Anything the teacher can provide in the way of presenting live music to the children will make them readier to accept the fact that music is an integral and important part of everyday activity available for all people and not just reserved for the few. It is wrong the pretend that there is only one style of music – that which you happen to like. Teachers should be ready to learn about styles which may be unfamiliar to them whatever they may be – jazz, pop, medieval, classical, romantic, modern, music of other cultures, etc. The children should know that the music industry is one of the largest in Great Britain, as large and important, say, as the steel industry (are *you* surprised by that fact?) and they should be aware of the many and varied possibilities of careers within the industry, always remembering that performers are only a minute section of musical personnel.

Inservice education and training

This form of keeping in touch with more recent educational developments is now considered essential for all teachers and is especially useful for those teaching music, for the obvious reason that usually in schools there is only one music teacher who is treading a lonely path. Courses give such teachers the opportunity, not only of consolidating their own knowledge, but also of sharing their views and experiences with other music teachers. Nearly all authorities now have a strong music advisory service, part of whose duties it is to plan such courses by engaging speakers on specific topics and by giving courses themselves in general developments. Details of courses are circulated to headteachers in addition to being advertised in local teachers' centre programmes. It is possible that sometimes these do not reach individual teachers: in that case they should make the effort to contact the music adviser personally and find out what is happening in the area. It may be that the adviser may not visit the school frequently – he often has 150 or more schools to visit in addition to managing general office routine, attending meetings, battling for 'music money', supervising probationary teachers, interviewing staff and would-be students, etc. – but all advisers will visit if asked. Many teachers think they have to put on a special show when the adviser is in the school, but this is the last thing the adviser wants to see. What he wants to know is the situation as it really is, even (perhaps specially) such unglamorous details as availability of rooms and whether the piano sounds at the back of the hall? He always wants to know of teaching difficulties, particularly with regard to curriculum planning and content. It is always a good idea to discuss with the adviser any real difficulties encountered and not to be afraid to make suggestions regarding the content of future inservice training courses. Courses are often mounted on certain topics which individual teachers suggest. It is always helpful for the middle school teacher to contact the music specialist in the secondary schools the children expect to attend. Frank discussion is of real constructive help to both teachers. Again these interchange visits can be arranged by the advisory staff.

Useful equipment
A wide range of good quality: chime bars (ideally one set per class), glockenspiels, xylophones, marimbas, varied beaters, melodicas, tunable and untunable drums, bass drum, tambour, tambourines, triangles, large cymbals, castanets, maracas, woodblocks, claves, jingles, resi-resi.
Home-made instruments: scrapers, shakers, coconut shells, bottle-top jingle-sticks, sandpaper blocks, etc.
Recorders: descant, treble, tenor, bass (possibly).
Orchestral instruments: violins, violas, cellos, flutes, oboes, clarinets.
Brass instruments: trumpets, cornets, trombones, perhaps brass-band instruments according to the bent of the teachers.
Record player, reel-to-reel tape recorder, cassette recorder, felt board, flash cards, etc.

Conclusion
An article of this length can do little more than underline some possibilities in general terms: it cannot provide an exhaustive amalgam of all available methods and material. I have tried to draw attention to those aspects in the development of musical awareness of children of this age group which I believe to be important. Music teachers, in common with other teachers, should constantly question their own aims and try to assess their

achievements towards the realization of these aims. Finally, I must say that success in the teaching of music, more than in any other subject, seems to depend a great deal on the personality, drive and interest of the teacher. It is demanding and exhausting, and, unfortunately, presupposes that the music teacher works through every lunch hour, after school and during many evenings and weekends. As with most problems in teaching, modest success brings rich rewards.

Useful further reading

DENNIS, B. (1970) *Experimental Music in Schools* Oxford University Press
DOBBS, FISKE and LANE (1974) *Ears and Eyes* Oxford University Press
HART, M. (1973) *Music in the Primary School* Heinemann Educational
LAND, V. (1973) *Music in today's classroom* Harcourt Brace Jovanovich
MAXWELL-TIMMINS, D. (1971) *Music is Fun* 1, 2 and 3 Schofield and Sims
MORRISH, D. L. (1900) *Basic Goals in Music* 1 and 2, New York: McGraw Hill
VAJDA, C. (1974) *The Kodaly Way to Music* Boosey and Hawkes

3 Social learning in the classroom

In a piece of ongoing research being carried out by the editors into the types of problems met by beginner teachers at the start of their professional careers, the most commonly recurring source of difficulty in the classroom was the individual problem child. Every classroom seems to have one, and if he (and they are invariably boys) leaves then another, hitherto unsuspected, takes his place. But as Joan Bird points out it is all very well to identify him, and even if the source of his particular problems can be diagnosed, it is still a far cry from the individual teacher and the school being able to respond in a reasonable way to the needs of the child concerned. The teacher and the school face the inevitable dichotomy of responding to the needy individual without jeopardizing the opportunities of the group. It is suggested that this can only be done where the school maintains a caring attitude and a flexible structure for both its pupils and teachers. For there are also problem teachers who need just as much care given to the selection of their timetable commitments and the children for whom they will be responsible – a matter often overlooked.

In a pluralistic society children are presented with complex conflicting systems of values and behaviour. Too often children appear to be abandoned to make their own choices and society is called on too late to clear up the resulting chaos. For the teacher, therefore, knowledge of the development of children's moral thought is central to the understanding of the individual child and the group. Colin Alves points up a number of recent studies which set out to establish conceptual frameworks which can be used to aid the teacher interpret the data on children's moral thinking. Indeed these studies should be prescribed reading for all those concerned with teaching the child, for the ultimate aim of moral education is to raise the level of moral judgment and consequent behaviour, or in other words to help children learn to choose.

The area of training for choice in the classroom is a complex one, for children can only practise choosing when alternatives are presented to them in a way which allows decision making in a punishment-free situation. Armin Beck and Eliezer Krumbein examine the area of simulations and games in the classroom. They claim that the teacher is always faced with the problem of providing direct experiences for her pupils within the confines of the classroom. For the most part the experiences have to be gained vicariously but they suggest that simulation enriches the learning situation bringing to it heightened commitment from all those concerned and a whole range of planned outcomes. A simulation is a model of a real situation or thing, but behavioural scientists would suggest that the particular characteristics of this type of model are that it is capable of being manipulated. To take this further, the operational model permits the teacher to highlight certain aspects of human behaviour and to examine them in the comparative calm not normally found in the complex human relationships of real life. The authors, writing of their experience in the United States, are surprised at the slight impact simulation and games appear to have made in British schools, and they readily supply examples of experience-based learning suitable for the middle years child in a multicultural and multiracial society.

3.1 Children with behavioural problems

Joan Bird

Behaviour problems generally are believed to be on the increase. Reports in the press and other news media suggest that parents are becoming less able to control their children and that schools are finding discipline harder to exert. While many of these reports refer to adolescents and to behaviour which is directed in an aggressive manner towards society, there are disturbing suggestions that younger children are being affected and are now more likely to suffer from depression and anxiety or to express a general malaise by becoming less manageable and amenable to control. Concern by the old for the behaviour of the young is by no means a modern phenomenon and it may well be that we are unduly anxious. However, there is no doubt that the middle years age group is a very important one to study and in which to intervene if possible, for problems of personality or behaviour unresolved in the middle years are likely to become far more serious and difficult to control during adolescence.

There is a fairly considerable body of writing dealing with problem behaviour: this tends to fall into different categories according to the particular interest and field of study of the author. There are those books which concern themselves largely with the personality and ego development of the child, attempting by an analysis (the word used here in a general sense) of his behaviour to understand his motivation and hence to help him to adjust through some kind of therapeutic treatment which may, or may not, involve professional intervention. *Children under Stress* by Sula Wolff (1973) is a helpful and readable book of this kind which gives not only the psychological viewpoint but also a comprehensive examination of stressful situations which might be experienced by a normal child. Another category of writing offers methods of identifying and classifying problem behaviour and personality types. *Studies of Troublesome Children* by D. H. Stott (1966) and *The Social Adjustment of Children* by the same author are particularly useful to the teacher. The latter is the manual to the Bristol Social Adjustment Guides which themselves provide for a detailed analysis of behaviour while being comparatively simple for the teacher to use. R. B. Cattell, M. Rutter and M. Chazan are other writers who have produced books and articles dealing with a similar point of view. Alec Clegg and Barbara Megson (1968) in *Children in Distress* draw attention to the significance of child poverty, broken homes and parental neglect with their effect upon behaviour, and no reader seriously interested in causation of problems in school should ignore *How Children Fail* by John Holt (1970). Finally any recommendation for reading must include the Underwood Report (Ministry of Education) which, although published as long ago as 1955, still provides the basis for much work.

The psychologist, the sociologist and the educationalist, then, all have an interest in behaviour problems and teachers will find it useful to be well read from all these angles. However, the teacher has a difficult task which is uniquely his own; while becoming more and more conscious of adverse home background or undue emotional stress upon his pupils, he cannot act as social worker and psychotherapist in any full sense of the word because his business is with his whole class. While he may be fully alert to individual needs he nevertheless must keep the welfare of the group in the forefront of his mind. He may find himself open to the accusation that he is ignoring the withdrawn, unrelating child in the back row but his energies are fully engaged in dealing with the more disruptive members of his class and, at best, he must settle for a compromise, playing the role of moderator, as far as he is able, between the problem child with his special needs, the requirements of the other children, and the expectations of the school. His prime task is education, not therapy, and acceptable behaviour must, for him, be interpreted as that which allows for profitable, enjoyable and cooperative learning situations within a school setting. It is with this aspect in mind that I want to explore further the behaviour problems of the middle school.

What do we mean by behaviour problems?

We label a child a problem if he consistently fails to behave in a way which is considered appropriate by the community within which he lives. Much as we may like to pay lip-service to independence and originality of thought and action, the stability and security of any society depends very largely on the degree to which its members are prepared to conform to its established norms. Deviant behaviour causes anxiety to other members of the group who then put pressure on the miscreant in order to bring him into line. The normal child is helped to respond because he possesses a strong natural desire for what Stott (1966a) terms *social attachment*. In the early years this shows itself as a need for attachment to the adult parent figure; later it is extended to include the peer group. The child behaves in a way which he hopes will gain approval and hence strengthen the bonds of attachment. In the course of this process he learns to defer gratification of his immediate desires and to adapt to a world in which he is not the only member. He learns to share, to wait his turn, to serve and to receive help from the group, to be both self-sufficient to a degree and yet aware of his dependence on others. Paradoxically, however, this self-denying activity is not enough. Kelvin (1971) points out, 'Socialization, in the broadest sense, consists of learning the norms of one's society and coming to conform to them; one of these norms, and a very fundamental one, is the norm of nonconformity.' So, presumably, we do want the child to be independent and original after all, but only within certain decreed limits. How is he to sort out what really is required of him? Briefly, he must learn. Kelvin again has emphasized how little of man's behaviour is genetically 'built-in' but is rather a result of experience and learning. Very important is the ability to observe and to sense the modes of behaviour which are most acceptable to the group and, at the same time, to realize the second of the needs which Stott (1966a) has identified, that of *personal effectiveness*. This concerns the skills which the child develops to master his environment, both material and human; practice of these skills enables him to feel 'in control'. Success in effectiveness gives confidence and breeds further success while failure increases feelings of inadequacy and often leads the child to retreat still further from an overdemanding situation.

So far, then, two factors concerning behaviour have emerged. First, the significance of the customs and expectations of the community which the child is motivated to observe through the exercise of his drive for social attachment. These may be clearly defined and easily understood, as among the family or in small isolated groups; or they may consist of highly complex collections of rules for conduct and manners, varied according to situation, which can take a lifetime to master. And second, the needs of the individual and the strength of his drive for effectiveness. There is, however, a third factor: the part played by the adult who, either openly or by his attitude, passes judgment upon the child's activities and upon whose degree of tolerance the child's success in coping may well depend. In school unacceptable behaviour may stem from any or all of these three factors; too difficult a situation, inadequacy on the part of the child, or too high a standard set by the teacher. How do these breakdowns occur in the middle years and can they be ameliorated?

Inadequate response from the child

The Underwood Report (1955), in its definition of maladjustment, groups the symptoms of the condition under six headings:

1   Nervous disorders – fears, withdrawal, depression, overexcitability, apathy, obsessions.
2   Habit disorders – speech, sleep, movement, feeding, incontinence, nervous pains, allergic conditions;

3 Behaviour disorders – unmanageableness, aggressiveness, jealousy, demands for attention, stealing, lying, truancy, sex difficulties;
4 Organic disorders – conditions following head injuries, encephalitis, epilepsy, chorea;
5 Psychotic disorders – hallucinations, delusions, extreme withdrawal, bizarre symptoms, violence;
6 Educational and vocational difficulties – backwardness not accounted for by dullness, inability to concentrate, inability to keep jobs.

Children who show these symptoms are not necessarily maladjusted. It is a matter of degree and the suggestion is that intervention is needed at the point when the child is prevented from leading a normal life. For the sake of brevity, and perhaps keeping closer to the day-to-day experience of the average teacher, I would offer three general headings under which particular cases can be examined:

1 Innate disorders: organic, psychotic or resulting from personality traits which are likely to make it difficult for a child to conform; for example, hyperactivity, oversensitiveness.
2 Inappropriate behaviour resulting from the child's having learnt unacceptable responses or having lacked the opportunity to acquire favourable ones. Social disadvantage and 'spoiling' – overindulgence – would be included in this category.
3 Disorders resulting from adverse background experience – broken or inadequate homes. Children affected have suffered illtreatment or neglect and, feeling themselves deprived in some way of basic needs, react in an unacceptable way in their attempts to meet their requirements.

Innate disorders
Looking first at what I have termed innate disorders, the teacher of this age group is unlikely to come across extreme cases for these should have been recognized in the child's first school and referred for specialist attention. However, because of the less demanding atmosphere of infant classes and the attempts of teachers of young children to retain a homely approach, some children may have managed to get by with less than adequate behaviour. The hyperactive child may have been allowed considerable freedom of movement and leeway in making frequent changes of occupation. The excessively shy child may have taken refuge in the Wendy house or book corner and have avoided the activities which would reveal his lack of selfconfidence. Much nuisance behaviour may have been tolerated, in the hope that the child will prove to have been merely a slow developer, which can no longer be allowed as the learning situation becomes more formal.

Geoffrey was such a child. Coming from an inadequate home with a family reputation well known to the school, his infant school teachers had been anxious not to prejudge him. His attention span was practically nil, but during story times he was allowed to follow his own devices, wandering freely round the school and occupying himself as he saw fit. At first he showed little interest in the other children but later he began to molest them, developing considerable skill in pinching, kicking and spitting. But by this time Geoffrey was practically a school institution and members of staff, teaching or otherwise, were constantly ready to intervene by removing him from situations where he could disrupt, even to the extent of escorting him home some time after the other children had been dismissed. Geoffrey's transferral to the middle school revealed the degree of abnormality which his behaviour had reached. Although the school was far from being formal, he could not be allowed his previous freedom nor were there staff available to give constant individual attention. To the distress of his first middle school teacher, who felt she had failed him, he was referred to the school psychological service and was classified as subnormal and in need of special schooling. It is interesting to note that it was not until Geoffrey had, in effect, been rejected by his group that outside agencies could intervene and he could be given the very specific help he needed.

More common than Geoffrey are those children whom we may term 'temperamentally vulnerable'. Any deviation from the norm is obviously towards extremes, therefore failure to adjust satisfactorily to a situation will be demonstrated by either over- or under-reaction and the pre-liminary classification of behaviour problems is frequently made in these terms. But why does this happen and what decides the direction towards which the individual tends? Is this reaction the result of learned behaviour (in which case one hopes it could be unlearned) or is it inherent – a quality which the child must learn to live with? Stott believes that the explanation is to be found in terms of neurological function and that such conditions as lack of social attachment or personal effectiveness can be traced to impairment of neural structures. This theory by no means eliminates the importance of early experience, which has been clearly shown to have considerable effect in influencing behaviour, but helps us to understand why some children seem to be so much more at risk than others.

Stott, too, was not satisfied with the simple division of cases into the two types. Many questions remained unanswered as to why the withdrawn child acts in this way. Is it because he cannot muster the strength to make the effort required to establish social contact, does he lack the experience of how to go about it, or does he simply not care for people? The answer to these questions is obviously important if any constructive effort to help is to be made. The case of Linda is relevant here.

Linda, ten years nine months at the time she was referred, was of normal build and average intelligence. Her father was a local government clerk, her mother a housewife. She had one sister very similar to herself in characteristics. The family was reserved and uncommunicative; one or other of the parents was usually on the sick list with some vaguely defined ailment. Linda attended a lively and progressive school where the children worked largely on assignments and projects in which they were expected to show a good deal of initiative and responsibility. Linda made no positive attempt to attach herself to any activity but relied on the teacher to assign her to a group. She would then depend on the group leader to allot her a task and to direct her as to how it should be done. Her performance would be correct but extremely slow and painstaking. Gradually the children lost patience with her, not so much it seemed for her inadequacy as for the gloom which she somehow managed to spread around her. Her teacher admitted that he found it difficult to like the child or to spark off any response from her. Linda then began to resort to a number of physical ailments to enable her to avoid participation. She pleaded colds or stomach upsets to excuse her from any form of exercise, including drama. Headaches, she said, prevented her from writing or listening. Notes from home supported her complaints but when a medical certificate was asked for the doctor was unable to find evidence of physical illness. She retreated to the quietest corner of the highly active and somewhat noisy classroom and sat primly, causing no nuisance, but doing nothing. Appearances suggested that Linda found this particular school environment far too taxing and could not cope with the noise, the pace, or the need for showing initiative. She was seen by the educational psychologist who recommended her removal to a smaller, formal school. Here her tasks were clearly defined and limited in scope. Her capacity for neatness and her unfailing obedience constantly won praise – the fact that she waited to be told what to do became a virtue and she began to respond to the approbation of her new teacher with an occasional smile and to make gestures of friendship to children as retiring as she was herself. Unfortunately the family refused further help from the educational psychologist, who had hoped to help Linda to recognize the use she was making of physical ailments to relieve her anxiety, but at least she was sufficiently helped to enable her to transfer reasonably happily to secondary school when the time came and eventually to take a job in a small office.

Linda was a child who seemed to share with her family a natural lethargy and a lack of personal effectiveness. Given a supportive environment and a chance to react at her own pace she proved quite capable of making adequate adjustments and social contacts. The steps taken by the middle school were crucial in ensuring this, for had help been deferred until the start of adolescence it is highly likely that Linda would have opted out of school altogether.

The over-reactor inevitably produces more stress in the classroom than the unforthcoming child. His purpose is to gain attention and to do this he is prepared to disrupt the whole class. He has an insatiable need for constant reassurance that he is being noticed and this overrides any rational knowledge that his behaviour is totally unacceptable. Such a child was Martin, aged eleven years and ten months. Extrovert and active, he was the third child in a family of five and consequently never qualified for either the privileges of the older children or the petting of the younger ones. He was possibly the most intelligent of the family. His behaviour in the class was disruptive in the extreme. He would interject witticisms during teaching or discussion sessions, cause 'accidents' to material during craft periods or to people during physical activities, and constantly be in the wrong place at the wrong time. He made imaginative and exciting suggestions for class projects, particularly where drama work was concerned, but he could not be relied upon to carry out the ideas he had evolved and this infuriated him, causing him often to destroy the very things he cared most about. By the time he was eleven his classmates rarely found him even mildly amusing and his teachers had reached the end of their patience, yet his attempts to increase his prestige had reached a pitch approaching frenzy. He had earlier been referred to the school psychological service but pressure of demands from cases considered more urgent had meant that he had not been interviewed. At this point, however, treatment seemed essential, and with therapeutic help, which involved not only the school but also the parents and the child guidance clinic, a scheme was worked out whereby it was hoped to give Martin the assurance of personal identity which he so badly needed and, at the same time, a chance to develop sensible and sensitive reactions to the demands of the community. The exercise was a slow and painful one but was ultimately successful. Again intervention was vital at this age for with the added strain of adolescence Martin's antisocial behaviour might well have become delinquent in terms of the law.

As with the unforthcoming child, the attention seeker, although easily recognizable, is not all of a kind. Martin's behaviour was not hostile; he rarely hurt another child and damage to property was effected when he was in a rage and was not deliberate. Even his poor, long-suffering teachers would find themselves at times as overwhelmed by extravagant efforts to oblige as they were by his misdemeanours. His drive for personal effectiveness included an equally strong desire to be socially acceptable and he was potentially a natural leader. Teachers will be only too familiar with far less attractive children, whose means of gaining the limelight range from tale-telling to physical assault. As long as they are noticed by the group they appear to be indifferent as to whether they are liked by it. The Bristol Social Adjustment Guide lists symptoms categorized as showing qualities of hostility, anxiety, or rejection; these may be directed towards adults, towards other children, or towards both. For instance, the child who in early years has been let down by his parents may react with open or concealed hostility to his teachers but may be anxious to be held high in the esteem of his contemporaries. The teacher is faced with the arduous task of slowly breaking down the attitude of mistrust. Understanding the nature of the child's plight may help him not only to find the right approach but also to bear with patience the many rejections which will be made.

One more behaviour disturbance attributable to innate characteristics is that termed by Stott (1966a) *inconsequence*. Children learn to moderate their behaviour in the light of its effects. In response to the desire for adult attachment they start by adopting those actions which will please their parents, and as their understanding increases they include others in their considerations. But this, Stott points out, requires a sense of time and cannot be achieved by animals or very young children who live only in the present. Suppose, however, the child is lacking in what Stott calls temporal integration. Not only will he take little heed for the consequences of his actions but his learning will be affected for he will see no purpose in acquiring knowledge not of immediate use and he will lack concentration and perseverance. He will be easily distractible, responding only to immediate situations.

Michael spent most of his schooldays in remedial classes. At ten he could barely read and his mathematical skills were minimal. Yet his teachers felt he was far from dull. If confronted with a new activity he was often the first to see its possibilities or to grasp the functioning of some new piece of equipment. He devised and executed original schemes for serving school dinners, mixing paint and clay, and imaginative games, some of which were highly successful and some utterly disastrous for he seemed incapable of stopping to consider the results of his actions; nor, although he was frequently stimulated by opportunities for learning, could he persevere long enough to develop any skill. He was unpunctual, untidy, inattentive and impervious to punishment. At the same time, he brimmed over with goodwill towards his fellows and never remembered an injury long enough to bear a grudge. Grievances were forgotten as rapidly as duties. Throughout his schooldays Michael remained lovable but completely incorrigible. By the time he was eighteen he had been dismissed from more jobs than he could remember, had three illegitimate children all by different girls, and had been committed for trial for a string of offences all resulting from a complete disregard of other people's property or convenience.

Could Michael have been helped before adolescence? Psychologists are now taking a great interest in the syndrome of inconsequence but so far the prognosis remains very poor although the symptoms may diminish as the child grows older. Those children who combine inconsequential behaviour with antisocial tendencies are thought to be potential delinquents. Yet one feels that the caring community of a school should have something to offer the Michaels of this world. Perhaps, as understanding of the condition grows, community support may be enlisted so that responsibility can be delegated and some kind of watch maintained to protect the child from the effects of his thoughtlessness.

Inappropriate learned behaviour
The acquisition of behaviour skills, then, may be affected by temperamental deficits in the child. Many children cope because they are fortunate enough not to be exposed to situations which will test their weakness; others may be severely tested by their environment. Among these are children who have not learnt what is expected of them, or have developed habits in early life which later have to be broken. Norms of behaviour have been built up slowly, by consensus of opinion, over the course of time and the human child, with his prolonged infancy, has a considerable period allowed him in which to become familiar with these norms. At first he only has to comply with the expectations of his home where he is known and loved and where he is granted a great deal of licence. Demands made upon him increase steadily as he grows older. We have already mentioned the way in which the infant school attempts to cushion the child's entry into the wider social world of school; what then is expected of him by the time he reaches the middle school?

Susan Isaacs (1963) says:

> From the age of seven or eight to eleven or twelve ... the child enters upon the most stable and well-organized period of his emotional life, a stability largely lost with adolescence and not regained until full maturity. Such difficulties as do occur in this phase tend to take the form of adventurous defiance; wandering, stealing, lying and other mild delinquencies.

Sula Wolff (1973) says of this age, 'His (the child's) energies become diverted from the intimate relationships within his family and are invested in two main activities: peer relationships and learning.' This learning should include the learning of social techniques. Some of the more obvious expectations that we have for the eight year old, when he is promoted from the first school, are:

1 That he will have mastered physical skills such as tying his own shoelaces and managing simple implements – scissors, writing implements, keys and latches, for instance. (The middle school teacher who takes this for granted may not appreciate the amount of hard labour the first school teacher has had to put in on getting the child to this point!)

2   That he can attend, within reason, to his own physical needs.
3   That he can get to school unescorted by his parents (unless, of course, transport is essential) and is accustomed to doing some shopping on his own and running errands.
4   That he can take care of his own property and has some sense of responsibility for it.
5   That he can state his own needs and ask for help if he is in trouble.
6   That he does not too easily resort to tears and is not too dependent on the continual proximity of the teacher.
7   That he can work and play with his peers with a fair degree of cooperation.
8   That he 'knows what school is for' – that is, he is reasonably willing and anxious to learn. Together with this come other expectations regarding his ability to sit still, to concentrate, to be amenable to discipline and comparatively obedient.

During the course of the middle years period we expect him to become more proficient in all these respects and also to develop a good deal of social knowhow. These are the years when he will discover the significance of rules, not only by accepting the dictates of others but by formulating his own. It is a great time for the invention of highly complex games which rarely get started because the players are far too busy arguing about the rules or declaring, in varying degrees of stridency, that 'it isn't fair'.

Socially, too, the middle school child has demanding tasks to contend with. Up to seven or eight years of age the approval and support of adults is of predominant importance. As long as the child can placate parents and teacher he is able to function fairly happily. However, as his peer group takes on a significance in his relationships he has to learn increased and more complex skills of reacting. Very many of the behaviour difficulties of this age group arise from the child's ineptness at judging between the claims of his teacher and his peers for his attention. He 'plays to the gallery', using any ploy to raise a laugh from his classmates, and going from strength to strength in his bravado in baiting the teacher. Then, suddenly aware that he has gone too far in diverting his contemporaries, he will swing to the opposite extreme and be equally infuriating in his efforts to oblige, constantly and noisily volunteering for classroom duties (which he will probably not perform unless there is an audience present) and ingratiating himself with any visitor to the class. Well may he be asked, 'Do you *mean* to be cheeky?' Although intended as a rhetorical question, it could well be a real query. By twelve or thirteen, however, he should have developed a sense of situation and some mastery of register. He should appreciate that the light-hearted repartee which he exchanges with the lollipop man is possibly not acceptable for his headteacher; that there is classroom language and behaviour and playground language and behaviour and, indeed, many other modes with which he must become familiar if he is to be socially acceptable.

We are rarely fully conscious of the value we put upon social acceptability until we are confronted with its opposite. John Holt (1970) describes watching a retarded child of thirteen at a concert making a great effort to behave 'correctly' as she had obviously been trained to do. He felt at first that she would be less distressing to watch if she had romped and played in a manner fitting her mental age but then 'sensed very vividly the horror that this would arouse in all who saw it'. A child's actions may be in no way morally wrong or socially harmful but may nevertheless be extremely distressing if they are not appropriate to his age and stage of development. Thus we accept temper tantrums in a two year old and doubtful table manners in a four year old but we cannot condone them in the nine year old. This is understandable if we consider how group survival depends upon the ability of its members to mature and take their share of responsibility in due course. No community can support too many inadequates.

Jenny was the kind of child who had not learned how to behave. She was the only child of middle-aged parents who adored their precious daughter. She was intelligent, pretty, and had an appearance of sophistication in advance of her nine years but she rarely worked and was cordially disliked by her classmates. She expected, and demanded, the best of everything; the place next to the teacher, the newest equipment, the first choice of occupation and constant attention. She helped herself indiscriminately to the property of others and was surprised when they objected. Like Linda, she laid claim to a wide variety of ailments if pressure was put upon her, but her appearance of radiant health belied her protests. She had everything money could buy – and yet Jenny was a deprived child. She had never been given the chance to 'grow up' as a person. Her parents were completely satisfied with their daughter as she was; she fulfilled their need by accepting their indulgence and continuing to depend on them to intervene between her and the outside world. Her petulance and egocentricity were making her progressively less acceptable to the group towards which she should have been transferring her attention but she was enclosed in a vicious circle which could only be broken if she could be motivated to try to gain the approval of others besides her family. As things were, this seemed unlikely to happen. The term 'spoilt' child is perhaps more true than we would like to believe.

Joan Tough (1973) gives an excellent illustration of how a child may be handicapped by lack of learning experience in the home. She relates the messages given by two five-year-old boys to their teacher:

Jimmy: Not got to have my milk.
Teacher: Why not Jimmy?

Jimmy: My mum says I haven't to.

And the following:

Michael: Could I stay inside today?
Teacher: Why don't you want to go out Michael?
Michael: I've got a cold you see. It makes me cough outside 'cos it's
           very cold.

Joan Tough comments:

> The first is a bald statement which makes no attempt to reconcile the
> rival authorities of parent and teacher. It makes no attempt to
> anticipate the effect the form in which the message is cast might have
> on the teacher. The same form would probably be used to convey the
> information to another child. The second message, on the other hand,
> is sensitive to the teacher's authority and the language selected makes
> no challenge to it.

The fact that these children were only five should serve to strengthen the
impact of the story although we are dealing here with the middle years age
group. Already by the age of five the child is able by his manner of speaking
to antagonize those in authority over him. Even if Jimmy's teacher is
extremely insighted and sympathetic towards him she must, for his own
sake, remonstrate and get him to rephrase his message. Michael's would at
once be accepted and treated as communication between people with a
shared understanding of each other. Jimmy must *learn* what is second
nature to Michael and in the learning may well feel that both he himself
and his family are being depreciated.

Teachers who are troubled by the attitude of their pupils in this respect
would do well to try to meet their parents. John, aged eleven, the son of a
professional man of some standing, was admitted to a new school when his
family moved into the neighbourhood. On his arrival he announced to the
much loved and indispensible caretaker, 'Don't you start telling me what
to do, my man. My father has just been made a manager of this place and
he will get you the sack!' So great was the outcry in the school that John
was ostracized by his fellows for several days and his father visited the
school for an explanation. As a result of this John was forgiven, by the staff
at least, and his father's service as a manager was the shortest ever known!
Justice seemed to have been done; nevertheless, John suffered a rejection
which can only have been distressing for him and was probably not fully
deserved. Children who, in school, have to cope with different social and
cultural standards from those of the home, whether this is due to differences
in social class background or racial difference, are likely in due course to

adapt to the new setting. But in the meantime they may acquire a sense of failure or unacceptability which can take a long time to disperse and which may gain for them the reputation of being disobedient and uncooperative, a reputation that they may continue to live up to.

Adverse childhood experiences

Few, if any, teachers these days can be unfamiliar with the kind of behaviour problems that are found in children from broken or unhappy homes. The book *Children in Distress* deals with this aspect in a way which no short article could hope to do. Clegg and Megson (1968) point out not only the heart-rending distress caused by poverty and squalor but that resulting from situations where the child is neglected, treated as the family drudge or scapegoat, or used as the target for the displaced hatred of the parents for each other. Sometimes the plight of the child is so desperate that outside help must be called in; even so, it is unlikely that he will be removed from school and the teacher is left to cope with symptoms which may include attention seeking, hostility, restlessness, lack of concentration, frequent tears, enuresis, extreme timidity, theft; the list seems inexhaustible and whatever the sum total of any particular child there is almost always one common element – he is unlikable. As one teacher once remarked, 'The child who most needs to sit on my knee is the one with the wettest pants.' This unlikableness is the first hurdle which the teacher has to overcome in himself and most of us are best helped to do this if we can at least understand why the child behaves in this way and why he so often rejects our well-intentioned advances.

Psychologists have shown us that behaviour is always purposeful in that a child acts in a way which will achieve for him certain ends though he may not consciously know what these ends are or have given consideration to his mode of achieving them. A good deal of study has been done in attempts to identify the goals of behaviour and to classify them in terms of needs. Most generally acknowledged are the primary requirements for physical survival (food, warmth, etc.), affection, approval, security and recognition. Mia Kellmer Pringle (1973) in an article exploring the roots of violence and vandalism, adds the needs for new experience and responsibility. Anthony Bolger (1973) uses as headings for classifying problem behaviour in schools the needs for attention, power, revenge and escape. The child from the broken home usually has many unfulfilled needs and once we feel that we have discovered what we think he is trying to gain from his behaviour, we are on the right road to helping him. Eventually we hope not only to recompense him for what he has missed, but also to show him a more appropriate life style for the future.

Clive, aged nine, after an outburst in which he destroyed a great deal of property and turned the air around him blue with his language, said, 'I did it because I wanted them to know I was in the world.' Clive had been rejected by his father from birth, often with violence, and his mother, in mortal fear of her husband, had locked the child in his bedroom for long hours and had done her best to ignore his presence on the occasions when he had to be visible. He had been conditioned not 'to be in the world'. The fact that he could express this in school so openly was a tremendous step forwards in his own growth to health and a great compliment to the school itself that had given him sufficient security to be able to voice his feelings in safety. Had he been punished for this explosion of feeling it could have been a long time before he was able to try again to communicate.

It is not always easy to discover the real cause of the child's distress. Sally, aged eleven, was the child of divorced parents who had both remarried and started second families. They continued to live in the same town and Sally was passed back and forth between the two households, spending alternate months in each. Her behaviour in school was extremely disturbed; she was aggressive towards the other children, disobedient and disruptive in class, and had wild fits of temper followed by floods of tears. A certain amount of petty stealing had been going on and her teacher was convinced that she was the culprit although she had managed to avoid being caught. Neither of her parents answered invitations to come to school to discuss her troubles and the staff could find no way of getting through to the child. It was felt that she must be feeling rejected – neither family having her all the time – and insecure because of the need to readjust constantly to the change of home. Some sibling jealousy seemed likely with a toddler in each house to compete for attention and as both parents were known to be hot-tempered it was more than possible that rows were the order of the day. Her teacher tried to give Sally opportunities to discuss her problems by leading her conversations in this direction but with no noticeable success. A chance event served at last to show that the original assumptions had been quite mistaken. The school welfare officer came to give Sally's class a talk about his work and afterwards invited the children to question him. Sally, who had followed every word with uncharacteristic attention, wanted to know what happened to children whose parents could not afford to feed and clothe them. She showed great interest in the local authority children's home and was invited to visit it later in the week. Shortly after her visit she said to her teacher, 'I wasn't half glad to see that home. It's a good one, you know. I'd been worried to death what I'd do with those two kids if both my dads got out of work at the same time.' From that time on Sally's behaviour showed almost unbelievable improvement. Her concern had been one for very basic needs.

It would be quite impossible to give a case history to illustrate every kind of disturbance that children from broken homes may suffer. Many are far more seriously affected than Sally. However, I have chosen her case because it shows so clearly the need to search behind the symptoms for the real cause and also the danger of jumping to the wrong conclusions. Children are not only unpredictable, they are also extremely resilient, and a little reassurance and support in the right direction is often enough to see the child through a difficult period.

The problem child within the school setting

We have looked at a very few examples of children who show problem behaviour. Allowing that the teacher can find out what troubles the child and has the desire to help him, what can be done within the school situation? How far must the teacher's position as leader of the whole group defeat his attempts to assist the individual? Burt and Howard (1952) refer to a long-held belief that, 'The *primary* causes of maladjustment . . . are to be found within the individual and in the structure of his relations with the rest of the family, especially as they operate during the first five years.' Although the school may appear to be the root of the trouble, the real cause is that 'a hidden disturbance has become manifest in response to school stresses'. But, these writers go on to add, in their experience a change of school has often effected a complete and permanent disappearance of the symptoms. What are we to believe? What is to be understood by 'a change of school'?

The first requirement is very often for a change of attitude towards behaviour problems as a whole. Many headteachers are still unwilling to admit to having difficult children within their school at all and fail to make referrals to the school psychological service or to appeal for extra ancillary help which might well be forthcoming. To have a child transferred to another school is regarded as an utter disgrace although, as we saw in Linda's case, this may be a positive and logical step with no value reflection upon either of the schools concerned. Class teachers who are quite prepared to confess to difficulties in teaching skills to their children feel that they are admitting serious inadequacy if they cannot control a child's behaviour. Traditional school organization, with its isolation of classes, contributes to this situation.

Miss J, in her probationary year, felt that she was failing completely. She found her class extremely hard to control and was so exhausted at the end of each day that she felt she must give up teaching, particularly as none of the other staff complained of the disobedience or noisiness of their classes. It was pure chance that allowed her one day to look in on a lesson taken by one of the senior staff and to see that, in fact, her discipline was well in keeping with that required by the school. This she still felt to be less than desirable but, relieved of a feeling of personal inadequacy, she was able to do something positive about it.

Understanding of the symptoms and causes of problem behaviour is the starting point for an altered attitude. Once the teacher appreciates that it is highly unlikely that he is solely responsible for transforming a normal, reasonable child into a mute or a demon, he can take what measures he is able to remedy matters and, if these fail, he can without loss of face ask for outside help. This help can well come from minor adjustments within the school.

Some problems can be alleviated by careful allocation of children to classes. Streaming by ability has been strongly criticized in recent years and in many schools children are now placed in classes according to age or by almost random selection. This open situation obviously exists only where there is a fairly large intake but here, at least, it can allow for some sharing out of children according to temperament and need. Mr A said of his ten year olds: 'They are very difficult to manage. Nearly half of them are continually demanding my attention. Most of them come from broken or unhappy homes and they really need care and assurance but if I show special interest in any one I must to some extent neglect the others and they are wildly jealous of each other. Anyhow, which one am I to choose?'

A reasonable balance of over-reactive and under-reactive children with, if possible, a high proportion of children with normal needs, would have allowed Mr A to give more help to individuals in the way they needed. He would probably still feel that he was failing to do them full justice but his class as a whole would benefit more than he might think if they could rely on his fairness and impartiality. Some of his children might well need to be referred for special, individual therapy but he would still be doing invaluable service by assisting them to come to terms with working within a group. This no educational psychologist has the scope to do.

Often the atmosphere of the whole class can be improved by the transfer of a single child to another class which is less easily disrupted and can tolerate a troublemaker. Heads of schools for maladjusted children are very aware of the need to limit the number of violent or aggressive children in any group and take this into account when making admissions. Normal schools could well take a leaf out of their book.

The personality of the teacher himself is another factor which more often could be profitably taken into account. Mr X may be skilled at providing challenging outlets for hyperactive children but find that the unforthcoming child irritates him beyond words. Miss Y can cope easily with tears and tale-bearing but be threatened by noise and destructiveness. Both would benefit by having in their classes the children with whom they could most easily relate. The benefit to the child is obvious, yet although we take it for granted that a teacher should specialize in his own subject we are generally wary about letting him do the same where personality is concerned.

Team teaching and vertical grouping, now more common in schools, often allow for a child to remain in close touch with one teacher for longer than would have been possible where yearly promotion is the accepted rule. Once a difficult child has formed a positive relationship it is important that this should be maintained for as long as it is needed, and one of the advantages that the middle school age grouping offers is that the child has one or two extra years before he has to cope with the many relationships that subject specialization involves. The new system is not yet sufficiently widespread, nor has it been in existence long enough, for any valid estimate to be made regarding its effect upon adolescence. However, there is a great deal of evidence to show that with certain behaviour problems, especially, for instance, school phobia, the breakdown point occurs at transfer to secondary school. The middle school could well provide the vulnerable child with much needed extra time to cope with pubescence in a less demanding setting where he is already well known. Children's needs where learning is concerned can be very different. Linda, as we have seen, was lost in a cooperative, open environment where individual initiative was expected but blossomed where the routine was strict and protective. Formal teaching methods can have a number of very specific advantages for the disturbed child: he knows exactly what is required of him; he knows when each task is finished; the degree of success he achieves is usually clear, and demands upon his imagination are limited (a state of anxiety is not likely to produce creativity). Children who are potentially able and whose behaviour problems stem largely from boredom are likely to respond to a more demanding situation where they have, as Mia Kellmer Pringle (1973) recommended, responsibility and the stimulation of new experiences. Discovering the right environment for each child may well be a matter of trial and error and, though it may eventually result in a change of school, it is obviously better for all concerned if the same school can provide for differing needs.

Not all schools are large enough to allow leeway for the difficult child to be placed in a class where both teacher and method of teaching will meet his particular needs. However, smaller schools can offer advantages of greater communication between staff and shared responsibility for problem children. Theory informs us that praise is more effective than punishment in reinforcing behaviour and that troublemakers, whose aim is to be noticed at any cost, should be ignored rather than reprimanded. The teacher who sees young Fred apparently prepared to cut his classmate's throat or do irreparable damage to school property can hardly allow himself the luxury of looking the other way. However, a scheme whereby he can be sent with a message to some understanding member of staff, who will keep him cooling his heels long enough for peace to be restored in the classroom, can save a riot. It also gives Fred an element of the attention he needs without this being at the expense of the other children. One school found their caretaker invaluable in this respect; he was always ready to find some physically testing task for hyperactive youngsters and was often able to strike up an informal friendship with them in a way that the class teacher, with his need to impose some kind of discipline, could not yet manage. In the same school the kitchen helpers did much the same for some of the shyer children who, not daring to assert themselves in the classroom, were delighted to be given prestige tasks in the dining room. A by-product of this was the growth of a strong feeling of purpose within the school. Members of staff, teaching and otherwise, frequently compared notes about the children, shared a common interest in their development, and vied with each other to be helpful. Once again, the middle school has opportunities for this shared involvement which the secondary school would find impossible.

The importance of cooperation and communication where young and inexperienced teachers are concerned is inestimable. Many who start their teaching in difficult schools say that they cannot control their classes for long enough to have a chance of speaking to the children, let alone getting to know them. Miss G, placed for her probationary year in one of the toughest schools in the district, found after six days that all she had managed to say to her class of deprived and disturbed children was, 'Sit down and be quiet. When you are quiet I'll give you something exciting to do.' As that happy circumstance had never arisen, the children remained unrewarded and unmotivated. Meanwhile, behind the classroom racket, they had become conditioned to the plaintive voice begging for silence. Obviously Miss G had to break this nonproductive pattern and withdraw with what dignity she could muster from a contest which she stood no chance of winning. Mr K in a different, but equally difficult, school had the same problem, and both decided that their negative attitudes must be ended and that, no matter what happened during the trial period, they must only reinforce acceptable behaviour (which both admitted did just exist in isolated pockets in the classroom!). Mr K's headteacher gave him full support for trying out these methods and very slowly but surely he was successful. 'The children just got fed up with baiting me when they found there was nothing in it for them. Then we began to make friends.' Miss G was not so lucky. Her headteacher was not prepared to accept the increased volume of noise which was bound to ensue while the children redoubled their efforts to get attention in the traditional way and senior members of staff were constantly sent to subdue hubbub. While Mr K's class came to respect him for his consistency and to rely upon his calm, Miss G's children were reinforced in their belief that she could not control them. Experienced teachers can give invaluable help by supporting and reassuring their younger colleagues, especially in admitting to their own earlier difficulties, but intervention is rarely effective.

To offer lists of helpful hints to teachers on how to deal with classroom problems not only smacks of presumption but is not of great use. Ultimately the resolution of the problem lies with each individual teacher who can only relate to children in the ways which his own personality dictates. Children are quick to sense insincerity and though many good teachers can 'put on an act' it will be ineffective unless it reflects genuine feeling. However, on the credit side, the tendency is towards normal, healthy development and children are remarkably resilient, even when exposed to quite traumatic experiences. They are also surprisingly sensitive to each other's problems and are less likely to resent special attention being given to a child in need than many teachers fear. Firmness, consistency, fairness and a genuine liking for children will take the teacher a long way on the road to helping the individual and controlling the class.

Let the last word come from an ex-problem child himself:

My ideal teacher should be able to control me and I would like her to help me in my every-day troubles. If you fight, the teacher must group you together and sort things out before blaming a child. They must be quiet and NOT blow their top. They must forgive you for making a mess, and not let you talk if you are a chatterbox which I am. Teachers should be helpful and kind and have a sense of humour. One very important thing is that they should enjoy teaching very much. P.S. I hope I'm not asking too much!!

References

BOLGER, A. (1973) 'Problem behaviour in schools' in *Therapeutic Education* Autumn

BURT, C. and HOWARD, M. (1952) in P. Williams (Ed) (1974) *Behaviour Problems in School* University of London Press

CLEGG, A. and MEGSON, B. (1968) *Children in Distress* Penguin

HOLT, J. (1970) *How Children Fail* Pitman

ISAACS, S. (1963 reprint) *The Psychological Aspects of Child Development* University of London Press, Institute of Education

KELLMER PRINGLE, M. (1973) 'The roots of violence and vandalism' in *Therapeutic Education* Spring

KELVIN, P. (1971) 'Socialization and conformity' in *Journal of Child Psychology and Psychiatry* October

MINISTRY OF EDUCATION (1955) *Report of the Committee on Maladjusted Children* (Underwood Report) HMSO

STOTT, D. H. (1966a) *Studies of Troublesome Children* Tavistock

STOTT, D. H. (1966b) *The Social Adjustment of Children: Manual to British Social Adjustment Guides* University of London Press

TOUGH, J. (1973) *Focus on Meaning* Allen and Unwin

WOLFF, S. (1973) *Children under Stress* Penguin

Useful further reading

CLEGG, A. and MEGSON, B. (1968) *Children in Distress* Penguin
HOLT, J. (1970) *How Children Fail* Pitman
KELLMER PRINGLE, M. (1975) *The Needs of Children* Hutchinson
STOTT, D. H. (1966) *Studies of Troublesome Children* Tavistock
WOLFF, S. (1973) *Children under Stress* Penguin

3.2 Moral education in the middle years

Colin Alves

'Moral education ought never, in any circumstances, to be rational.' This was the orthodox view of the matter among the inhabitants of Aldous Huxley's *Brave New World*. As such, it was obviously a view unacceptable to Huxley himself, yet it would presumably have been acceptable to many of Huxley's own contemporaries, inherited by them from the Victorian tradition which simply identified morality with obedience to authority. It is a happy coincidence that the year in which *Brave New World* was published (1932) also saw the publication of Jean Piaget's psychological study of *The Moral Judgement of the Child*, for Piaget's book subsequently stimulated a wide series of studies of moral development all of which have given support to the idea that children can, and ought to, be *educated* in this field, not merely 'trained'. These studies have all regarded growth in morality as very much a matter of growth in 'rationality', not just the development of blind habit or the unthinking absorption of attitudes. Clearly anyone who feels in any way responsible for the moral development of the pupils of his school must grapple with this central issue before he embarks on planning any practical activity. What is the nature of 'real' moral development? In what does moral maturity consist? What aims and methods are therefore legitimate in moral education?

In a fairly recent book Douglas Graham (1972) identifies the three main theories which have influenced thinking in this area over the past few decades – psychoanalytic theory, learning theory and cognitive development theory. Both the first two (which he identifies, respectively, with the names of Freud and Skinner, amongst others) he suggests 'have taken a basically hedonistic view of men as motivated to maximize their pleasure or satisfaction by reducing the "tension" associated with the internal stimulation which arises from "instincts" or "needs"'. In other words men become moral because the very act of being moral itself reduces tension within them.

Tensions of this sort arise from the pressure of what is popularly called conscience, and this in its turn arises from one of two sources. According to Freud and the psychoanalytic school, conscience is the result of early relationships in the child's development, particularly relationships with his parents, and of the child's own awareness of himself as open to criticism by others. The child wants to be accepted by others, and so he makes his behaviour acceptable to them. In time he 'internalizes' the expectations and demands of others. From then on he needs to be accepted just as much by himself as by others, and so he makes his behaviour conform to what he had learnt (consciously or unconsciously) to be likely to bring approval from his parents and childhood friends. If he fails to do this, his conscience is troubled and he fails to achieve the inner state of satisfaction which is so necessary to him. According to Skinner and the behaviourist school, on the other hand, what we call 'conscience' is basically a collection of conditioned responses acquired over the years as a result of specific punishments and rewards handed out (or arising from natural consequences) following on certain patterns of behaviour. The complexity of the mechanisms by which these responses are acquired does not really alter the fact that, on this argument, moral development is a very simple matter of 'upbringing' or social control of behaviour.

It would be foolish indeed to ignore the insights available to us from an approach to the problems of moral development from either of the two stances just described. And schools cannot deny that their work has to do with relationships and with systems of punishment and reward. Nevertheless, the more essential business of a school is with the cognitive development of its pupils, and it is therefore to the third of the theories identified by Graham that we shall devote the bulk of our attention.

Piaget (1932) set out the results of three interrelated enquiries. He believed that 'all morality consists in a system of rules'. He therefore investigated children's evaluations of a system of rules which impinged directly, even if not very significantly, on their lives; namely the rules governing the game of marbles. He also investigated the criteria by which children judged actions to be good or bad, particularly whether they regarded motive and intention to be of greater importance than the consequences of an action. And thirdly he investigated the ideas of 'fairness', particularly in regard to punishment.

His findings (in a very simplified form) were as follows:

1   The young child's first real concept of 'rules' is that they are 'not only obligatory, but also inviolable' – 'sacred absolutes' as Norman Bull (1969) calls them – handed down by an unchanging and unchangeable tradition. At about the age of ten, however, 'the rule of a game appears to the child ... as the outcome of a free decision (by the players) and worthy of respect in as far as it has enlisted mutual consent'.

2   The young child judges the 'badness' of an action by its consequences –

often in terms of any punishment that might follow it. It is worse to break a tray full of cups by accident than one cup on purpose, because more cups actually get broken in the first case. Some children of this age, Piaget claims, 'look upon lying as naughty because it is punished, and if it were not punished no guilt would attach to it'. But a change occurs, again at about the age of ten, and lying is then seen as wrong because it undermines mutual trust; deliberate damage is seen as wrong because it is an 'antisocial' act. (Piaget did note, however, that some younger children who had been specifically taught by their parents to pay attention to motives rather than consequences, reached the point of judging by motive and intention at a very early age. The significance of this will be seen later.)

3   For the very young child the question of 'fairness' does not present itself, but when it does (at about the age of eight, according to Piaget) it is seen primarily in terms of equality – everyone getting equal shares (unless they've been naughty!). From about eleven upwards this strict egalitarianism gives way to the more mature concept of equity, which takes due account of individual needs, etc.

Interpreting these findings Piaget drew on ideas from the fields of philosophy and sociology. First, from philosophy he took the distinction between *heteronomy* and *autonomy*, terms which had been central to Kant's thinking. Heteronomy, 'government by others', was a form of morality dependent on authority and external control; the 'goodness' of an action was defined by others, and one performed these 'good' actions because one was told to and would be punished if one failed to conform. Conversely, autonomy, 'self-government', depended on internal forces of self-control; one freely decided for oneself what was good and acted accordingly. For Piaget, as for Kant, autonomous morality was the only true morality.

This view was reinforced by Piaget's dependence on Durkheim's theories about the social bases of morality: 'Society is the only source of morality'. In the case of heteronomous morality, however, society (or at least the mini-societies of family, school or church) imposed its moral code upon the child. With autonomous morality, the child developed his own inner morality by free *interaction* within the society of his friends and playmates. And so Piaget claimed that the natural movement of the young child's moral thinking was from 'other-directed' to 'self-directed', a movement from the false morality of conformity and obedience to the true morality of cooperation and free intention.

Piaget's interpretation of his findings has been criticized on a number of grounds, but perhaps the most significant criticism has come from researchers who have compared Piaget's tests of moral judgment with his own findings from other areas. For example, the work of R. B. Stuart (1967) and then of P. M. Crowley (1968) suggests that the younger child's apparent inability to judge by motive and intention was caused, in Piaget's test situations, by 'centration', a term which Piaget himself has elsewhere defined as 'a tendency to concentrate on some striking aspect of an object or a question, to the neglect of other more relevant features'. In his famous experiments involving the pouring of water from tall, thin glasses into low, wide dishes the children 'centred' on the striking difference of shape and so were unable to see that the volume of water remained the same throughout. In just the same way, Stuart and Crowley argued, when Piaget told his story about the two people breaking cups, the younger children being questioned were so struck by the enormous number of cups broken in the first instance that they were unable to 'focus' on the intentions of the people involved. Another argument leading to the same conclusion is that if the children had been told about someone breaking *one* cup by accident, and someone else breaking one cup on purpose, they would not then have been faced with the complex intellectual problem of balancing out 'good intentions plus bad results' against 'bad intentions plus bad, though not quite so bad, results'. To say that the young children found the problem too complex is a perfectly legitimate conclusion to draw from the experiment. It is not legitimate, however, to say that the children were only able to take account of consequences.

The majority of researchers who have followed up Piaget's work have suggested a much more complex framework than he did for the developing moral judgment. They also reject his simplistic belief that heteronomy is bad and autonomy is good. Bull (1969), for example, argues that heteronomy is a necessary and vital step forward from the complete amorality of the young child, and that without it autonomy will not develop: 'It is only through learning that he "must" that the child can ever come to know that he "ought".' The purpose of external rules, backed up by a system of rewards and punishments, is 'the control of impulse'. Fear of punishment when rules are broken develops into guilt under similar circumstances and guilt develops into conscience. Bull also makes the point that even when conscience develops, fear and guilt are not left behind. He cites the example of a motorist:

> Even on one and the same journey he may, according to circum-
> stances, behave on different moral levels. At one time, he may be
> guided purely by impulse; at another, by fear of the law; at another,
> by respect for public opinion; at another, by his own inner principles
> of behaviour.

In America, Kohlberg (1963) has also modified the Piagetian position in a roughly similar kind of way. His research has led him to identify six types of judgment about how to behave. In type 1 'good behaviour' is that which avoids punishment and/or censure by 'important people'. In type 2 it is that which contributes to the satisfaction of specific personal needs. In other words, both these types are basically egocentric, type 1 in a negative way, type 2 in a positive way. Kohlberg classifies them together under the general label of *pre-moral*. The next two types he jointly labels *conventional role-conformity:* type 3 is what he describes as a 'good-boy morality of maintaining good relations', based on specific approval by others, while type 4 is more concerned with maintaining social order for its own sake. For type 3 the reward of good behaviour would be 'acceptance'; for type 4 the equivalent would be the actual feeling of having done one's duty. The final pair reflect a more consciously thought out type of morality. Kohlberg labels them *self-accepted moral principles*, and describes type 5 as a 'morality of contract and of democratically accepted law', while type 6 is a 'morality of individual principles of conscience', a fully autonomous morality.

Kohlberg believes that a pattern of moral development can be traced which moves gradually 'upwards' through the six types and yet, like Bull, he believes that the lower types are never entirely left behind. Among seven year olds, for example, he found that over 70 per cent of their moral judgments were of the punishment-avoiding type 1; about 25 per cent were of the specific need-satisfying type 2; and virtually all the rest were of type 3. Among ten year olds, the pattern of response was much more mixed. Punishment-avoidance still predominated, but only just, with 32 per cent as compared with 27 per cent for specific need-satisfaction; acceptance by one's group (type 3) motivated 22 per cent of the responses, while a sense of duty (type 4) was reflected in 16 per cent of the responses; the remaining 3 per cent were classifiable mainly under type 5, though type 6 was not entirely absent. On moving on to thirteen year olds a dramatic shift in the pattern could be seen. It was type 4 (sense of duty) which now pre-dominated with 32 per cent; this was followed by type 3 (winning approval) with 25 per cent; type 6 (democratic contract) now came third highest with 15 per cent, and types 1 and 2 had dropped way down the list with 11 per cent and 13 per cent respectively (though it should be noted that this still meant that virtually a quarter of all the responses, even at thirteen, were of a *pre-moral* character); type 6 responses were still fewest in number, with 4 per cent, but at least they had increased much more rapidly between ages ten and thirteen than they had between seven and ten.

Kohlberg agrees with Bull, then, that none of the early stages are left completely behind as moral growth occurs. He disagrees with Bull (and Piaget), however, when he asserts that the evidence we have is not strong enough to substantiate the claim that 'attainment of each mode of thought is prerequisite to the attainment of the next higher in the hypothetical sequence'.

Williams and Williams (1970) have also played down the sequential claims of earlier investigators. Their analysis of moral judgment is fourfold (with a fifth category of *amoral* or *uncontrolled response*, a response which shows no regard for either expedient or altruistic considerations). These four modes they describe as follows:

Self-considering
A situation is evaluated in terms of its consequences, but these consequences relate to the subject himself. They may be matters of naive expediency – thinking in terms of rewards and punishments – or they may have a more sophisticated element, in which case the subject is thinking of his own emotional or social discomfort (guilt-avoiding, or shame-avoiding).

Self-obeying
The problem is not evaluated, but is simply referred to an internalized rule or criterion. In this group we place the inhibiting aspects of conscience and comparison with an ideal self (ego-ideal).

Other-obeying
Again the problem is not evaluated, but is referred to an *external* authority. We distinguish between various types of authority, which range from a personal authority figure to the social or peer group, and to such abstract embodiments of authority as the law.

Other-considering
The problem is evaluated in terms of its consequences for other people. In this group we find empathic, altruistic, utilitarian and rationally generalized forms of moral thinking.

After setting out these four modes Williams and Williams comment that (as in the case of Bull's motorist) most moral judgments involve all four modes:

Most of us refrain from stealing from a shop. Naturally, since the reader is a sensitive and intelligent person, this is because he has worked out that the consequences are harmful to the shopkeeper and, if his example were followed, to society in general. But it is *also* because he would go to prison if he were caught; *and also* because authority is against it; *and also* because he would be ashamed of himself if his friends knew; *and also* because he just feels it wouldn't be right. And so on.

They also note that this mixture of responses is as typical of the child as of the adult, though to a lesser degree. This supports Kohlberg's view that the various modes could well be parallel operations rather than sequential stages. Evidence is presented that even four-year-old children are perfectly capable of altruistic thought, even though of a very simple type. ('Why is it wrong to steal?' ' 'Cos they might be looking for it.') It is also suggested that the development which undoubtedly occurs as the child grows older, bringing increasing complexity and flexibility to his thinking, occurs *within each* of the four modes (although the self-obeying mode may be an exception). Certainly it is easy to see how the other-obeying mode develops from 'because Daddy says so', through conformity to one's peer-group, to an abstract 'respect for the law' – which can only develop when the child reaches a formal-operational level of thinking, to use Piaget's term. Similarly the self-considering mode moves on from simple expediency (based on considerations of punishment and reward) as the child becomes intellectually advanced enough to hypothesize both about possible long-term, and also about less concrete, consequences.

The question now arises whether developments such as these are equally possible in the case of every individual. Clearly the speed of development, and possibly its extent, does depend to some degree on the individual's intelligence. The research findings point firmly (though not unanimously) in this direction. Graham (1972) sums the matter up in this way:

> There seem to be two main ways in which intelligence is relevant to moral development:
>
> 1 It enables children better to judge what the probable results of their behaviour are likely to be...
> 2 It enables children to acquire more abstract linguistic and conceptual tools in terms of which to judge behaviour.... As far as feelings of guilt and remorse are concerned, it would seem that intelligence is less likely to be directly relevant.... Relatively high intelligence does not guarantee a high level of moral conduct; and, where the moral level is low for other reasons, intelligence may simply operate to enable a rascal to indulge in more sophisticated roguery, with a better chance of succeeding in his evil design and avoiding the consequences.

In other words, a person with low intelligence will not reach the higher levels of moral judgment, but the possession of high intelligence does not inevitably lead to a developed moral sense. For 'other reasons' the 'moral level' may be low.

What might these reasons be? As we saw at the very beginning of this survey, the psychoanalytic and behaviourist schools of thought claim that the capacity for moral judgment is affected by experiences of childhood relationships and/or of social control. These could predispose a person to a preference for one mode of response rather than another.

There may also be a certain measure of truth in the long-established theory of 'personality-types', interpreted in terms of moral characteristics.

For example, Havighurst and Taba (1963) identify five such types: the unadjusted, the defiant, the submissive, the adaptive and the self-directive. In another study Peck and Havighurst (1960), while keeping the number of types to five, used a different set of labels: the amoral, the expedient, the conforming, the irrational-conscientious and the rational-altruistic. Despite the fact that Peck and Havighurst comment that these five were 'each conceived as the representative of a successive stage in the psychosocial development of the individual', the crucial difference between this approach and that of Kohlberg (1963) or Williams and Williams (1970) is that the latter work from specific, separable 'responses' (*all* of which can often be found in the make-up of one single individual at one given time), whereas the 'personality-type' approach suggests that certain individuals consistently (and, possibly, unalterably) respond in one particular manner, and remain 'true to type' at least over a long period of time, if not throughout their lives.

The most generally accepted application of 'personality-type' theory is in connection with sex-difference. It is commonly held that girls are more likely to be moral than boys are. This question, however, is not nearly as clear-cut as popular opinion might suggest. Admittedly Norman Bull's (1969) findings indicate that girls are consistently more honest than boys, at least between the ages of ten and seventeen (and particularly around the age of thirteen), and the Eppels (1966) found four times more boys than girls who were 'dominantly materialistic'. But many other tests in the general area of social values and moral judgments show little difference between the sexes other than those which arise from a general conformity to traditional sex roles (girls tending to be more humanitarian, more 'motherly', 'softer'). In terms of Kohlberg's six types it has been suggested that among those (many) adults whose normal responses are restricted to types 3 and 4 (conventional role-conformity), women 'stabilize' within type 3, men within type 4. Kohlberg comments:

> Personal concordance morality (i.e. the maintenance of good relations) is a functional morality for housewives and mothers; it is not for business men and professionals. Adult moral stabilization, then, appears to be a matter of increased congruence between belief and social role.

This opens up the whole sociological perspective on the question of moral development. Development is not something which depends solely on inner unfolding; it is very much affected by upbringing. Williams and Williams directly relate their four modes of responses to four different forms of moral constraint exercised upon children. They quote 'four mothers', each having told their young child not to pull his sister's hair, and each having been asked 'Why not?' The first gives the answer,

'Because I say so'; the second, 'Because you mustn't'; the third, 'Because I'll smack you if you do'; the fourth, 'Because it hurts her and makes her cry'.

It is often suggested that these forms of constraint are used in different proportions according to the social class of the families concerned. Certainly there are research findings which suggest that individuals from different classes exhibit markedly different and characteristic moral responses which cannot be accounted for in terms of intelligence differences. For example, E. Lerner, back in 1937, found that children from 'high-status' homes took more account of circumstances and motives when making moral judgments than did children from 'low-status' homes. This was confirmed by the work of Leonore Boehm in the 1960s, though the class differences, according to her findings, seemed to diminish considerably from about the age of ten upwards. She also reported (in contradiction to Lerner) that where 'independence of adult authority-figures' is concerned it is working-class children who score more highly.

The existence of class differences affecting the rate of moral development, and possibly even the direction of development, inevitably raises sociological issues regarding the *goal* of moral education. In recent years a great deal of criticism has been levelled against schools for 'wishing to impose middle-class morality on working-class children'. This is usually seen in terms of schools preferring behaviour which is characterized by quietness and tidiness, genteel ways and an unassertive manner, rather than the cheeky robustness, noisy spontaneity and 'healthy lack of respect' supposedly displayed by the working-class child. But to look at it this way is to pitch the argument on the wrong level. The real argument is not just about whether to encourage or discourage certain styles of classroom behaviour. It is to do with much more fundamental questions.

Williams and Williams, as we have seen, have identified four different modes of moral response, and they class as *amoral* only those responses over which no control of any sort is exercised, responses which are 'impulse-governed, directed to the gratification of one's own (immediate) desires'. Even judgments based on nothing other than 'naive expediency' are still labelled as 'moral' judgments. Similarly 'conformity to social norms' is accepted as a 'moral' response, a use of terms which would have been unacceptable to Piaget, who regarded 'conformity' as something quite different from 'morality'.

Williams and Williams did not actually differentiate between their 'four mothers' on the basis of social class (and indeed they went on to suggest that all four sanctions will often be used by one and the same mother during the rearing of her child). However, the work of Lerner and Boehm suggests that the mother who says 'Because it hurts her and makes her cry' is more likely to be a middle-class rather than a working-class mother. Does this mean that 'other-considering' morality is simply a middle-class morality, different from but no *better* than the self-considering morality of 'You've bloody got to look after number one in this world, mate' or the other-obeying morality of 'What would the neighbours say!?'

Further sociological evidence which might be deemed to be relevant has been summarized by Barry Sugarman (1967). He suggests that 'those who live in the subculture of the lower-status group, with their less adequate intellectual comprehension of the world around them, tend to find the world extremely confusing, uncertain and with little patterning or orderliness'. This in turn leads to a greater degree of fatalism and a greater concentration on rewards to be extracted from the present situation, rather than any reliance on the possibility of long-term rewards being considerably larger (the 'deferred gratification' principle so characteristic of the middle-class view of life). Sugarman also suggests that lower-status parents are less likely to be consistent in their treatment of their children (thus confirming the lack of orderliness such children already find in the world). The picture which would seem to emerge from all this is one of children who are likely to live by impulse, controlled only by the force of adult authority, and even by that only when it is physically present. This is a picture not of one of the Williams' four modes rather than another, but of their *amoral* category. To put it another way, it is not that there is one sort of morality among the middle class and another sort among the working class; rather is it that the conditions which prevent the formation of *any* stable form of morality are inevitably more frequently the lot of the working-class child than of his middle-class contemporary.

To say this, however, is not to say that the children of *typical* working-class parents are amoral, nor that amorality *characterizes* the lower status groups. In the National Opinion Poll Moral Education enquiry in 1969 over 50 per cent of the (random) sample expressed the view that moral training was either the most important or second most important aspect of the education of secondary pupils. This refutes any suggestion that the majority group within our society exhibits a lack of concern about morality. In any case, the evidence of everyday experience shows that the middle class do not have a monopoly of altruism. Nor are prudential, expedient and conformist responses the monopoly of the working class. 'You've bloody got to look after number one' translates easily into 'Well, one has to take the necessary steps to safeguard one's standard of living, doesn't one?' and concern for what the neighbours think is as prevalent in *Waggoners' Walk* as in *Coronation Street* (if not more so!).

It is not even as if there were a problem of a conflict of moralities along the line of majority versus minority, irrespective of class. At first sight this may appear to be the case. There is plenty of evidence to show that Kohlberg's type 6 morality is only found among a very small group of people. Kohlberg and Kramer (1969), for example, found that the normal changes in moral judgment which occur beyond the age of thirteen consist of considerable further reduction in the pre-moral responses, but a continuing domination of type 4 thinking ('sense of duty') among men, or type 3 ('good relations') among women, with some further growth of type 5 but hardly any of type 6. But the argument at this point can become confused if one uses the general term 'rational-altruism' for Kohlberg's type 6 and then identifies this with the 'other-considering' morality we have been discussing. What specifically characterizes type 6 is its *rationality*, not its altruism. Altruism can be rooted quite as readily in type 3 and type 4 levels of judgment – in which case a form of altruism can be seen as the morality of the majority. The only point at issue is whether it is a rationally *developed* altruism. In most cases it is not, and in this sense 'rational-altruism' is a minority stance. But this does not mean that in trying to encourage rational-altruism the schools are trying to impose a 'minority view' onto the children of the majority. The question of numbers has nothing to do with the argument. It is not a question of conflicting moralities; it is a question of the level of development to which the common morality can be extended.

This leads us to a philosophical consideration of what developed morality, mature morality, the moral ideal, should be. The general ideal towards which liberal education as a whole is striving has been crisply defined by R. F. Dearden (1968) as 'a personal autonomy based on reason', and he amplifies this by now familiar phrase by suggesting that such an ideal will involve us in (among other things) being 'fair in our dealings with others'; 'personally responsible for our choices', and avoiding 'self-deception or the deception of others'. This echoes very closely (even if not exactly) the definition of 'moral maturity' given by William Kay (1968):

> The morally mature person must be rational; he must be altruistic; he must be responsible; and he must be morally independent. Here one has four primary moral attitudes all of which in a fully developed form mark the morally mature. It may be argued by some that a rationally moral man is morally mature. But is he if he is not altruistic? Again others may say that an altruistic, responsible man is morally mature. And again it must be asked, 'Is he, if he is not reasonable?' Indeed, it is clear that moral maturity is not only indexed by rationality, altruism, responsibility and moral independence, but consists of their co-existence in a developed form.

Another way of approaching this issue is used by Graham (1972). Rather than trying to define the 'morally mature' man he concentrates on defining 'moral education' itself, in a passage which is worth quoting at length:

The ultimate aim of moral education is to raise the level of moral judgment and consequent behaviour, in such a way that judgment and behaviour are based to as great an extent as possible upon generalized principles. These are principles concerned with the proper consideration of the rights and interests of others. They require that rules or laws which are applicable to some should be applicable to all, except (in so far as) ... special rights may be allowed to those with special responsibilities or with special handicaps.... By the general application of moral principles we mean that no person can claim for himself special privileges *except* in respect of special extenuating circumstances.... Although factors like limitations of intellect mean that by no means everyone can reach the highest levels of development, and constitutional factors and/or early experience may predispose to psychopathy or 'consciencelessness', we must aim at getting everyone to as high a level as possible, and at having as many people as possible capable of thinking about moral problems and principles, and about ways in which principles should be applied to new and changing circumstances.

In case readers feel this is an approach to the problem which overstresses the intellectual aspects (for example, especially, in the last couple of clauses) it should be emphasized that Graham speaks of 'moral judgment *and consequent behaviour*' in his first sentence. What exactly is involved in this compound of decision-based action? This is the question to which John Wilson (1973) has been devoting careful and considerable thought over the past few years. He has suggested a list of 'components' of moral action, which he has implied in a series of questions about the hypothetical person 'S':

(a) What rules or principles does S think he ought to follow? What feelings or emotions does he have that support his belief that he should use these concepts and principles? (He may think in a general or theoretical way that he ought to use the concept of 'honour', but have no feelings attached to it – not feel remorse when he fails to deploy it, for instance.)

(b) What knowledge or awareness does S have of the surrounding circumstances? This would include (i) S's ability to identify his own and others' emotions; (ii) S's knowledge of the relevant 'hard' facts.

(c) What social skill does S have in dealing with people?

(d) Does S bring the above to bear on those situations with which he is actually confronted? Does he use the principles he claims as right so as to make a sincere *decision* to act in a certain way?

(e) Does S actually *act* in accordance with his decision?

In an earlier book Wilson had identified a somewhat simpler list of components, giving them names derived from the first syllable of a number of classical Greek terms. The major difference between the two lists is that, whereas in the earlier version he assumed that S would be motivated by a form of altruism, allowing 'other people's feelings and interests actually to count and weigh with one' (what Graham would call 'the proper consideration of the rights and interests of others'), in the later version quoted above he is very careful not to prejudge *which* principles S ought to follow. As an alternative to an altruistic base he suggests the possibility of using principles drawn from a 'personal honour' ethic, such as that upheld by Japanese samurai, and many other basic sets of principles could be listed: for example, a 'nationalist' ethic in which the overriding consideration is service to one's country; or a 'creative' ethic, such as that passionately held by many artists, where nothing can be allowed to take precedence over the processes of creativity; or a Marxist ethic, in which the first consideration must always be the advancement of the future communistic society; and so on.

But, having drawn our attention to the possibility of other bases, Wilson then reminds us that a moral *educator* (i.e. someone who wishes to affect his pupils' behaviour, even if only in the very unspecific way described above by Graham) will need to decide what general principles are going to underlie his approach. So, for much of his illustrative material, Wilson starts from the rational-altruistic principle generally accepted within liberal education, i.e., the principle of being fair in our dealings with others. Probably the most memorable illustration he has produced of this approach is his analysis of the thought and behaviour of a 'morally educated person driving a car' (I have supplemented the original Greek-derived labels with cross-references to the list of questions listed above):

He identifies with other people sufficiently for their sufferings or inconvenience to count with him (PHIL: a). He knows how aggravating it is if one is held up by an unnecessarily slow driver (EMP: b(i)). He knows that if, say, he drives his car at a steady thirty miles per hour on a crowded main road, most people will want to pass him, because most cars cruise at more than thirty (GIG: b(ii)). Putting these together, he formulates and commits himself to a rule – 'It is not right to drive at only thirty under these circumstances (DIK:d). He is then capable of acting on the principle, not overpowered by fear of going too fast, or a desire to be obstructive or anything of that sort, and increases his speed (KRAT:e). (*Note:* In the later developments of this scheme Wilson identified three or four subdivisions within each of PHIL, EMP, GIG and KRAT (for example, distinguishing 'knowledge that' from 'knowledge how' within GIG) and reduced DIK to one of the subdivisions of KRAT.)

There is widespread agreement, then, among these writers that 'mature/educated morality' consists in a combination of altruistic intent (at least in the sense of having an overriding commitment to respecting the rights of others) with informed awareness of the facts of the situation, plus the intellectual skill and psychological freedom of decision to apply one's principles correctly to the circumstances confronting one. This is the preferred model, as it were. It may be true that in practice the majority of people are content with a conformist type of morality, for the simple reason that this seems to work quite well without need of very much thought. But it works well only in situations where the twin dangers of totalitarianism on the one hand or anarchy on the other are no more than very distant possibilities. Unfortunately societies which are able to arrive democratically at a lasting consensus on all moral questions are few and far between. In other societies, such as our own present society, positive steps have to be taken to help people cope with the lack of consensus. As Graham says, in a continuation of the passage quoted earlier:

> Moral principles are not rules of behaviour. . . . In the case of a society where values are relatively static, there is in general less distinction between principles and rules. The appropriate conduct in various circumstances tends to be generally agreed, and therefore it is easier for people to learn applicable rules, and apply them effectively. This is because most people's expectations are more or less the same, and situations involving dilemmas or uncertainty as to how one should behave are less likely to occur. In times when traditional rules have to an appreciable extent ceased to be generally accepted, especially among younger people, the learning of rules prescribing and proscribing behaviour is less likely to be effective . . . as an adequate guide for behaviour. Hence in these circumstances it is more important to try to educate as many people as possible, not in the old rules, but in the capacity for examining principles and weighing up current practice to see how far it is compatible with principles.

This capacity has been defined by Peter McPhail (1972) in simple terms as the capacity to *choose*. By setting this capacity within a general framework of altruism (as do all the other writers we have considered) McPhail is able to define the overall aim of moral education as being 'to help boys and girls learn to care and to choose'. This phrase comes in the opening paragraph of the 'teacher's book' from the Schools Council project in moral education of which McPhail is the director. Notice that the phrase is not 'to leave the boys and girls free to choose'. Such an aim could hardly be described as 'educational' at all. Pupils have to be helped to *learn* how to choose. And yet McPhail is as insistent as Graham, Wilson *et al* that moral education must basically concern itself with principles, not with rules:

> Rules may have moral functions and conventions may be expressive of consideration for others as well as having a value as a means of reducing the number of conscious decisions which I have to make in relatively unimportant daily situations, but rules and conventions are not what morality is about any more than to obey such rules and conventions is necessarily to be moral. We want boys and girls to learn to choose, to decide what in particular situations they will do, so long as it is only consistent with taking the needs, interests and feelings of others into consideration as well as their own.

But as well as needing help in learning to choose, pupils need help in learning to care. Being considerate to others is not something which comes automatically to everyone. They may not feel motivated to act considerately, and even if they do (even if their intentions are right) they may not have the sensitivity and insight, or the background knowledge, to see what is actually 'considerate' behaviour in a given situation. There is truth, for example, in the adage that sometimes one has to be cruel to be kind, and one has to learn through guided experience when this truth applies – *and* when it doesn't.

Sensitivity and insight need to be developed, in any case, in a more fundamental way. McPhail has identified a complex of *skills* and *abilities* which a person needs to exercise when he is responding morally to a situation. This complex is made up of elements of 'choosing' as well as 'caring', and has many points of contact with the list of questions devised by Wilson. But McPhail's emphasis here is very much on sensitivity and insight in the *inter-personal* situation, rather than on the abstract consideration of moral issues – i.e. Wilson's question (c) comes to the fore much more strongly than in any of the examples we have quoted so far. McPhail puts it this way:

> The establishment of an 'I-Thou' relationship requires that we develop four abilities:
>
> 1 *Reception ability*, meaning the ability to be, and remain, 'switched on' to the right wavelength, to listen, to look, to receive the messages sent out by others.
> 2 *Interpretative ability*, meaning the ability to interpret accurately the message which another person is sending, what he really means, what he really wants.

3 *Response ability*, meaning the ability to decide on and adopt appropriate reactions – to meet another's needs. It involves decision-making, evaluation, the use of reason as well as psychological knowhow; the calculation and the prediction of the consequence of actions, of possibility and probability.

4 *Message ability*, meaning the ability to translate appropriate reactions into clearly transmitted unambivalent messages.

These abilities need to be analysed as well as practised, practised as well as analysed. Pupils need to become *consciously aware* of what 'being considerate' involves; but as well as being conscious of these skills they need to have plenty of opportunities for exercising them appropriately, both in real life situations and in simulated conditions (most obviously in drama work).

We need to remind ourselves at this point of what the more recent findings of developmental psychologists have suggested, namely that children even of preschool age can exhibit the full range of moral responses, but that each type of response is capable of considerable development as the child matures. However, without denying what has just been said, our greatest concern, if we accept the view of the moral 'ideal' held by McPhail etc., will be with the fourth of Williams' modes. We will ensure that the two self-related and the 'other-obeying' modes are not left at an infantile stage of development, but we will concentrate particularly on the fullest possible development of the 'other-considering' mode. This development is obviously dependent on general intellectual development, but can be speeded up or retarded by the treatment the child receives from adults. Take, for example, the ability to give due regard to motive when judging the rightness or wrongness of a person's actions. Lunzer and Morris (1968) see this as central to their analysis of 'growth towards maturity'. They suggest that the very young child learns 'to distinguish between things which he does accidentally and things he does on purpose because the reaction to the situation is different when it is done intentionally'. From this basis of self-knowledge he is then able to 'distinguish between the intentional and accidental actions of others'. They point out that this process is not idle observation on the part of the child: 'Attention to motives has functional value in so far as it enables the child to predict reactions to his behaviour.' It is therefore crucial for the child's development that adult reaction to his behaviour is consistent, and does indeed distinguish between accidental and intentional actions. The parent or the teacher who punishes a child without listening to his explanations of what happened – i.e., without appearing to take any account of even the possibility of an 'accident' – is seriously hindering the child's moral development in a very crucial area, for the child is being taught to persist in the infantile method of judging the 'worth' of all actions solely by their consequences. The results of such teaching eventually manifest themselves in the 'moral viewpoint' that 'a thing is only wrong if you get caught'.

I have used the word 'teaching' in the last sentence quite deliberately, even though it refers to an act of punishment, not to an act of formal instruction. Punishment does not merely reinforce (or counteract) habit, operating solely at the behavioural level; it contributes directly to the offender's intellectual understanding of right and wrong. And it is not only punishment which does this. Any and every aspect of an adult-child relationship is *teaching* the child something about modes of moral response, teaching that it is a good thing to be considerate of others, or else teaching the opposite. As McPhail says repeatedly, a school must be conscious of what it does to its pupils through the relationships which exist in the school, and through the structures which support these relationships. (*Note:* The impact of school structures on the moral health of its pupils is such an enormous question that it needs an essay to itself. Just a few of the matters to be discussed would be the decentralization of the school 'to produce psychologically viable groups', the involvement of the pupils in 'some degree of self-government', the design of the school's reward system so that it supports success of as wide a variety as possible. (These, and other related items, are listed in Wilson, 1973, page 410.) Derek Wright (1971) comments that 'if we are to take moral education seriously, and even more if we take the autonomous character as the ideal to be pursued, then it is no use supposing that moral education is something that can be tacked on to the existing curriculum as an extra; on the contrary, all aspects of school life must be looked at in its light, and it must enter centrally into our concept of what a school is.' See also Sugarman in *Moral Education*, September 1969.)

Treatment by others during childhood and adolescence is the greatest formative influence on an adolescent's style of life. As children develop verbally, arguments of increasing complexity may be advanced to justify action; but the springs of action – the motivation of action – are generally to be found in the treatment which the individual has enjoyed or suffered.

Examples of adult behaviour which inhibit the growth of other-considering responses among their pupils could produce a formidable list. Just a few of those quoted by the adolescents interviewed by McPhail were as follows: orders without explanation, criticism without positive suggestions, personal remarks, exhibitions of temper, manifestly unfair punishment, refusal to listen, petty verbal nastiness and sarcasm. McPhail sums it up by saying that 'bad' behaviour, 'inconsiderate' behaviour, was any behaviour which had unpleasant consequences for the children, '*and which made them feel less like people*' (my italics).

Any consciously adopted formal system of moral education in a school will fail completely unless it is supported by an equally conscious effort on the part of *all* adults in the school (non-academic as well as academic staff) to exhibit in practice the considerate style of life which the school is seeking to encourage among its pupils: 'If teachers do not earn respect by their own adherence to moral principles, these principles are likely to be discredited and appear as of little importance in the eyes of the children.' 'Our behaviour, our treatment of others, is far more eloquent than any statements we make about morality.'

But statements we must, and should, make. Moral education is not *only* a matter of relationships, however important these may be. Traditionally, school assembly has been the place where 'moral statements' have been made. Sixty per cent of the schools whose staffs were consulted by McPhail claimed that assembly was one of 'the areas of school life which they thought contributed most to the moral development of their pupils'. The pupils themselves did not see it quite the same way. Occasionally assembly was felt to be helpful ('I look forward to *her* services because she talks to the pupils more than any others and connects our lives in with it.') but of much more value in the eyes of the pupils themselves were opportunities for group discussion. Too often, however, one hears accounts of discussion which fails to engage the pupils' attention, and which proves a waste of everybody's time. What seems to be needed to make discussion successful is that the subject matter should be controversial. This is even more important than the relevance of the subject matter to the children's own experience, though such relevance will naturally bring added involvement. Kohlberg's comments on this point are as follows:

> I have found that my hypothetical and remote but obviously conflict situations are of intense interest to almost all adolescents and lead to lengthy debate among them. They are involving because the adult right answer is not obviously at hand to discourage the child's own moral thought as so often is the case. . . . The pat little stories in school readers in which virtue always triumphs or in which everyone is really nice are unlikely to have any value in the stimulation of moral development. Only the presentation of genuine and difficult moral conflicts can have this effect.

Kohlberg speaks of 'adolescents' being interested in his material, but the principle he is discussing applies to younger children as well. One of his colleagues used some of the same material with twelve year olds, in an experiment which incorporated a form of teaching. Each twelve year old had one of Kohlberg's stories read to him and was then 'asked to play the part of the main character in the story and to ask advice concerning the issue posed'. This advice was then supplied by the experimenter, and the sort of comment which was most effective in influencing the subject's general moral thinking proved to be comment couched in terms appropriate to the moral stage just *above* that displayed by the subject in a previous test. When that earlier test was re-administered a significant number of the subjects improved their rating as a result of the role play they had taken part in. It should be noted that the subjects were not tested on the material involved in the role playing. They did not just *learn* a new solution to one specific problem. 'They learned to *apply* a more mature form of argument' to problems in general.

Another colleague of Kohlberg's took a class of children once a week for three months and explored 'hypothetical moral conflicts' with them. He got the children to put forward their own solutions to each problem as it was presented, categorizing these solutions (*without* telling the children, of course) as 'stage 2', 'stage 3' or 'stage 4'. He then took one of the stage 3 solutions and set it side by side with one of the stage 2 solutions, discussing their respective merits with the class. He then did the same with the stage 3 solution and one of the stage 4 solutions. Finally he put forward a stage 5 solution of his own for discussion. After three months he found that 45 per cent of the children in the class were now normally offering solutions one stage higher than the ones they had been offering at the beginning of the experiment. (In a control group there had only been an 8 per cent improvement over the same period.) (*Note:* Anyone adopting this technique may find it useful to be warned in advance that Bull has come up with evidence which suggests that thresholds in moral development may be specific to different moral issues – for example, heteronomous judgments predominated in his sample up to the age of thirteen where *lying* was concerned; to the age of eleven about *stealing*, and only to the age of nine about *cheating*. One should therefore not be discouraged if there appears to be occasional 'regression' in the group's moral insight as the discussion moves from one issue to another.)

Of course, if one follows the Williams and Williams account of moral development, then it will not be enough simply to contrast 'stage' with 'stage', or 'mode' with 'mode' in this structured type of discussion; one will have to identify the *level* of the children's answers *within each* of the four modes, and compare these answers one with another. The complexity of such a comparison is probably beyond the capacity of all but the most intelligent children within the middle school age range. Indeed many teachers may be sceptical of embarking on *any* form of discussion of moral issues with children of this age. But, given that the 'discussion group' is *small* enough (and this should not be difficult with modern methods of classroom management), even the younger children will benefit from being given the opportunity to talk with an adult about issues which have emerged, say in the stories they have been reading. With older children material can be introduced with the deliberate intention of provoking discussion (whether it be discussion of the highly structured type suggested by Kohlberg's colleagues, or of a more general introductory type aimed simply at facilitating verbalization of ideas and awareness of conflicting viewpoints). Such material can be drawn from books, films, tape recordings, case studies, potted biographies or other 'situation-establishers' such as are provided by the *Lifeline* programme (McPhail *et al* 1972). John Wilson has suggested the use and study of games for the exploration of the function of rules. (Can the children make up a new game with its own rules? Can they improve on the rules of an existing game? What happens when opponents play to different sets of rules? etc. etc.) He also speaks of 'games' in a more technical sense, i.e. the acting out of simulation exercises (acting out a dictatorship situation, for example).

The use of simulation exercises and role play has already been noted in connection with McPhail's list of relational skills. There it was suggested that pupils needed not only to analyse, but also to practise these skills. The teacher concerned with moral education needs to discover not only the best means of stimulating, focusing and structuring discussion, but also the best vehicles for the *exercise* of morality within the school community. Role play and drama work generally can open up the emotions through the imagination, but a wide range of real life situations can also be provided by the school to enable its pupils to offer practical care and service towards others. The classroom hamster has its part to play in this; so has the school entertainment laid on for the local old-age pensioners, or even the collection of milk-bottle tops for some charitable cause (as long as this is not allowed to remain remote, impersonal and mechanical, as sometimes happens).

I have deliberately done no more than give a few examples of 'classroom techniques' because the techniques of moral education are for the most part fairly generalized techniques. The important thing to establish is the nature of the process in whose service the techniques are employed. It is appropriate therefore to close by summarizing once again the educational implications of the theories of moral development and the definitions of moral maturity which we have been considering.

If one follows Piaget, then all one's efforts as a teacher should be directed towards arranging the children's environment in such a way that their social interaction with one another hastens the process whereby heteronomy gives way to autonomy. If, by way of complete contrast, one follows Bull, then one will *use* the heteronomous characteristics of the middle years child as a means of establishing a firm pattern of moral expectations which will act as 'the seed bed of development in moral judgment'. If on the other hand one follows Williams and Williams, one will take steps to see that each mode of moral response is being constantly developed towards a maturer version of itself. One will also have to decide whether or not the other-considering mode needs particular cultivation, on the grounds that it is the *best* mode. The Williamses themselves are quite clear on this point:

When we say that no single one of these modes of thought is developmentally prior to the others, it does not follow that they are *morally* equivalent. On the contrary, most moral philosophers would argue that the other-considering or altruistic mode is the best, and perhaps the only proper, basis for moral action.

One will also have to help the pupils work out their own practical hierachy of values, and to establish stable interrelationships between the different modes of response. This is particularly important (if one accepts Kohlberg's findings) between the ages of ten and fifteen, when self-considering responses cease to dominate all others. It would appear to be at this stage that altruism can either be allowed to become permanently associated with rule-obeying and conformity (with all the dangers this brings in a rapidly changing society) or it can be harnessed to the growth of 'personal autonomy based on reason' and so be helped to develop into the fullest type of moral maturity of which each individual is capable.

References

BOEHM, L. (1962) The development of conscience: a comparison of American children of different socio-economic levels *Child Development* 33 575–90

BULL, N. J. (1969) *Moral Judgement from Childhood to Adolescence* Routledge and Kegan Paul

CROWLEY, P. M. (1968) Effect of training upon objectivity of moral judgment in grade school children *Journal of Personality and Social Psychology* 8, 228–32

DEARDEN, R. F. (1968) *The Philosophy of Primary Education* Routledge and Kegan Paul

EPPEL, E. M. and M. (1966) *Adolescents and Morality* Routledge and Kegan Paul

GRAHAM, D. (1972) *Moral Learning and Development: Theory and Research* Batsford

HAVIGHURST, J. and TABA, H. (1963) *Adolescent Character and Personality* New York: John Wiley

HUXLEY, A. (1932) *Brave New World* Penguin

KAY, W. (1968) *Moral Development* Allen and Unwin

KOHLBERG, L. (1963) *The Development of Children's Orientation Towards a Moral Order* New York: Vita Humana

KOHLBERG, L. and KRAMER, R. (1969) Continuities and discontinuities in childhood and adult moral development *Human Development* 12, 93–120

LERNER, E. (1937) *Constraint Areas and Moral Judgment in Children* Manasha, Wisconsin: Banta

LUNZER, E. A. and MORRIS, J. F. (1968) *Development in Human Learning* Staples Press

McPHAIL, P. (1972) *Moral Education in the Secondary School* Longman
McPHAIL, P. *et al* (1972) *Lifeline* Longman
PECK, R. F. and HAVIGHURST, R. J. (1960) *The Psychology of Character Development* New York: Wiley.
PIAGET, J. (1932) *The Moral Judgment of the Child* Routledge and Kegan Paul
STUART, R. B. (1967) Decentration in the development of children's concepts of moral and causal judgment *Journal of Genetic Psychology* 111, 59–68
SUGARMAN, B., WILLIAMS, N. and WILSON, J. (1967) *Introduction to Moral Education* Penguin
WILLIAMS, N. and WILLIAMS, S. (1970) *The Moral Development of Children* Macmillan
WILSON, J. (1973) *A Teacher's Guide to Moral Education* Chapman
WRIGHT, D. (1971) *The Psychology of Moral Behaviour* Penguin

Useful further reading
BULL, N. (1969) *Moral Education* Routledge and Kegan Paul
HIRST, P. H. (1975) *Moral Education in a secular society* University of London Press
KAY, W. (1975) *Moral Education* Allen and Unwin
LORD, E. and BAILEY, C. (1973) *A Reader in Religious and Moral Education* SCM Press
LOUKES, H. (1973) *Teenage morality* SCM Press
MAY, P. (1971) *Moral Education in School* Methuen
SCHOOLS COUNCIL (1972) *Moral Education Project (13–16+)*. *Lifeline* Longman
WILSON, J. (1973) *A Teacher's Guide to Moral Education* Chapman

3.3 An approach to experience-based learning in the middle years through simulations and games

Armin Beck and Eliezer Krumbein

Working side-by-side at the master's bench was the historically favoured method of instructing the young in new behaviours. When more skilled workers were needed than the apprenticeship system could provide, schools were organized to intellectualize the knowledge formerly transmitted by master to pupil, transform it into some kind of symbolic, generalized form, and thereby make the process of instruction less expensive of the master's time. Moreover, we are sometimes asked to believe that this nondirect, symbolic, lecture-book-laden form of the didactic is actually superior to the earlier direct apprenticeship. We do know that one by-product of the waning apprenticeship system was that the masters of their crafts ceased to be teachers, and so we had to create colleges of education and schools of education to teach teachers for the schools. Further, the constant task of the effective school teacher has been to create a model of reality in the classroom to substitute for real life. They have conceived ways of cutting life experiences down to size and into parts, so that they would fit through the doors of the classroom. Having achieved this they then have had to piece the real-life experiences together and reconstruct them inside the classroom for the pupils to see and study. Procrustes' bed provides an apt analogy.

Our task in this article is to explore ways in which teachers can use direct and indirect experiences in the classroom to enhance and enrich both the processes and outcomes of education. We will discuss relevant historical and contemporary literature, so that interested persons may read more widely. We will present our own model of experiencing, which deals with the confluence of three types of variables: types of experiences; multicultural and multiracial objectives toward which experiences are directed; and behaviour changes which are required in order to achieve the objectives. Finally, we will describe a number of games, simulations and educational experiences and suggest ways in which they relate to our model.

Some relevant literature
Separation of work and play in the curriculum
In *Democracy and Education* (1916) and *Experience and Education* (1938) John
Dewey expressed his concern over the growing separation of the worlds of
work and play. A goal of education, Dewey felt, was to motivate and
involve the student sufficiently so that he threw himself passionately into
his studies and work, as though they were play. John Holt (1975) is still
concerned with this artificial separation. He feels that when we involve
children in studies which are more akin to the worthwhile experiences of
life and which provide the absorbing satisfactions of play, it will effectively
set them on a path in which much of life is play and fun. Dewey, in his
attempt to focus on the classroom as he knew it, urged the enlargement of
studio and laboratory experiences in school. So he wrote *How We Think*
(1933), *Art as Experience* (1934) and *Experience and Nature* (1925) for
mathematics, art and science teachers. Dewey had hopes of reforming
education by working within the public educational system, while Holt
lays more emphasis on alternative educational formats.

Eric Berne conceived a method of understanding personality development and of influencing its redevelopment through a form of
psychotherapy which is chiefly accomplished in groups. Called Transactional Analysis (T/A), it has become well known through his books *The
Games People Play* (1966) and *What Do You Say After You Say Hello?* (1973),
and Thomas Harris's companion work *I'm OK – You're OK* (1973). T/A is a
developmental system of psychology, drawing liberally from
psychoanalysis and dynamic psychology. Like other American varieties of
personality theory, it espouses the concept that personality emerges in
interactions and transactions between the individual and significant
others. T/A presents personality as an aggregate of three ego states or
aspects of personality called Parent, Adult and Child. Each of the three is
ideally in homeostatic balance with the other two. For the individual to
have appropriate responses to environment, growth and achievement of
life's major goals he should come into increasingly closer touch with the
feelings associated with each ego state. Parent feelings are nurturing and
critical and include rules, values and laws. The Adult is devoid of feelings
and has the cognitive ability to array facts for decision- making. The Child
feels happy and sad, hungry and hurt. It is the seat of creativity. The Child
jumps and frolics. T/A's goals of personality development are intimacy,
spontaneous expression of feelings and awareness of self and environment.

In its therapeutic style, T/A builds and maximizes the Child ego state.
Thus, as one gets in touch with Child feelings one comes close to releasing
creative potential. Berne notes that most persons seem to do what they
'have to, what is required of them, what society demands' – all Parent-
laden concepts. So, for most persons, work is not an expression of Natural
Child but rather of Adapted Child, a Child which has been 'trained'

to do what it is told. James and Jongeward (1971) illustrate ways of evoking feelings associated with each ego state. Similarly, George Isaac Brown (1971) describes in detail the application of effective and experimental approaches in learning in order to heighten consciousness of feelings associated with ego states.

The word 'game' is used in Transactional Analysis to connote an interpersonal transaction gone awry. One or more parties in the transaction manipulate so that one will be winner and other loser, or in even greater pathology, so that both are losers. Berne decries games as competitive and manipulative arenas for human interaction. Rather, he espouses cooperative activities in which intimacy, spontaneity and awareness are the goals. While we do not use the word 'games' in Berne's technical sense, we do subscribe to a learning environment which maximizes opportunities for cooperation. In *Games Alcoholics Play*, Steiner (1971) describes how negative developmental influences tend to emerge in 'tragic scripts', resulting in personal distress. Haimowitz and Haimowitz (1973) likewise provide dynamic descriptions of T/A applications in learning. The sensitive teacher may learn much in these works about misuse of competition in interpersonal relations.

Cultural anthropologists describe childhoods of passionate play among South Sea islanders and North American Indians. Before the intrusions of 'whites', descriptions of these people speak of the idyllic blending of play into work. Herbert Kohl (1970) and Donald Erger (1973), in describing the ideal of the English infant school and the Open Hallway model of primary education, suggests ways to broaden and deepen experiences in education, so that the boundaries between work and play are blurred. The object of these models of study is to get the child 'turned on' to passionate involvement with fellow learners, with materials of instruction and with the environment of things and people. As advocates of the integrated day well know the open school may be achieved in three ways: by opening up space through opening doors and eliminating walls; by opening time through elimination of school bells and formal periods of instruction; and by opening up formal studies. These may be achieved by *providing students with options of subject matter* to be chosen from a wide range of choices, and by *providing freedom of the sequence* in which a pupil chooses to study his material. The open classroom ideally provides all three options. Less ideally, one or more of the three options may be achieved. In this chapter, we suggest experiences and methods which the teacher may select to move in the direction of open-ness, experiencing and blending of work and play. In brief, myriad students of human behaviour, over time, have sensed a kind of magic energy in childhood and its play. Each has sought to show the pedagogue how to direct that energy into activities. Our experience-based model, we feel, is a further step in this direction.

Social philosophy and social engineering in the curriculum

Ivan Illich (1971) advises the poor of the earth to withdraw their children from tax-supported schools. He reasons that since the schools indoctrinate conformity, their graduates will not be motivated to self-liberation. How shall the children of the poor, and adults too, then be educated? Illich recommends that learning webs be established in which individuals who want to learn, and who may have ideas about *how* they want to learn, declare their interests and register them at a neutral agency. Individuals who want to teach also make their declarations. A market-place of interactions and exchanges occurs. Illich and others, including the authors of this article, who have experimented with learning under such auspices, feel that the learning which results is closer to what many learners want, learning is more experience-based, and the learner is more in control of learning.

This type of development in education and training is quite recent. Operational research, which is a special application of simulation in which the factors under study (tanks, soldiers, factories, raw materials, personnel, transportation, finance, etc.) are quantified, was born in Britain during the Second World War when the teams of physical, biological and social scientists were assembled to study, on paper, the factors which would go into development of the Tank Corps in North Africa and Europe. Imagination was to substitute for war games and small wars. As computers became more generally available, simulations became more realistic and more successful in their power to predict reality. C. P. Snow (1961) has described such efforts in the development of the atomic bomb. In the early 1950s the U.S. Air Force contracted with the Educational Testing Service of Princeton, New Jersey, to develop simulations of administrators' in-baskets. These contained a simulated set of papers and stimuli which command the administrator's day to which the student has to respond. The Dutch, pursuing these experiences as new departures on the Harvard Business School's famous case study method of learning business management skills, developed business simulations. Their special contribution was calling recesses in the simulations so that participants could confer with Boards of Directors, Generals, Consumer Panels, Bankers, Cabinet Ministers, etc. Harvard, not to be outdone, developed real-life interventions at the conclusion of its case studies. Teams of students, with different solutions to cases each presented their findings to real-life officers and directors of the corporations being studied. The officers and directors then quizzed the simulation participants, made suggestions and chose their favourite solutions. Of course, only time would tell whose taste was best. Finally, Chapanis (1961) cogently and briefly analysed and described *models* and simulations as 'analogies of reality' which may have some flaws, and *theory* as 'a conceptual system which attempts to describe the real thing', in a manner which is helpful to model and theory builders.

Bloom (1971) suggested that a variety of approaches be used to improve learning in the classroom. These included academic games, experiencing, individual and group tutoring, provision of adequate time for students to learn at mastery level, and holding teachers and pupils accountable for pupil achievement. He proposed a 90/90 rule which he found true in his research: 90 per cent of pupils are capable of *mastering* 90 per cent of the school curriculum if they can be motivated to learn, using the modalities described above. Moreover, when pupils begin to master their studies they experience a growth in self-concept, which, in turn, leads to greater mastery.

James Coleman *et al* (1966), in a report of the largest study in educational achievement ever completed in the United States, suggest that such mastery of studies and school environment does lead to an elevation of self-concept among middle-class pupils. However, among poor, coloured and other racially isolated minority groups, they found measures of self-concept remain unchanged or show a decrease even when school achievement improves. The relationship between school achievement and pupils' self-concepts were studied further at two schools in Chicago. One school has a racial, socio-economic and ethnic mix which is purposely identical to the population of the rest of Chicago's schools – heavily minority and poor. The other, St Mary, is a private Catholic girls' high school with an ethnically, racially and socio-economically heterogeneous population. Both schools emphasize *experience-based* learning, make use of students' ethnic, socio-economic, racial and religious experiences in mutual teaching and learning, and make a conscious attempt to have the curriculum reflect the values and life styles of their students. Both schools have substantially more than 50 per cent minority group and poor pupils. Research showed that achievement levels and self-concept level rose over a two-year period. While achievement levels have been falling in the Chicago schools generally and many other major urban school systems, they have risen and exceeded national norms in the Chicago Archdiocese Catholic schools with a similar population mix. While we have not studied self-concept in the Catholic schools, many of these schools, by their very nature, reflect the values and life styles of their students. We would expect self-concepts to rise with achievement.

Why do these results differ from Coleman's studies and from the generally and continually deteriorating achievement picture in most large American and British urban school systems? It is our hypothesis that the curriculum, environment and control system of most schools is so negative to coloured, poor and other minority pupils that they actually reinforce their self-concept in a negative manner. This is true enough even though they may have been 'trained' or educated to master the academic material. Thus, the mutually motivating relationships of academic mastery and self-concept noted in Bloom's work do not have an opportunity to take hold. Beck and Beck (1972), in this context, describe the anguish of an Asian primary school pupil who is unable to see her own culture reflected in her school. The researches outlined above have much to say to those responsible for education in the world's large urban communities – the simulations, observations and reality-based experiences we describe in this chapter are selected to reinforce values of multicultural and multiracial society. From our experiences in applying each of them, they should equally reinforce the learnings and self-concepts of both majority and minority group children.

A theory of experiencing
The objective of this theoretical presentation is to place the views of the authors in context with the above review of relevant literature and at the same time permit the teacher to see clearly what the experiences are doing. We will examine objectives, behaviour changes, and types and sets of experiences.

A theory of experience-based learning should perform several functions:

1   It should suggest effective ways of motivating learning.
2   In order to do this, it should suggest ways of 'warming up' the teachers and learners so that they can better share their thoughts and feelings.
3   It should suggest ways of involving the teacher and learners on a continuing basis, developing a kind of pervading interest or passion. Longer learning contexts should lead to longer retention of effective knowledge and skills.
4   It should provide a variety of reference points to other reality. It should be accessible to the learner for him to make generalizations to other material of interest and concern to him.
5   It should provide a means whereby important meanings stand out clearly from unimportant meanings.
6   It should provide many-faceted opportunities to learn from other co-learners, not only from the teacher and formal learning materials.
7   It should provide a clear guide by which the learner or leader of learning can identify the principal variables and values under treatment in the experience. He can then, if he desires, select other experiences to complement and supplement what he already knows.
8   It should relate clearly to important values in the immediate and wider worlds of the learners: specifically, as we have emphasized, multicultural and multiracial values.
9   It should take account of the concepts of cognitive, affective and psychomotor learning which are part of the everyday working tools of the teacher.
10 Negatively speaking, the theory should provide an available set of standards which enable the teacher to weed out experiences as unrelated and undesired.

The theoretical framework which follows would appear to perform the functions enunciated above. It suggests the desirability of teachers and practitioners selecting experiences which reflect a confluence of three sets of variables. These include:

(a) Fourteen multicultural and multiracial educational objectives.
(b) Five behaviour changes required to achieve the objectives.
(c) Six types of experiences, including continua of active-passive, individual-group, and cooperative-competitive experiences, to help achieve the behaviour changes. In addition to these variables, we have identified three sets of experience-based learnings: *simulation experiences*, which use games and exercises as abstractions from reality; *social observer experiences*, in which the learner is on the sidelines of real-life activity, much like the 'social observers' who were innocent bystanders in early Hitchcock films; and *real-life experiences* in which the learner is an active participant in life's activities and cannot stop the action or easily withdraw from it. In tables 1–3 we have set out how each set of experiences may, in turn be related to (a) objectives, (b) behaviour changes and (c) types of experiences.

(a) *Multicultural and multiracial educational objectives*
Children from a variety of ethnic (national), religious, racial, and socioeconomic backgrounds are increasingly prevalent in schools. In Britain as well as the United States, the heyday of homogenous schools is rapidly passing. We have therefore chosen to emphasize multicultural and multiracial values. Thus, we suggest as objectives, in addition to establishment of a positive self-concept on the part of the learner, certain values, skills, and knowledge, as mentioned below. Well-executed experimental learning will meet many of these objectives:

1 To foster a positive self-concept in the learner.
2 To foster a high value placed upon cultural pluralism and variety. (This is the opposite of a blending or melting pot idea.)
3 To foster a high value placed on cooperation in learning and the achievement of life's goals. (This does not negate the presence of competition. It speaks rather to cooperation as a priority.)
4 To foster a high value placed on sharing of power.
5 To foster a high value placed on justice and the achievement of it.
6 To emphasize the acquisition of vocational skills.
7 To emphasize the acquisition of self-selected skills.
8 To emphasize acquisition of cooperation skills.
9 To emphasize acquisition of skills to oppose injustice.
10 To know your own life style.
11 To know your own value system.
12 To know your own cultural strengths.

13 To know your own learning style.
14 To know the facts and experiences of racism and social inequity.

The authors have utilized these objectives in a variety of educational settings, especially since they were enumerated by colleagues at the Equal Educational Opportunity Center of the National College of Education, Evanston, Illinois, U.S.A. They are the result of creative participation of staff from many different professional backgrounds, races, ethnic and religious and socio-economic groups under the leadership of a black scholar, Benjamin Williams.

(b) *Behaviour changes required to achieve objectives*
Most contemporary educationalists who set up behavioural objectives state the objectives in terms of general or specific behaviour changes which, when attained, constitute positive measures in assessment of learning: Krumbein (1974); Taba (1962); Bloom *et al* (1956); Tyler (1950). We have focused our attention on five behaviour changes which appear to be attainable in school learning; which figure prominently in the experiential learning with which we have been experimenting, and which are widely regarded in the literature:

1 *Information or concepts to be mastered:* this is a cognitive behaviour. It includes a full range from memory to complex intellectual functions. It is useful to consider a range of concepts before deciding on areas of emphasis.
2 *Attitudes to be developed:* developing attitudes are sometimes difficult to pinpoint, except as they become more pervasive changes in values. They may, indeed, be the mirror images in behaviour of underlying values.
3 *Values to be determined:* development of values is a complex function which involves more than the mastery of information. It depends upon attitudes towards oneself, others, social groups to which one belongs, and intellectual and aesthetic attitudes.
4 *Interests or concerns to be fostered:* these may also be the surface expression of more deep-seated values.
5 *Skills, abilities and habits to be fostered:* teachers often focus prematurely on the fostering and acquisition of complex skills which are properly dependent on prior learnings. For example, the skill of making choices may be dependent on skills in analysing problems, collecting facts and other data, organizing and interpreting data. Conjointly, the skill of decision-making may be related to ability to do independent thinking, to analyse arguments and propaganda, to plan for efficient use of time, receive feedback, foresee consequences of proposed actions, the abilities to modify proposed or past action in the light of experience or foresight, and skill in continuing to encourage feedback.

(c)   *Types of experiences*

As we have perused the literature on affective, humanistic, experiential education and group work, we have found six types of experiences:

1   Mind experiences: typically, experiences in which the individual works alone, separate from colleagues, in an attempt to identify and work with thoughts and feelings.
2   Discussion experiences: two or more persons talk things over, at various levels of depth, but no other significant physical activity is involved.
3   Individual physical activities: no interaction with others.
4   Participant-observer activities.
5   Cooperative physical activities.
6   Competitive physical activities.

Depending upon the objectives to be attained: (a) in learning; (b) in the characteristics of teacher and learners, and (c) in the social and physical limitations of the learning centre, one may feel free to select greater or fewer types of experiences. We have used each and all types in both formal and informal learning settings, with learners of all ages and social backgrounds and in settings as varied as nursery, university faculty, religious order, military hospital, and teachers. We recommend them to teachers of the middle years age group.

Sets of experiences

We have classified experiences into three sets. These are: (a) simulation or game experiences which are analogies of the real world; (b) social observer experiences, in which learners are asked to observe real-life activities and (c) real-life experiences in which learners participate as interns and are caught up in the rhythms of the field. In order to assist the teacher in deciding which exercises may be preferred to attain given objectives, behaviour changes and types and sets of experiences, we have developed in Tables 1–3 classifications of each of the three sets of experiences. These classifications will also meet the requests of teachers who want an easy means of determining which objectives, behaviour changes and types and sets of experiences they have been using, so that they may enlarge their repertoire of learning experiences.

Experiences

Twenty-eight experiences are briefly described below. The authors culled this list from sixty-three experiences they commonly use. Many more are available to any creative person who wants to plan on new ways to view old problems. Either directly or with some minor modification, these experiences can be used in classrooms ranging from primary school through to teacher training. The descriptions consider the resources necessary, the number of people who can profit from one experience, and the amount of time generally required to complete the experience.

In the previous section we mentioned three sets of non-traditional learning experiences. These are simulation experiences, social observer experiences and real-life experiences. The descriptions fall into these three categories. *Simulation* has the advantage of permitting the student to immerse himself into a life-like situation and pull back at a crucial time for the purpose of examining the developing situation. He can then analyse a series of alternative behaviours before proceeding. (See *Role play: urban student as outlaw*, no. 15 below.) An individual or group experience can begin or stop at any given moment: the class period ends, the teacher wants to emphasize a point, or a student wants to retrench.

At the same time, certain simulation exercises permit a group to move helter-skelter towards a solution without having to live with the outcome in real life. In a *Fifteen-minute Day* exercise (no. 7 below) performed at an administrative training workshop, a variation had the group of thirty participants working on a problem until a final solution was reached. In this case we knew the game was ended when the 'school superintendent' was fired by his governing board. Since it wasn't real life we could pick up the pieces of the conflict, analyse them, and put them back together.

Social observation experiences carry with them some dangers. If not careful, the observer can be viewed as a 'colonial anthropologist', as a student or a scholar who will study a portion of the community for the purpose of fulfilling an assignment, and will return nothing to the community. According to Beck (1972) there needs to be a reasonable return to the community for its willingness to impart information. The scholar, in other words, should either do his research at the behest of the community or should share his findings with the community for its own use.

The third set of learning experiences which we discuss are the *real-life* experiences. The participant has the obvious advantage of being neither a student of *life* (social observation) nor a student of *make-believe* (simulation), but of being an actor in life's reality. When a pupil begins to *Teach in a local jail* (no. 28 below) he is dealing with live inmates, not sociological statistics. He cannot stop action in the midst of an experience, as he can in a simulation, or cannot say that he is not a judge, only a scholar, as he can when he is a social observer. Nonetheless, his real-life experiences can be even more beneficial of those facts; he has no retreat from reality, he as no chance to go back to his wife or mother – or teacher – for support or sustenance. He is there on the front line, for better or worse.

In experiential learning, the grist for the pupil comes through the three sets of experiences discussed above. The learning itself is thus considerably enhanced through 'debriefing' exercises. The discussion that a class or the group has after its experiences are completed; the questions that are raised by themselves and by the group leader; the behavioural conclusions that are drawn subsequent to the experiences; these discussions markedly enrich the learnings!

Using 'experiences' as a primary method to teach groups, then, can be successfully carried out by teachers interested in trying, failing, trying, re-evaluating and trying again. We do not mean to say that 'anyone can do it', but we do say that, to some extent at least, all teachers can succeed. The literature on the subject, discussed earlier in this chapter, can be of great value in getting started. Brown (1971), for example, has a multitude of experiences to try, and ways to try them. The experiences described in this chapter can be used in the same way. It is important to remember that experiential teaching has nothing mystical about it; it is just hard work and imagination.

Finally, each experience described can be used for a variety of purposes. *Cross-generation communication* (no. 10 below), for example, can be used as a warm-up exercise wherein pupils get acquainted with each other. It can be used as a basis for analysis of non-verbal communication. It can be used by primary teachers as an experience that children or teachers can write about. The teacher and/or the pupils need to be properly focused on an outcome, and then a variety of experiences can be used.

The authors have used all of the exercises described below. The ideas for the experiences come from a variety of sources. We do not apologize for the fact that some of the examples go obviously beyond the child of middle years. We have included them to provide teachers with ideas. The best types of experience-based learning are provided by teachers taking up an idea and relating it to their own pupils and specific context.

SIMULATION EXPERIENCES

1   *Collage*

This exercise helps participants determine what it feels like, for them, to be a (middle class) (working class) (immigrant) (Irish) (white) (Catholic) (Welsh) person in England. Using magazines with pictures in them, large sheets of newsprint, scissors, paste and masking tape, the pupils make a collage or montage of pictures, materials and words to express the chosen subject. Then small groups of five or six analyse each other's collage. Large group discussion consists of each group writing statements of its own trends and differences on large newsprint, placing it on a wall, along with its collages, for a permanent classroom 'environment'. General discussion follows. The whole exercise takes about ninety minutes.

2   *Racism sort*

A series of statements about eight to twelve school and classroom situations dealing with racial interaction are devised and left unresolved. Groups of four to six people read them, analyse them, and determine whether the situation described is 'racist' or a manifestation of human nature. The small groups then report their findings and conclusions to the large group; questions and discussion follow. (Ten minutes for each question.) This is an example. Is the behaviour racist?

A group of coloured pupils block the stairway from whites. The coloured pupils are trying to get 'passing money'. The stairway becomes filled with pupils, both coloured and white, and a physical confrontation is imminent.

3 *Who am I?*

With a Polaroid camera a picture is taken of each participant at the start of the workshop or class period. The picture is placed on a preplanned poster, one for each student, approximately 12" × 20". The rest of the preprinted poster should include open-ended sentences for completion by the pupils:

I am...

My hopes for the class include...

What I bring to this experience...

Each pupil completes the sentence and tapes the poster to the wall. Through studying all the posters, the pupils find like-minded people and get acquainted with them. This can form the basis for further grouping. The exercise lasts between twenty and thirty minutes. Posters remain on the wall to help create an environment unique to the class group.

4 *Racism box*

This is similar in intent to no. 2 above. A box is presented to a group of five to twelve pupils, containing ten items that can have something to do with race or social class. The group discusses each item for racist content. After about twenty minutes, a large group discussion ensues. In the box would be such items as a swatch of cotton, an ethnocentric advertisement from a popular magazine, a golliwog, a football-club rosette, mustard seed or plants, Scottish tartan, piece of coal, cricket ball, a school tie or scarf, a tea bag, a working man's cap, etc.

5 *Mutual consultation*

This may be done in a 'fishbowl', wherein a group of six to nine pupils (the participants) sits in an inner circle, and the remainder of the group (the observers) form a circle on the outside of the inner group. A pupil brings a problem into the fishbowl. The problem can be anything that is pressing him at the moment. For five to eight minutes, the inner circle asks him penetrating questions regarding the problem. (It is not unusual for the nature of the problem to be considerably changed under the pressure of questions.) The leader's function is to encourage the individual to focus on one behaviour he can change in order to achieve his purpose. Each member of the fishbowl is invited to give the person suggestions for solution. The person is then asked what he heard, and if he plans to try any of the solutions. After he responds, another person's problem is brought before the group. Each problem takes between fifteen and twenty-five minutes. The person with a problem almost never goes away empty-handed. One rule, however: the outer circle may not speak; if they have something to say, they must enter the fishbowl, or inner group (there should always be an empty chair in the fishbowl).

6 Create a bad school

Considerable planning by the teacher is necessary for the success of this experience. The idea is to create, on paper, all the policies and practices that make up a bad school. Groups should range in number between four and eight, and there should be one group for each major area of the school's operation: curriculum, employment practices, maintenance of the physical plant, school rules, involvement in decision-making, etc. In the large group debriefing discussion, it is usually not necessary to talk about what should be in a good school: a school is bad only in comparison with one that is good. The experience will take about sixty minutes. Care should be taken to avoid stereotyping a bad school and thus making it ridiculous.

7 Fifteen-minute day

This experience simulates a 'wholistic' approach to a problem. We quote an example here as used by one of the authors in Washington D.C. recently. But problems of a similar character are common in all countries and thus allow the experience to be used. It dealt with the question: 'Should pupils from the District of Columbia (predominantly coloured) be integrated with pupils from the suburbs of Maryland and Virginia (predominantly white) immediately surrounding the District?' The participants were divided into the following interest groups:

White 'elite'
Black 'elite'
White community separatists
Black community separatists
Latin American Parents Defence Organization
School Administration/school board members
Commissioner of Education and two advisors
White politicians
Black politicians
Churches
Pupils
White community integrationists
Black community integrationists

The 'Commissioner of Education' called a meeting of these groups for the purpose of resolving the question. Each 'day' lasted fifteen minutes; a 'timekeeper' saw to that. In this case, the experience came to an end on the fourth day, when a 'Congressional Committee' agreed to hold open hearings on the question. A variation of this exercise ignores the time frame of fifteen minutes and proceeds until the question is finally handled. Immediately after completion, each participant should be questioned regarding his thoughts and activities, and his perceptions of others' behaviour. The experience and discussion may last from forty-five to one-hundred-and-twenty minutes.

8   *Teaching/learning network*
On 3″ × 5″ cards, each pupil is asked to write two or three things he would like to learn. These can either be limitless, or centred around a specific topic, as determined by the teacher. On a large prepared chart (one chart for every eight to ten subjects), the pupil then writes his topic and his name. Someone else in the group agrees to teach it to him, and in turn writes his name. The chart should be as follows:

Want to learn	*Subject*	*Want to teach*
William	To make a paper aeroplane	Jonathan

When each pupil's name is on the chart at least once, negotiations begin: When can you teach me? What materials should I bring along? etc. A broad variety of pupil skills will come to light. In a classroom a certain time each week can be given over to the network, and the beginnings of mini-courses or an open classroom can be made. Initial planning for a class lasts between twenty-five and forty minutes.

9   *School newspaper*
Classroom newspapers can be 'published' once a week,·if the teacher is willing to spend the time necessary. The rewards are high in language competence and morale. Whose cat had kittens? Whose sister got married? Who went to the cricket match? are questions that might be answered in the newspaper. Whatever each person contributes must be well done and everyone in the class must contribute: writing, art, layout, stapling together. Each week might see a different committee of editors. After the newspaper is printed on duplicating paper, or another inexpensive process, it can be gone through by the class: What was done well? What could have been done better? Daily or weekly 'radio broadcasts' can be handled in much the same way, using a cassette or tape recorder rather than a duplicator.

10   *Cross-generation communication*
Use of this experience helps participants gain empathy for people older or younger than they. One of the authors told a group of teachers whom he

was inservice training, 'Close your eyes.' (pause) 'Imagine a child whom you observed or taught recently.' (pause) 'Picture his dress, have a conversation with him; take a moment and explore your feelings toward him.' (pause) 'Now imagine the child that you were at his age.' (pause) 'How did you look? What did you do for fun? How did you feel?' (pause) 'Let the child that you were play with the child that you observed.' (pause) 'After a few minutes, open your eyes and share your experiences with the other three or four people in your group. Consider any differences between the conversations you had as a grown-up and the one you had as a child.' Variations abound; include parents or grandparents, neighbours, etc. The experience takes about fifteen to twenty minutes.

11 *What I want most for my children (parents, friends, etc.) this year*
This is a good exercise to use with parents and non-school adults, as well as with teachers and pupils. Each group of four to five pupils should make a list of four to five things in answer to the question. A spokesman should read this list to the large group. Finally, an analysis by the group should be made of the answers. Typically, the responses will show that the most important things are not reading, writing and arithmetic, but things that we don't consciously teach: getting along with each other, understanding society, learning to make their environment into a congenial partner. It takes between forty and sixty minutes.

12 *Urban fairy tale*
The large group compiles a list of twenty to thirty words that describe typical urban sounds, sights, smells, tastes and physical feelings. Using most of these words, each person writes a 250-word 'fairy tale'. The stories are either taped to the wall, or small groups read them to each other. The ensuing discussion is between city and suburb and rural areas, and impingements of these upon the educative process.

13 *Best/worst learning experiences*
Each pupil writes two paragraphs: one on what in his memory has been his best learning experience, either inside or outside of school; and one his worst. Small groups of four or five exchange papers and read each other's aloud. Discussion follows. In the large group debriefing, the best experiences often happen outside of schools and have to do with growing skill, independence and interpersonal intimacy; the worst often takes place inside the school. Twenty to thirty minutes should be sufficient.

14 *Blind!*
This is carried on in groups of two. One person is tightly blindfolded and spends several hours getting around alone and with the help of someone assigned to be his 'eyes'. The debriefing will deal with feelings toward yourself and toward other people with stigmas.

15   *Role play: urban student as outlaw*
The whole class participates, with certain designated people as the 'main actors'. Typical urban situations should be used. This is one from a school in Chicago described by Beck, Burns and Krumbein (1975), but teachers can easily create their own scenarios to suit their pupils and situation:

Dale, a bright pupil and a potential leader, has reading problems. He picks up the skills he needs quickly – so quickly that he becomes bored and impatient with other members of the class. Much of Dale's reading instruction is therefore done on an individual basis. This sometimes results in what Dale feels is too much teacher attention. When Dale feels he is losing his reputation with other students because of this attention he becomes loud and aggressive.
re: Dale   Although you did see Dale in school today, he did not attend your class. You are in the classroom between periods with another teacher when two girls run in screaming 'Dale's in the hall pulling his trousers down'. You investigate and find Dale in the hall with a group of his male friends. He is holding his trousers up at the waist. As you approach the group, it seems to you that Dale may be 'spaced out' on drugs.

The role play is around the question: What do we do now? As in no. 7 above, each pupil should be questioned regarding his thoughts and activities during the role play, and his perceptions of others' behaviours. Time is about forty-five to ninety minutes.

16   *Mirror*
The whole class divides into pairs. Each pair faces one another; one person is the leader and the other the follower. Without using words, the leader moves his arms, legs, body, head, etc. The follower mirrors his movements. After three or four minutes, the roles are reversed. The teacher asks, 'How do you feel?' The whole experience takes about fifteen minutes.

17   *Hello!*
The whole class divides into pairs. Each pair faces each other. 'Say hello with your eyes.' 'Say hello with your eyes and your hands, feeling free to touch anywhere on the hands, arms or shoulders.' 'Turn around. Rub backs up and down, back and around, saying hello only with your backs.' 'Back to back, each person looking straight ahead, say hello in words, do not turn round.' 'Face each other, say hello with eyes, hands and voice.' In saying hello, the participants should introduce themselves as well as they can. They can tell each other which way they liked better. Ten to fifteen minutes.

18   *Jail!*
This experience is tied in directly with nos. 24 and 28. It illustrates how one

set of experiences can be used in the social observer, simulation and real-life categories.

(a) The first part of the experience is to visit a local prison or institution. Find out the kinds of educational or vocational training needed, and which are provided. (Social observer)

(b) The second part of the experience has various groups in the class developing a set of educational experiences for the inmates. This, of course, must ultimately be done in conjunction with the institution authorities. (Simulation)

(c) Finally, teach or tutor in the institution. Keep a log of experiences; what happened while you were there and how you feel about it. (Real-life)

SOCIAL OBSERVER EXPERIENCES

19 *Observe classroom behaviour*
Visit another class, another school perhaps, preferably in a different part of town. Watch the way pupils interact with their teachers. Suggest to your pupils that they take notes on the different stimuli and responses to learning and behaviour. When they return there is plenty to talk about!

20 *Visiting nurse*
Make the rounds one day with a visiting nurse. Note how she elicits positive and negative responses from her patients. What can be learned about human nature from this experience?

21 *Community health centre*
Get in line and take a seat in a community health centre, especially in a poor neighbourhood. How are you treated? How are others treated? What can be learned about human nature?

22 *Complain to the town hall*
With the class, devise a hypothetical complaint against the town/local district council: rubbish collection, building heat, police behaviour, etc. Go through the whole procedure, starting with the local representative and carrying it all the way to the top. What are the blocks to effective government? Is textbook civics the same as real life? Can the two be made compatible?

23 *Compare*
Using two or more different neighbourhoods as the basis for comparison, secure census data and interview data on one or more of the following: food, clothing, shelter, heat, health, legal services, recreation, education.

24   *Jail!*
Please refer to no. 18 and no. 28 below.

25   *Teacher aide*
The idea is for the pupil to do the actual work of an aide, not observe or simulate it. In so doing, a log should be kept.

26   *Supervise young children*
Working as a supervisor of young children in a lunch room, for example, will give the participant the real-life experience necessary to round off some of his understandings. As with the above, the log is an important part of the work.

27   *Neighbourhood groups*
Pupils can organize a special-interest group in their own neighbourhood or school: i.e. a nature conservation club. Working with several other pupils he can plan goals, activities and evaluation possibilities.

28   *Jail!*
Please refer to nos. 18 and 24 above.

Conclusion
We have attempted to present a practical guide to the teacher on experiential approaches in the classroom. While, as we have said, some of our examples go beyond the child of middle years, we hold them to be of great value to teachers. For, if teachers are to reflect to their students and pupils an accurate portrait of life and the world, they must personally encounter simulation, observer and real world educational experiences which are appropriate to their own age and development.

Our model of experience-based education enables the teacher to select either simulation, social observer or real-life experiences to enrich her classroom work. Experiences in each of these sets may, in turn, be selected for different purposes:

1   The multicultural and multiracial educational objectives they are expected to serve;
2   The behaviour changes which the experiences should help to produce;
3   The types of experiences the teacher prefers on the continua of individual-social, intellectual-physical and competition-cooperation.

The teacher may assess the worth and efficacy of these approaches by determining, in a variety of ways: (a) whether students have engaged in the educational processes of various types of experiences; (b) whether behaviours have changed in expected ways and in sum; (c) whether objectives have been attained.

Table 1: Classification of experience-based learning

	Experiences	Objectives	Behaviour changes	Types of experiences
Number	Titles	Numbers	Numbers	Numbers
1	Collage	1, 12	3	1, 2, 3, 5
2	Racism sort	2, 14	1,5	1, 2
3	Who am I?	1, 7	2	1, 2, 3
4	Racism box	2, 9, 14	1, 2	1, 2
5	Mutual consultation	3, 8	5	1, 2
6	Create a bad school	2–14	1–5	2, 3, 5, 6
7	Fifteen-minute day	2–14	1–5	2, 3, 4, 5, 6
8	Teaching/learning network	3, 8, 13	1, 4, 5, 7	1, 4, 5
9	School newspaper	3, 8	1, 5	1, 2, 5
10	Cross-generation communication	2, 10	3	1, 2
11	What I want most for my children this year	3, 7, 8	3	1, 2
12	Urban fairy tale	1–14	2, 4	1, 2, 5
13	Best/worst learning experience	9, 10	3	1, 2, 5
14	Blind!	3, 8	5	1, 2, 5
15	Role play: urban student as outlaw	4, 9, 10	2	2, 4, 5
16	Mirror	1, 2	5	2, 5
17	Hello!	13	1, 5	2,5
18	Jail!	2	2	2, 5

Table 2: Classification of experience-based learning

SET II – SOCIAL OBSERVER EXPERIENCES

Number	Experiences Titles	Objectives Numbers	Behaviour changes Numbers	Types of experiences Numbers
19	Observe classroom behaviour	10	3	2, 4
20	Visiting nurse	5, 9, 14	2	2, 4
21	Community health centre	5, 9, 14	2	2, 3, 4
22	Complain to the town hall	5, 9, 14	1, 2	2, 3, 4
23	Compare	3, 5, 9, 14	1, 2	1, 2, 4, 5
24	Jail!	2, 10, 12	1, 2	2, 3, 4

Table 3: Classification of experience-based learning

SET III – REAL-LIFE EXPERIENCES

Number	Experiences Titles	Objectives Numbers	Behaviour changes Numbers	Types of experiences Numbers
25	Teacher aide	1, 2, 13	2, 5	2, 5
26	Supervise young children	2, 8, 12	1, 2	5
27	Neighbourhood groups	1, 2, 8, 12	1–5	2, 5
28	Jail!	1, 2, 5, 9, 11, 12	2, 5	2, 5

References

BECK, A. (1972) 'Professional Development in Cities' in H. J. Walberg and A. T. Kopan (eds) *Rethinking Urban Education* San Francisco: Jossey-Bass

BECK, K. and BECK, A. (1972) 'All They Do is Run Away' *Civil Rights Digest* August

BECK, A., BURNS, J. and KRUMBEIN, E. (1975) 'The Urban Teacher as Outlaw' *Journal of Negro Education* (in press)

BERNE, E. (1966) *The Games People Play – The Psychology of Human Relationships* Andre Deutsch

BERNE, E. (1973) *What Do You Say After You Say Hello? – The Psychology of Human Destiny* New York: Bantam

BLOOM, B. S. *et al* (1956) *Taxonomy of Educational Objectives: The Classification of Educational Goals Handbook 1: Cognitive Domain* Longman

BLOOM, B. S. (1971) 'Learning of Mastery' in B. S. Bloom, J. T. Hastings and G. E. Madaus *Handbook on Formative and Summative Evaluation of Student Learning* New York: McGraw Hill

BROWN, G. I. (1971) *Human Teaching for Human Learning – An Introduction to Confluent Education* New York: Viking Press

CHAPANIS, A. (1961) 'Men, Machines and Models' *American Psychologist* 16, 3, March

COLEMAN, J. *et al* (1966) *Equality of Educational Opportunity* Washington: U.S. Department of Health, Education and Welfare, U.S. Government Printing Office

DEWEY, J. (1916) *Democracy and Education* New York: Macmillan

DEWEY, J. (1925) *Experience and Nature* La Salle, Illinois: Open Court Publishing Company

DEWEY, J. (1933) *How We Think* Harrap

DEWEY, J. (1934) *Art as Experience* New York: Minton, Balch and Company

DEWEY, J. (1938) *Experience and Education* Tiffin, Ohio: Kappa Delta Pi

ERGER, D. (1973) *Understanding British Infant Schools* PO Box 551, Farmingdale, N.Y.: Carley Publications

HAIMOWITZ, M. L. and HAIMOWITZ, N. R. (eds) (1973) *Human Development* (Selected Readings) Third Edition, New York: Thomas Y. Crowell Company

HARRIS, T. A. (1973) *I'm OK – You're OK* Pan

HOLT, J. (1975) *Escape from Childhood* Penguin

ILLICH, I. (1971) *Deschooling Society* New Yord: Harper and Row (Harrow Books)

JAMES, M. and JONGEWARD, D. (1971) *Born to Win – Transactional Analysis with Gestalt Experiments* Reading, Massachusetts: Addison-Wesley Publishing Company

KOHL, H. R. (1970) *The Open Classroom – A Practical Guide to a New Way of Teaching* New York: Vintage Books

KRUMBEIN, E. (1971) 'On the future of simulations in the schools for teaching, evaluation and research'. Paper presented before the American Educational Research Association, Interest Group on Simulation in the Schools, New York, 5 February

KRUMBEIN, E. (1974) 'How to prepare a resource unit and learning experiences', College of Education, University of Illinois at Chicago Circle, mimeograph

STEINER, C. (1971) *Games Alcoholics Play: The Analysis of Life Scripts* New York: Grove Press

SNOW, C. P. (1961) *The New Men* Macmillan

TABA, H. (1962) *Curriculum Development: Theory and Practice* New York: Harcourt Brace and World

TYLER, R. W. (1950) *Basic Principles of Curriculum and Instruction* Syllabus for Education 305, The University of Chicago

Useful further reading

There are a number of books now available dealing with the techniques of simulation and gaming in a number of contexts:

LONGLEY, C. (1972) *Games and Simulations* BBC Publications

TANSEY, P. J. (1971) *Educational Aspects of Simulation* New York: McGraw Hill

TANSEY, P. J. and UNWIN, D. (1969) *Simulation and Gaming in Education* Methuen

TAYLOR, J. and WALFORD, R. (1972) *Simulations in the Classroom* Penguin

WALFORD, R. (1969) *Games in Geography* Longman

WARD, C. and FYSON, A. (1973) *Streetwork: the exploding school* Routledge and Kegan Paul (This is a particularly useful source book for the teachers of all age groups. The section on 'Sources and resources' contains a full and valuable list of teaching and information materials available from the different agencies for those teachers wishing to explore the possibilities of experienced-based learning as discussed in this chapter.)

4 Perspectives on the middle years

Brenda Cohen sets out to examine the polarity between primary and secondary education in terms of aims, methods and curriculum. It is argued that there are legitimate reasons for the differences that exist between the two sectors, and that middle schools should aim to provide a bridge between the two. This will involve seeking a compromise between such aims as the full development of the child as an individual, and that of equipping the child with knowledge and skills valued in the world beyond the school; between the ethos of cooperation and equality and that of competition and differentiation of function. In terms of methods, it will mean making a compromise between the flexibility of the primary school and the high degree of organization characteristic of the secondary school; and in terms of curriculum, it will mean searching for a way of mediating between an integrated and undifferentiated curriculum and finely defined subject specialization. To avoid the inherent danger of confrontation developing between the advocates of either set of approaches, rather than the compromise which a 'bridge theory' implies, the solution advocated is one of accepting the validity of elements in both approaches, and incorporating these elements into a new and distinctive type of institution, which would be characterized by the balance it achieved between the two sides of the polarization, mainly by its deliberate and planned adoption of mixed and varied approaches.

Nicholas Tucker draws together for us a profile of the middle years child, stressing his essential 'middleness' between infanthood and adolescence. The period is often referred to as the latency period, as it is looked on by many as a time of relative calm (though not all teachers would agree with this perception of their pupils), of consolidation and growth during which the child makes important steps forward in all areas of his development. He appears to turn away from the family and adults in general, seeking more the familiarity and security of the peer group. It is a trying time for the child and equally so for the adults in his life. The teacher is invited to play a vital role in the development towards a healthy adolescence, which requires a sympathetic and empathic understanding of the child's problems and concerns. The classroom interaction, which is dealt with more fully in the next article, sets the scene and tone for later years, and it is important that teachers provide a stimulating variety of learning experiences to cater for each individual in her charge.

Terry Sexton in his article on the sociology of the middle years stresses the importance of this as a period of transition. It is a time when the child must learn a new set of understandings about his relations with others in society. Whilst rightly avoiding laying the foundations for yet another special area of sociology, he suggests that the subject does have something useful to say about the child, the classroom and the school during the middle years. He considers the perception of age differences as an important factor in the lives of children in a way it is not in the lives of adults. This is true paradoxically although this is a period of time when more than any other they are segregated into age-matched groups. In our schools eight year olds work with eight year olds, and twelve year olds with twelve year olds. However, in society, he argues, age does not hold such an importance. As the pupil or student emerges into adult life he finds that his new 'peers' are of all ages. In another context (Raggett 1975) we pointed out that:

> ... the beginner teacher has to look to a different set of significant others.... In college as in his previous experience, his 'peers' who acted as a reference group were normally a homogeneous age group in whom he might readily see himself reflected. Now he has to accept that his 'peers' or 'colleagues' are as a social group dependent rather on a common occupation.

It is this necessary change in perspective that begins to take place during adolescence, a time which may commence during or shortly after the middle years period. The theme of transition he believes is implicit in the concept of middleness and he sees it as the keynote for the article. In more primitive cultures the transition to adult life is ritualized and initiation is preceded by a period of schooling in the concepts and perspectives of the adult society. So in our education system the middle years are an important strand in this schooling for initiation into our own much more complex society. Sociologists, as he points out, study 'what holds social groups together or tears them apart'. In this case, then, it is of extreme interest to see what in the middle years is acting as the cement and what the destructive agent. This thoughtful and penetrating essay offers us some ideas to begin the discussion.

Michael Eraut points out that evaluation is a word that has emotive undertones for many teachers. It smacks of cost accountancy and an overconcern with outcomes, many of which are felt to be best left undefined. It appears to involve measurement and aspects of making judgments about values and having clearly defined things to measure and criteria by which to measure them. It all appears threatening, mechanical and contrived. But teachers evaluate all the time. In the day-to-day work of the classroom the teacher is analysing a whole variety of matters, judging results, effectiveness, suitability, progress, etc. with a mixture of intuition – inspired or otherwise – guesswork, knowledge, experience and a whole hierarchy of personal priorities. But it is this process of teachers, individually and in groups, making decisions at all levels that is important. It is argued that the processes involve three tasks: the collection of evidence, the analysis of that evidence and the making of recommendations to the decision makers – though there are those who would not see the last process as part of evaluation. But the article stresses that the mechanics and techniques of evaluation are less important than creating an attitude within the school where it can readily take place. The most important characteristics are 'clear thinking, perceptive observations, empathy and consultation'.

Reference

RAGGETT, M. (1975) 'Teachers' professional socialization' *The London Educational Review* 4 1 Spring

4.1 Philosophical thinking and the middle school years

Brenda Cohen

Philosophy, characteristically, deals with issues in their most abstract and general form, uncluttered by the concrete particularities of time, place and circumstance. In general, these particularities could only be held to distract the eye from the apprehension of pure truth. The approach of philosophers who have concerned themselves with education has on the whole been consistent with this observation, in that the reflections they have offered on the basic principles of education have been applicable to education in general and not confined to any particular age group. Some justification is needed, therefore, for raising philosophical issues in relation to a specific age group and possibly even to a particular type of school. Such a justification can be found, however, when one turns to the way in which philosophers of education have actually put forward their ideas on the principles underlying the educational process, as opposed to merely considering those principles themselves. Plato and Rousseau, for instance, widely different though their approach to fundamental principles may have been, both took care to describe their practical approaches strictly in association with the ages and stages of human development as they saw them. In particular, the period between infancy and adolescence was early recognized as having its own special characteristics, and hence as meriting its own special educational approach. It would seem, then, that there are long-established precedents in seeking to relate basic educational principles to the practices associated with a particular phase of childhood.

When account is taken of the way in which schools actually operate within the British school system, it is clear that, in practice, for somewhat arbitrary historical reasons, the natural and obvious unity of the middle period of childhood has been obscured by a state system of education in which a break at eleven years of age has normally been favoured (in contrast to the private sector where thirteen is more common). This may well be one of the factors that has led to an increasing polarity between the theory and philosophy of the primary school and the theory and philosophy of secondary and later education. It is clear that if due consideration is given to the findings of psychologists in the recognition of a distinct period of childhood with its own characteristics and qualities, as well as to sociological findings which point to other recognizable aspects of the middle years of childhood, then a strong case exists for the independent development of a distinctive set of both methods and aims for these particular years, although whether this recognition demands institutionalization in a separate establishment, the middle school, is a more open question, and one to be determined by the practicalities of the situation rather than *a priori*.

A major part of the motivation for the creation of middle schools has come in fact, from practitioners who felt not only the claims of this age range to special considerations, but also the need to provide a bridge between the culture of the primary school and that of the secondary school. The Plowden Report (DES 1967) appeared to favour this point of view when it argued that;

A school with semi-specialist accommodation shared between cognate subjects, and teachers skilled in certain areas of the curriculum rather than in single subjects, could provide a bridge from class teaching to specialization, and from investigation of general problems to subject disciplines. The influences of semi-specialist teachers primarily concerned with the older pupils might be reflected in more demanding work being given to nine and ten year olds, while the primary tradition of individual and group work might advantageously be retained for a longer period than at present and might delay streaming.

This statement might well be taken as a succinct but definitive statement of the theoretical justification for the middle school. In passing, it may be noted, however, that the Plowden Report does not adhere with strict consistency to the spirit of this observation, since it goes on to argue less for a 'bridge' than for a predominantly primary ethos in the middle school:

If the middle school is to be a new and progressive force it must develop further the curriculum, methods and attitudes which exist at present in junior schools. It must move forward into what is now regarded as secondary school work, but it must not move so far away that it loses the best of primary education as we know it now ... we do not want the middle school to be dominated by secondary school interests.

In addition to the theoretical considerations suggested in these two slightly divergent paragraphs, the report adduced two other types of justification for the change to schools specifically for children of the middle years. First certain arguments of a practical nature were presented for changing the structure of education, such as, for instance, the argument that the introduction of middle schools would help reduce the size of comprehensive schools. Secondly, a developmental argument was introduced, to the effect that a break at eleven cuts across a definite and recognizable phase of learning and of attitudes to learning, a result which has particularly detrimental consequences in relation to creative and expressive subjects such as art and drama. As far as the practical arguments are concerned, these should not, of course, be allowed to determine the case, since most practical objectives can be attained by a variety of means, the introduction of middle schools being only one of a number of alternatives, political will and financial opportunity playing an equally important part in deciding which option will be selected.

The developmental argument, however, whilst being mainly dependent on examination of the psychological facts, does raise certain issues of a philosophical nature which it will be relevant to consider, but in the context of a wider discussion of what might well be described as the 'bridge' theory of the middle school. The basic theoretical arguments as presented by Plowden are very briefly described and fraught with questionable assumptions. In so far as the second Plowden statement quoted above implies a conflict between primary and secondary education in which 'primary' is equated with 'progressive' and in which 'secondary school interests' are regarded as an insidious threat, this second observation, sparse as it is, seems to detract from the even-handed approach of the 'bridge' theory implied in the first statement. It seems likely that it is the 'bridge' theory that the report, given the general tenor of its comments, more strongly represents, and it is this theory that will be taken as the most fruitful view of the purpose and style of the middle school for consideration here. If we take it that the intention of the theory is to point to a set of needs which do not fit readily into either the exclusively primary or exclusively secondary framework of response, then it should be possible to clarify this ideal by examining in more detail the polarization that is implied. By comparing the aims, methods and curriculum of the primary level with those of secondary education, observing how different goals produce different methods and approaches, it should be possible to see to what extent a 'bridge' theory of the middle school is genuinely viable.

Although it is not possible within the limits of this discussion to offer an exhaustive account of the aims, methods and curriculum of both primary and secondary education, it is possible to indicate, within these areas, some points of contrast between the two systems. The theoretical position, in both cases, will be inferred to a large extent from common practice rather than from written statements. In fact, however, written statements as to the aims of primary education abound, from the brief statements of official reports to the more considered and qualified statements of philosophers. R. S. Peters' (1966) general definition of education as initiation into worthwhile activities or modes of thought or conduct must inevitably form a starting point, but precisely because of its general nature cannot contribute to the contrast between primary and secondary education, being fundamental to both. There are, however, a number of ways in which what is deemed to be worthwhile in the education of young children differs from what is held to be worthwhile in secondary education, and may therefore be taken as a goal of aim, distinctive to the one or the other.

First, many statements of aims begin by focusing on the allround development of the child: intellectually, physically, emotionally, socially. This tends to be stressed to a much greater extent in connection with primary than with secondary education, perhaps because the end product of the process of primary education is still a child, whereas practitioners in the secondary field are aware of their charges emerging into the adult world at the end of the secondary phase, and so have their aims in respect of the child's development conditioned by their perception of the needs of society and the needs of the child in relation to the outside world. In both cases, however, there is likely to be stress on the need to develop initiative, independence and judgment in the child. Secondly, where, as is increasingly the case, non-selective systems of secondary education apply, the primary ethos tends to be one of equality and cooperation, in contrast to the secondary sector where the differentiation between pupils, and hence competition rather than cooperation, will appear as legitimate, or, at least, necessary goals. This explains, of course, why subject specialization and streaming are so frequently considered essential to secondary education, and are so much more easily avoided in the primary school. Primary education, too, places much stress on the value of freedom as an objective, in a non-formalized way; whilst the secondary sector, in contrast, is much more able to accept work with a formalized or conditioned ideal of democracy and the structured introduction of democratic procedures and participation rather than an unqualified notion of freedom.

This point, however, leads directly from the realm of 'aims' to that of 'methods'; and it is here that the freedom of the child to control the shape and content of his work, and to engage in activities he has to some extent at least selected for himself, is a value espoused by primary theorists. The possibilities for developing this type of approach in the secondary phase are, on the other hand, much more limited; here the explosion of subject-matter and a desire on the part of at least some pupils to acquire expertise which stands up objectively in the eyes of the world (usually through the testimony of an externally validated examination system) takes over from the desire simply to follow interests and investigate in any self-selected direction. Hence the primary preference for 'discovery' methods and a problem-centred approach, with the personal 'dossier' as the preferred type of record and assessment, as against the secondary stress on the acquisition of established and systematized knowledge by the quickest and most effective (rather than most stimulating or interesting) means available. If this distinction is pursued, a further contrast becomes apparent between primary methods as conditioned by the aim of flexibility, and secondary methods as conditioned by the aim of optimal organization and system. In practice this means a primary system largely opting to work on an untimetabled or loosely block-timetabled day (the 'integrated day' approach) for the sake of achieving maximum flexibility, whilst the most distinctive feature (for the child making the change) of the secondary school is the day divided into rigid periods scheduled for work in prearranged areas of the curriculum – a system designed to achieve the maximum degree of organization for the given end of imparting specialized knowledge. To this end it is not even unknown in the secondary sector for a computer to be considered a necessary resource in coping with the vast timetabling problems which, in large schools offering pupils some degree of choice of subject, appear to have got beyond the reach or control of the mere human mind.

Apart from these contrasts in aims and methods, the area of curriculum itself presents a contrast between the primary and secondary sectors, but here the most significant point is that while the primary school curriculum needs defining in broad categories only (and Dearden (1968) has offered perhaps the clearest and most elegant working-out of such a curriculum), the secondary school, starting from the same categories, divides and refines. This is simply an aspect of the familiar truth that the more one knows, the more distinctions one is able to make: only a degree of familiarity with economics, for instance, enables one to appreciate the distinction between macro-economics and micro-economics. At this level, Hirst's (1965) logical analysis of the 'forms of thought', in which he provided by the double criterion of (a) methods of validation, and (b) distinctive sets of concepts, a yardstick for separating out the essentially distinct areas of possible human knowledge, provides, whilst being fully consistent with Dearden's primary analysis, a more complete basis for working out a secondary curriculum. (To recognize that there are perhaps six or seven irreducible and distinct areas of human knowledge is to see that there is at least a presumption in favour of ensuring that pupils can operate intelligently within each of these areas. It may also suggest an *a priori* case against teaching in such a way that the logical lines between these areas become blurred.) Other theorists, such as Phenix (1964) and O'Connor (1957) make different distinctions, but the principle that such distinctions exist and are important for curriculum planning is widely accepted. What emerges, then, is a contrast between, at primary level, a leaning towards unity and the avoidance of unnecessary distinctions, manifested in the ready success of 'integrated' topics or projects, and making problem-based inquiry a real possibility; and, in the secondary field, a need as knowledge increases to recognize and accept essential distinctions. This necessity is, in its turn, manifested in increasing specialization and a tendency for interdisciplinary projects to be of less universally accepted value, frequently in practice confined mainly to pupils at a lower level of understanding.

These are the obvious contrasts, then, between the two systems as they have evolved over recent years. It may be argued that the contrast is over-drawn, in that many primary schools are by no means as 'progressive' as has been assumed here, and at least some secondary schools are considerably less orthodox and traditional than has been assumed in order to point the contrast. As far as the latter point goes, it might be urged that there is at present a veritable influx of revolutionary ideas (on deschooling, for instance, or, less extremely, in rejection of the conventional curriculum, conventional methods and conventional aims, following such educational Pied Pipers as Illich, Reimer and others) which is shaking the very foundations of secondary education as it has existed to date. All this must be conceded, but in effect what these secondary trends do is to represent to some extent the meeting-point of the progressive primary view with its secondary antithesis, and they in fact give some indication of the strains and conflicts to which the middle school, as the physical meeting-place of these traditions, will necessarily be subject.

Accepting, then, that the fluctuating fashions of the educational world make it impossible to pin down any particular notion as entirely typical, the picture of the two extremes that has been developed here can nevertheless be used to suggest three possible directions in which middle schools might go, as well as pointing to some of the issues which will confront them in their emergent state. The first possible direction, at one point hinted at in the Plowden Report, and the one that seems in fact to be largely influential in practice, is the further development of the primary ethos. Where this trend is followed, middle schools will be innovative institutions – usually open plan, employing team-teaching methods, an integrated day and sometimes even vertical grouping. In the case of new buildings the architectural design would tend to favour this approach, but would in any event considerably affect educational possibilities. The second possible direction, which, judging from what parents in the private sector are willing to pay for, might well be acceptable to many, and would certainly meet complaints and doubts expressed by some secondary schools dissatisfied with the literacy and numeracy of their primary intake, would be for the middle schools to become institutions where more formalized and specialist teaching was introduced earlier than is possible with the conventional break at eleven, and where more clearly defined standards were developed in terms both of academic attainment and discipline. The third possibility, which was expressed in the first of the quoted passages from the Plowden Report, and which has clearly influenced many local authorities in favour of setting up middle schools, is to allow each tradition to modify and mellow the other, thus providing for the child a bridge from one way of working to the other. Of course, whilst the administrator or organizer of an education system may favour the compromise inherent in such a notion, it would be a mistake to overlook the point that has already been suggested: that as pointed out by Michael Raggett and Malcolm Clarkson in their article on curriculum planning, the place of benevolently-intended compromise may very easily become a battleground for competing ideologies, particularly when, as is the case here, the proponents of the rival views have been accustomed for many years to doing battle by means of sorties and sallies from the security of their respective institutions. Undoubtedly, to bring the matter down to a personal level, the team-teaching of many of the open-plan middle schools will have to be operated by groups of individuals whose own views are at one extreme or the other, and who entirely repudiate each other's point of view. Indeed, the very notion of a compromise suggests recognition of the fact that the two extremes to be reconciled each have valid elements of their own. And yet the recognition of value in an opponent's position may be very hard to come by. For instance, the extreme progressive is at his most vehement when attacking examinations and the pursuit of purely academic goals, and at his most vigorous when pursuing goals of social integration and, increasingly, social justice. At the same time defenders of academic standards are grouping into organized movements and pressure groups to resist the erosion of their concept of education by the influence of the progressives. The stage might appear to be set for confrontation rather than for compromise.

Because of the difficulty of securing agreement for either of the first two alternatives for middle schools, however, it is to the third alternative that one must turn for a working solution. But if a 'bridge' theory is to work as the justification for the middle school, some demonstration of how these competing goals may be reconciled is necessary. Some attempt, therefore, must be made to identify the issues that may arise by returning to the three areas of contrast that have already been discussed.

The first of these areas is that of aims. Fortunately, it seems clear that the aim of full development for the child – physical, social, emotional, moral and intellectual – is one that can be subscribed to by all educationists. Similarly initiative and individuality are likely to be regarded as acceptable goals by most western educators at whatever level. It is only when these overall aims are converted into behavioural objectives that conflicts begin to develop. Does, for instance, appropriate intellectual development entail being able to perform certain mathematical operations at a given age, or simply manifesting an attitude of intellectual curiosity when presented with certain sorts of problems? Does it involve attaining certain standards of spelling and grammatical presentation, or rather an ability to write at infinitely greater length without regard to technical details of presentation? It is only when aims have been interpreted in terms of specific objectives of this sort that the real extent of agreement or disagreement can be gauged, and it is clear that within the middle school these issues will need to be thrashed out in considerable detail. Methods will follow to some extent from the behavioural interpretation agreed upon, as will curriculum and actual syllabus-content. For instance, discovery methods will appear more likely to develop the quality of intellectual curiosity if this is the agreed objective, while rote learning methods may aid certain types of mechanical arithmetical computation. If the latter skills are valued, appropriate methods will be employed for their attainment, even if this means a return to apparently discredited methods. Similarly, formal carefully prepared English exercises, possibly followed through consistently in a textbook designed for the purpose, will be necessary for guaranteeing given standards of written work, while the provision of stimuli for creative writing would be a method more likely to be adopted if the agreed goal were writing fluency irrespective of presentation.

Decisions on these matters would, of course, be immediately reflected in the curriculum followed by the school. A timetable biased heavily towards creative subjects such as art, music and drama would suggest that creativity is valued more than formal skills. Where, on the other hand, a solid proportion of the day is scheduled for specific activities relating to formal skills, creative aspects may be assigned a lesser status. In primary schools these evaluations may depend to a considerable extent on the attitude of an individual class teacher and on how he or she chooses to programme the day; in secondary schools teachers' functions are defined before they arrive: as teachers of physics, of history, art or drama, the proportion of time spent with particular children working in these particular areas is a matter for overall planning. In the middle school, however, while planning is very much less likely to be a matter for individuals, positions are unlikely to be as clear-cut as in the secondary sector. Here, then, is one area for reaching agreement, avoiding extremes, and recognizing that the school day is long enough to encompass both creativity and formal skills. The middle school's aim must be balance, in a way which may not be necessary or desirable earlier, and may not be possible later.

As far as the aim of full intellectual development in its widest sense is concerned, it will be necessary to take seriously the need to lay a sound basis for work in every fundamental area of human knowledge, moving from the very broad conception of that appropriate in the primary school towards the finer distinctions of the secondary school. It is worth noticing that in practice this may well mean a more positive adoption of the technological adjuncts of education, with foreign language work supported by language laboratories, more systematic study of science requiring the provision of laboratories and apparatus, the use of television and possibly programmed learning aids. At the same time, in other areas of the curriculum, older children will be reaching a stage of ability to deal with conceptual and abstract issues, particularly in relation to matters of reasoning and morality. As far, then, as the aim of the full development of the child's potential is concerned, there seems to be no reason why, in spite of differences of emphasis, this aim should not be translated into agreed behavioural objectives, with appropriate methods devised to secure these objectives, and reflected in a balanced middle school curriculum. The individual teacher within the middle school should undoubtedly play a part in determining the emphasis in his particular school, and there would seem to be no reason why different middle schools should not develop, within the limits of this requirement of balance, their own distinctive character and emphasis.

The second type of aim mentioned is of a different nature, and forming a bridge between the ethos of cooperation and that of competition may be more difficult a proposition. This area is, however, crucial, since extremely basic matters of organization depend on what is decided here. Will children work in groups, for instance? Will they use assignment cards? Will organization centre round class teaching or team teaching? What part will examinations and other methods of assessment play in the working of the school? Without agreement here it is clear that the school literally cannot operate, and yet it is here that views are most likely to be strongly held and least open to compromise. In practice, of course, a school will tend to exist, in advance of the recruitment of any particular individual teacher, as either an open-plan team-teaching institution or as one geared to the closed classroom. However, although it has already been conceded that architecture can be very influential, it cannot finally determine the use to which a building will be put. There are many examples of teachers committed to certain aims successfully resisting the geography or topography of a school; in many old primary schools, for instance, an open-plan atmosphere and teaching system has been created by the astute use of and integration of corridor-space; similarly, teachers in architecturally open-plan buildings have been known to use bays as traditional classrooms in order to pursue more conventional aims than the designer of the school envisaged.

It is agreement on aims, then, that is fundamental, with the overt methods used following on from this. When attention is focused on the two basic and apparently conflicting aims of cooperation and competition, of the two cooperation tends to sound a more laudable educational objective. Indeed, competition has long been frowned on by progressives. Rousseau's Emile, for instance, in eighteenth-century France, was encouraged only to measure himself against his own progress and not against other children; later Froebel attacked competition amongst children, and Dewey, too, early this century, opposed the use of grades and examinations, commending the cooperative aspect of group work. More recently, it has been with expressed relief, on the whole, that the primary schools have turned from the competitive atmosphere generated by the eleven-plus examination, towards the greater curricular freedom resulting from the absence of inter-school assessment and rivalry. At the same time a strong ideological cult of equality, which attributes differences in performance entirely to environmental factors has significantly affected attitudes to competition. It will be difficult for teachers sympathetic to these ideas to concede that there is anything to be said on the other side. However, alongside the feeling of relief at the end of the eleven-plus examination there exists a suspicion that a falling-off of standards may be not unconnected with this development, and that possibly as a general rule the competitive effects of examinations exert a favourable influence on education. Adopting a less rosy view of human nature than the progressives, those whose sympathies lie on this side of the debate would argue that not all academic goals can be achieved by reliance entirely on intrinsic rather than extrinsic motivation. They would argue, too, that competition more faithfully reproduces the nature of the world outside the school and, conceivably, that winning and losing are essentially connected with the Protestant work ethic which is fundamental to the success of the type of society in which children are growing up. Here the links between education and political arguments become apparent, since the supporters of cooperation would be likely, if they conceded the last point, to claim that this is in fact an undesirable feature of society, and that in a more just and more equal society the ethic of competitive warfare would be replaced by one of neighbourly support.

It is clear that total commitment on one side or the other will frequently be found on these issues. Nevertheless, when the points made on either side are viewed impartially and with an open mind, it becomes apparent that there are in fact significant and important – and not necessarily incompatible – elements on either side. For a useful analogy and an indication of the form that compromise might take, the field of sport provides a good illustration. Here competition undoubtedly adds to the quality of performance of participants and provides additional interest and a new dimension to something which is nevertheless essentially justified by its intrinsic appeal; neither does the possibility of being compared with others rule out the alternative of taking pleasure in one's own progress and attempting to improve on one's own performance. Very often too, apparently objective standards may be set (for example, the four-minute mile) which are implicitly derived from competition, but in which the element of pitting oneself against other people is less obtrusive. It must be admitted that these compromises are facilitated by the fact that in the field of sport there are virtually no egalitarians or extreme environmentalists. Nevertheless, the analogy does demonstrate that there is no *necessary* conflict between the ideals of cooperation and competition, at least in the sense that neither needs to be adopted uniquely to the complete exclusion of the other. Judiciously interwoven, they may in fact complement each other. Although there need not be a conflict, however, it cannot be denied that in practice there often is. Translated into classroom practicalities, the two aims may well generate very different educational methods and result in quite divergent programmes. For instance, the ideal of cooperation may be expressed in a classroom arrangement in which more able children are grouped with less able children in order to help them and work with them. Vertical (or 'family') grouping is another alternative which increases this element by adding an age difference, as well, to the disparity. The type of work set will have to be such that work in a group as opposed to work as an individual is a possibility, and therefore the teacher will need to prepare work and assignment cards to guide the activities of the groups. The ideal of competition, on the other hand, is more likely to result in homogeneous groupings, the most familiar of which is streaming, in order to help children make progress academically to the limits of their ability. The preferred teaching method is more likely to be (though need not necessarily be) class teaching, thus facilitating the provision of a curriculum which features the development of taught skills (foreign languages, for instance) and the building-up of bodies of knowledge.

Here, at the level of methods and curriculum, the middle school does have a real choice to make. Nevertheless, the possibility of compromise on aims should suggest that compromise on methods and curriculum too is a real possibility. It should, indeed, be strongly questioned whether the adoption of just one approach to all work could possibly be the right solution. Mixed methods have been working on a large scale in the primary sector, and some secondary schools have also attempted to vary their approach by introducing interdisciplinary project work on an experimental basis. The middle school, as a relatively smaller unit, free from the administrative and timetabling millstone that hampers so many of these secondary school experiments, and with a more carefully balanced staff than is normal in primary schools, could very easily be an institution in which children work in a variety of groupings using a variety of approaches to their work to attain whatever specific objectives are agreed upon in any particular area of the curriculum. In practice this may mean that special abilities will be developed further and that gaps will widen between different children in relation to the same subjects (for example, in a foreign language, in music or in mathematics). Doctrinaire resistance to this type of inequality cannot be justified, if only because the ideal of cooperation itself involves recognition of the fact that inequalities (whatever their origin) do in fact exist, and in the right context can be used to everyone's advantage. The possibility of using these differences to promote successful and interesting group work is only a small-scale mirror of society's ability to profit from the varying talent of its members, once these are developed by the educational system to their maximum. Middle schools, then, should aim to overcome the apparent conflict between the ideals of cooperation and competition and to produce, as in the case of the aim of developing the individual's full potentiality, a system in which the right balance is achieved between the types of goals that have hitherto been characterized as predominantly primary and those that have been seen as predominantly secondary.

Turning to the aims of freedom and democracy, the possibility of compromise is easier to see, since here the developmental argument comes into its own. The freedom offered in the primary school is freedom offered to a child who is still essentially dependent on adults for the framework in which he operates, whether that dependency takes the form of conformity or resistance. The involvement of older pupils in secondary schools in the procedures of running the school (with participation as a pupil-governor the culmination of this process) is, on the other hand, participation offered to autonomous human beings, able to take responsiblity to a considerable extent for their own actions and decisions. The middle school is ideally placed to supervise this transition from, in Piaget's (1932) terminology, heteronomy to autonomy, since it spans the period in which children's attitudes to rules undergo the radical change that enables them to become independent moral agents. In terms of practice, this will undoubtedly mean seeing that older children have a role and responsibility within the school, but it is more likely that this will be in respect of discipline and ancillary matters rather than curriculum. The framework in which this responsibility operates will need to be more carefully defined than is the case in schools with a younger age range. This particular point leads to a more general observation. From a wider point of view, it would be possible to say that this transition from childhood to adolescence is in fact the developmental key to the middle-school phase of education, and that from the point of view of the ideal of freedom, the middle school should be better placed for providing a rational and structured form of freedom, and thus meeting to some extent the adolescent desire to be recognized as an independent being, than is normally possible for a large secondary school. Again, then, in the area of freedom and participation it is possible to see how the middle school might operate as a bridge from primary to secondary education.

In three basic areas of the aims of primary and secondary education, then, it has been argued that the middle school can and should be a place of compromise, and that the validity of the aims of both sectors can be recognized in a middle school which sees itself not as a continuation of the primary school, nor as an early secondary school, but as a bridge between the two, developing its own distinctive ethos and character, in which elements of both the other sectors will be incorporated. Separate discussion of methods and curriculum becomes unnecessary, since it has been shown how compromise in these areas follows from a successful reconciliation of aims. Where this reconciliation has been achieved, for instance, independent discovery work will have as valid a part to play as examination-oriented work; there will be an appropriate balance between flexibility and organization; a gradual transition from undifferentiated work to increasing specialization will not rule out the inclusion of deliberately planned interdisciplinary projects, and each child will have the opportunity, on different occasions, of working as an individual, as a member of a small group, and as a member of a class. Given this approach, the antithesis between the child-centred primary school and the subject-centred secondary school will vanish in an institution which is indeed innovative, but only in the best sense of the word. The intrinsic interest and discipline of the subject-matter which is the object of education will not be lost sight of in serving the needs of the child who is the *subject* of the educational process. And last, but not least, the need to divide child from child by offering the project-based curriculum to some and a specialist examination-oriented curriculum to the most able will vanish in the mixed economy of the middle school that consciously sets itself the task of functioning as a bridge from primary to secondary education.

It may be useful, in finishing, to review the course of the argument, summarizing the main points. To begin with, it was suggested that there are well-established precedents for discussing the underlying principles of education at a particular phase of development. In particular the period between infancy and adolescence is a clearly recognizable special phase, although the British system's break at eleven obscures recognition of this fact. It was suggested that failure to identify this period might be partly responsible for the polarity which exists between the philosophy of the primary and of the secondary school. Bridge-building between the two was taken as a prime justification for middle schools, and the Plowden Report's statement of this theory was taken as a model, although it was noted that the Plowden Report tended to favour a primary bias for the middle schools. A comparison of the two sides of this polarization was undertaken in order to throw light on the 'bridge' theory. It was seen that the aims of the primary school emphasize the personal development of the child in an atmosphere of equality and cooperation, while the secondary school emphasizes preparation of the child for the world outside school, and hence differentiation of function and competition. It followed that in its methods, the primary school emphasized freedom, self-direction and discovery, while the secondary school tended to stress the acquisition of knowledge and the public validation of this acquisition (mainly by the examination system). The first system, it was pointed out, lends itself to flexible methods; the second requires a high degree of organization. It was suggested that the curriculum of the primary school needs defining in broad categories only, while that of the secondary school necessarily divides and refines; and that, in practice, this tends to mean that the first type of curriculum can be forwarded by integrated subjects, while the second tends to specialization in relatively narrow fields.

Having recognized these contrasts, it was argued that the middle school was faced with the three alternatives of (a) following the primary pattern; (b) following the secondary pattern, or (c) providing a bridge between the two, with distinctive characteristics of its own. In adopting the third alternative, it was recognized that there was a danger of confrontation developing rather than compromise. The areas where contrasts had been identified were taken as indicating the issues where agreement would need to be reached in developing the middle-school ethos, and it was argued that in all these areas compromise was in fact possible. For instance, it was pointed out that the aim of fostering creativity would entail the use of 'open' teaching methods and a curriculum in which creative areas were substantially represented, whilst the aim of laying a foundation for advanced academic study would entail a systematic approach to cognitive areas and a full use of efficient modern teaching aids where appropriate. Here it was argued that a balanced programme was essentially the answer, but that it would be feasible for different middle schools to develop distinctive emphases. Similarly, it was suggested that the aims of cooperation and competition were not mutually exclusive, even though they might entail widely different teaching methods, and that the emphasis in the middle school should be on a variety of methods and approaches for different curricular goals. Finally, it was suggested that the aims of freedom and democracy could be readily reconciled in the middle school, spanning, as it does, the transition from childhood to early adolescence and from dependence to independence of judgment.

The conclusion reached here, then, has been that the middle school should be essentially a place of compromise, where the validity of the differing aims of primary and secondary education can be recognized and incorporated into a new and distinctive type of institution, with is own aims, methods and curriculum, derived from the other sectors but not wholly identifiable with either. To have the best of both worlds is a legitimate and not necessarily impractical aim for middle schools.

References

DES (1967) *Children and their Primary Schools* (Plowden Report, Volume I) HMSO

DEARDEN, R. F. (1968) *The Philosophy of Primary Education* Routledge and Kegan Paul

Hirst, P. H. (1965) 'Liberal education and the nature of knowledge' in R. D. Archambault (Ed) *Philosophical Analysis and Education* Routledge and Kegan Paul

O'Connor, D. J. (1957) *An Introduction to the Philosophy of Education* Routledge and Kegan Paul

Peters, R. S. (1966) *Ethics and Education* Allen and Unwin

Phenix, P. H. (1964) *Realms of Meaning* New York: McGraw Hill

Piaget, J. (1932) *The Moral Judgement of the Child* Routledge and Kegan Paul

Useful further reading

Archambault, R. D. (Ed) (1965) *Philosophical Analysis and Education* Routledge and Kegan Paul

Bantock, G. (1952) *Freedom and Authority in Education* Faber and Faber

Cohen, B. (1969) *Educational Thought: An Introduction* Macmillan

Gribble, J. (1969) *Introduction to Philosophy of Education* Boston: Allyn and Bacon

Hirst, P. H. (1974) *Knowledge and the Curriculum* Routledge and Kegan Paul

Hirst, P. H. and Peters, R. S. (1970) *The Logic of Education* Routledge and Kegan Paul

Hooper, R. (Ed) (1971) *The Curriculum: Context, Design and Development* Oliver and Boyd

Peters, R. S. (Ed) (1969) *Perspectives on Plowden* Routledge and Kegan Paul

Peters, R. S. (Ed) (1973) *The Philosophy of Education* Oxford University Press

208

4.2 Teachers and children in the middle years: the psychologists' constructs

Nicholas Tucker

Up to now, the middle years of childhood have been rather neglected by psychologists; there is still no introductory text to this particular period one can recommend, and interested readers will have to dip into more general works to get some idea of what is going on. Even so, research into a number of specific areas at this age is still hard to come by; on the whole, psychologists have been more interested in the rapid developments around infancy, or the dramas of adolescence. This has sometimes led to quite a false impression that nothing very much happens in the middle years: Rynolds (1939) describes them as 'a quiet and happy period', whilst Sullivan (1953) sees them as 'one of the most tranquil phases of human life'. And so they may be, but such a generalization is bound to cause, at best, a wry smile amongst teachers who have experienced some of the less tranquil aspects of this age. It certainly is a very energetic time, in terms of sheer activity, including noise, and developmentally there is a great deal happening to make this a very crucial period indeed.

The development of the child

Physically, whilst there may not be any startling growth, at least until adolescence starts, there is a large increase in muscle strength in both sexes. This means a child of this age can withstand fatigue and physical stress more than ever before. Restlessness, fidgeting and sheer physical agility may also result from this. It has been said that, 'Youngsters at ages nine to twelve don't walk when they can run, they don't run when they can jump, and they prefer to perform whatever demands the greater physical effort'. Dearborn and Rothney (1941). With all this energy there is usually a steady improvement in motor skills, from performance in games to the finer manual tasks. To begin with, the average boy is taller and heavier than the average girl, but this may reverse around the age of eleven or so, with the girl's adolescent growth spurt coming two years or so ahead of the average boy. Some girls may begin puberty as early as ten years old, although the usual age for the menarche is still around thirteen years old.

Intellectually there is a very large change indeed, from the intuitive reactions of an infant to the more considered logic of a pre-adolescent, culminating with the beginning of abstract thought in early adolescence itself. How much of this development is linked with the maturation of the brain is still not clear, although this undoubtedly plays an important part. But for a closer understanding of the different stages of this intellectual development, we must turn to the work of Piaget, who has contributed most to this subject.

Up to seven years or so, an infant tends to react to surface appearances, and is not likely to draw many logical conclusions from his experience. He will find it difficult to see things from any other point of view than his own. If he meets a foreigner, for example, he may talk to him in English, oblivious to the possibility that this might not be understood; after all, if he (the child) understands English, shouldn't everyone else? In terms of money, he may think a large coin worth more than a smaller one or a bank-note, merely because it looks more to *him*, and that is again the most important criterion. In his fantasy world, he may confuse a wish for the deed itself; thus he may come to believe a story he makes up as something that has actually happened. In the same way, his whole notion of the universe is imbued with his own wishes and desires: all objects in it are made for the express use of man, and everything is organized along moral, planned principles. Thus if a thief is running away with his booty over a bridge that breaks, this breakage will be because the thief didn't deserve to get away. And, on another tack, it wouldn't matter what reason the thief had for stealing, even if it was to feed his starving family against the wishes of a tyrant landlord. Attitudes to laws at this age are very severe indeed, and actions are judged on their surface appearance, rather than on the motivation of those concerned.

It is important to know something of this infant world view to appreciate quite what the older child is growing away from. And, of course, elements of this type of thinking will persist throughout childhood, and even make an occasional appearance in adult behaviour. It is certainly a mistake to see any developmental stage as a hard and fast step forward; human development is notoriously uneven, and a child may be logical in one direction and blissfully unscientific in another all at the same time. Yet at around seven years old, Piaget (1952) does see the child as beginning to enter another intellectual stage with the onset of what he terms as 'concrete operational thought'. This type of thinking is much closer to an adult's, and perhaps can be best illustrated by a practical example drawn from Piaget's best-known experiment. A child is faced with two flasks, one long and thin, the other short and fat. Into these he pours water from two identical beakers. Although he will be quite sure that there was the same amount of water in the two beakers, a younger child will tend to say that there is now more water in the tall flask than in the short flask, simply because it looks more to him. If the water is emptied back into the beakers and is seen to be the same amount, never mind. For a child, at (in Piaget's terms) this pre-operational stage, the change in form can quite easily produce a change in amount. For a child at the stage of concrete operations, however, the situation is more complex. He is able to see, for example, that although one flask is taller, the other one is wider, and thus one dimension may be compensating for another in the final result. Even if the long flask looks as if it has more water, the child will be able to retrace the steps by which the water got there in the first place (a younger child cannot often manage to 'reverse' a situation in this way, going back from the end to the beginning again in his mind). Remembering the two identical beakers, he will by logic now realize that there cannot be more water in one flask than another, as no further water was added or subtracted at any other stage since. And so the child will argue the case through logically, very much as he may set about his parents at home, with that new-found, sometimes inexorable logic that is now capable of catching out an adult who might once have got away with a fairly blatant inconsistency.

This is not to say that the child is always able to think and argue logically at this age. Take the following proposition: Edith is fairer than Susan; Edith is darker than Lily; who is the darkest of the three? An older child, entering into what Piaget calls the stage of formal reasoning, may be able to think in more abstract terms and thus take this sort of problem in his stride, even though it is about something not immediately observable in front of him. But before the age of thirteen or so, a child is better able to think logically about objects rather than verbal propositions; thus Piaget's phrase 'concrete' operations, i.e., things that exist, sometimes actually in front of the child, as in the experiment with the two flasks.

With this growth in logical thinking, there is an accompanying sophistication in concept formation, by which a child puts his thoughts and impressions into a more coherent pattern. A small child may group things in his mind quite arbitrarily; thus because *he* moves, talks and is human, other things that move must also be able to talk and have human feelings. Or else he may group things according to common by irrelevant principles, such as putting different animals into 'families' according to whether he thinks they will like each other or not, rather as to what species they belong to, or some more scientific criterion. An older child will discriminate better when it comes to looking for common characteristics, and can therefore generalize far more meaningfully in a way that other people can follow; much of his former egocentricity may no longer be apparent now. At the same time, he may be able to use two principles of generalization simultaneously; thus categorizing flowers according to height *and* colour, or motor vehicles according to size *and* speed. He may also learn to reason ahead, as in number series such as 1, 3, 2, 5, 3, 8 . . . He will be able to define words more in terms of how they link conceptually with other words. For example, he may see now that a plum and a cherry are similar because they are both fruit (a younger child may say they are both round or that you can eat them both; answers that are also correct but do not get so close to a specific concept.) He may also now be able to manage some of the harder verbal questions that occur in intelligence tests, such as describing in what ways two objects are the same and also different in the one answer – a combination that may well defeat the less subtle intelligence of a younger child.

This type of intellectual development may not be easy without the enrichment of vocabulary that also happens at this age, where a child becomes better able to converse with another in terms they can both understand (a younger child can still be using a type of semi-private language that is not always very clear to others). His sentences may become more complex, both grammatically and in vocabulary, and thus better suited to express complex ideas. Thus he may be able to construct sentences that integrate several points of view, through being able to express contrasts, alternatives and so forth. At the same time, he may now be able to understand irony and humour much better in speech, through being able to see beyond the surface structure of a sentence towards double meanings and verbal absurdities. Similarly, he can start understanding metaphors, similes and proverbs; where he will not be able to look beyond the superficial meanings of the words to what is implied at a deeper level.

This growing objectivity in the child can be found in other developing skills at this age. In his drawings he will start recognizing the rule of perspective and rely less upon his subjective perception, unlike a younger child who may draw two visible eyes in a side-on profile of a face, simply because he *knows* every face has two eyes. Where spatial conception is concerned, Piaget (1956) has a neat experiment where a child is shown an artificial model of a landscape, composed of three hills crowned by a house, a tower or a church respectively. A small doll holding a toy camera is placed in front of the landscape, and its position systematically changed, so that it views the hills differently from the one view of the child observing the experiment. The child is then given several pictures depicting the landscape as it has been 'photographed' by the doll from its various positions, and has to match these positions with the appropriate photograph. A younger child cannot do this, dominated as he is by his particular view of the landscape. An older child, better able to coordinate different points of view, in this case quite literally, may be more successful.

There are many other discoveries Piaget made about the age group, all in the direction of children learning to perceive objects more realistically and thus coming better to grips with the world around him. Rather than multiply any more of these, it might be better now to try to assess the broader significance to the child of this progress, and how it ties in with his overall social development.

Some of the growing skills I have already described may not always seem in themselves very important; does it really matter, for example, that a child is no longer confused about the amount of water in two dissimilar flasks, or that he no longer thinks that 'killing two birds with one stone' should be taken literally? But when taken together, something of the magnitude of this step forward should become more apparent. Basically, the development of logical thought means the child is no longer so much at the mercy of his immediate environment, to be diverted by any odd stimulus which may or may not be significant. Now, with his growing powers of concentration, he is able to classify his everyday experience more logically, and devise effective rules and laws for understanding the workings of his immediate environment that do not share the magical thinking common at an earlier age. In other words, the big world outside now loses some of its mystery; to a certain extent it, and the adults who organize it, can now be properly understood. An arbitrary, confused and confusing world now gives way to a universe of more familiar facts.

Perhaps partly as a result of this new confidence, the child should become ready at this age to loosen ties with the family in order to strengthen his contacts with the outside world, in particular, the child's own contemporaries, his immediate peer group. This process may well involve him in a general attitude of revolt against much adult authority: it has been called the time when 'the nicest child begins to behave in the most awful way', and referrals to Child Guidance Clinics are at their peak at this age. If the child has his own bedroom there may now be that menacing 'Keep Out!' sign defiantly pinned up; inside, he and his friends may plot, converse and joke in language and over subjects that may distress the more faint-hearted parent, if they are indiscreet enough to eavesdrop.

But it would be unwise to try to work too much against the influence of the peer group at this age. It at least can offer the child company at his or her own social and intellectual level, and does not tire at the constant energy and noise so common at this age. It is also a far more realistic setting for the child than that provided by the family or other adults alone. Other children will not necessarily accept someone who is used to having it all his own way; learning to play with others at this age is a valuable social lesson. Within the group, a child finds other children faced with the same situation that he is going through; how they cope with it will be of constant interest to him. For example, at this age a child starts establishing a firmer idea of his sex-role; each sex will tend to keep to its own more than ever now, and will be eager to pick up any hints – from parents, friends or the wider social world – on what is the nature of a true male or female. For boys, this may lead to an exaggerated phase when neatness and cleanliness are despised as 'soft' or 'girlish', and toughness in language and action is at a premium. There may be physical and verbal aggression towards girls, but this may be most pronounced amongst boys still rather uncertain about their new masculinity, and eager to prove their worth whenever possible. Amongst girls, this may be a time for great activity within their own group. One type of girl may take to emphasizing her growing feminine charms, and become very fussy about dress, hairstyle and so on. Other girls may act the tomboy rather more, but in both cases this new behaviour may help the child become more independent of the mother at home, whilst possibly remaining an interesting figure to some of the boys. In fact, whatever children may publicly avow at this age, there can already be a great attraction between the sexes, though usually kept secret or laughed off in a would-be casual way.

At a time when traditional sex-roles are themselves very much under question, parents may well dislike some of the excessive polarizations that take place in children's interests at this age. But one cannot look for sophistication in the young; there may be time enough for this later, but since all children one day have to leave the family and grow independent of their parents, this reaching out into a wider social environment, however crude it may sometimes seem, is entirely healthy. Parents who may groan at the change in their child's vocabulary, tastes and fashions, and resent being told they should do things on the authority of another child down the road, should still remember that this is a normal stage of development. In fact, most children are not nearly so subservient to the whim of their gang as many parents imagine; it's only the very insecure child who may be overconformist in this way.

But with the best will in the world, parents' attitudes towards this new independence will not be wholly favourable. Parental attitudes towards a three year old and a nine year old show a pronounced decrease in warmth and understanding, where the parent has to change from being physical helper and restrainer to something far more subtle. Basically, parents have to provide a secure enough base for a child to explore the world from, confident that he can always dart back if things get too hot for him outside. If parents encourage overdependence, they may end up with a timid child, possibly too afraid to leave home and mother even to go to school. If the parents do not offer enough warmth and understanding, they may produce a child too dependent upon his own age group for emotional support and protection – just the sort of victim whom other children may take advantage of when it comes to someone else having to carry the can or commit some silly misdemeanour.

In other words, parents have a difficult job to do at this stage, but then so do teachers. Discussing the developmental tasks of middle childhood, Havighurst (1952) recognized three main 'thrusts' for growth: 'There is the thrust out of the home and into the peer group, the physical thrust into the world of games and work requiring neuromuscular skills, and the mental thrust into the world of adult concepts, logic, symbolism, and communication.' The first of these tasks may well be the province of the home, although schools enter into it as well; the other two are more clearly the responsibility of the teacher. Perhaps it is now time to consider some of the significance of this intellectual and social development for the classroom, and ways in which it might be fostered, other things being equal.

The task of the teacher

Here is one of the many possible recipes for learning: 'an individual must want something (be motivated), notice something (receive stimuli from within or without), do something (respond to these stimuli), and get something (satisfaction of some kind)' (Strang 1959).

So far so good. Such a formula may well be quite easy to apply to a normal child with normal abilities. Find the interest, set the appropriate lesson, then sit back and wait for it all to happen. But of course, it is never as simple as this. For one thing, is there such a thing as a normal child? The developmental pattern so far described refers to trends and probabilities at this age. An individual will never completely fit into this generalized picture, there will always be areas that are inconsistent, contrary or downright mysterious, both to other people and possibly to the child as well – and this is a child with normal advantages, both in himself and with his family. What about the child from a deprived background, the child from divided, quarrelling parents, the child who is in some way handicapped? Can there ever be a learning formula that applies to so many different conditions of children?

Obviously in the space here it would be impossible to take on the whole spectrum of the underprivileged, emotionally disturbed child, and the special problems they present to teachers and to themselves. I leave this area of study to Joan Bird in her article on problem children. Rather, I will continue to concentrate on the more or less normal child at this age. Some of the special problems he can face the teacher with may be found in a more chronic form in some of his less fortunate counterparts.

Basically, a child may get the most out of school if he starts by liking the place. This may seem an obvious statement, or even an unnecessary one – can there be any children now who do not enjoy school, what with all the informal methods and relaxing of authoritarian attitudes? Yet a study by Moore (1966) suggested that 80 per cent of children experienced difficulty in adjusting to infant school, nearly half of which seems to be of moderate or marked severity. This is not an auspicious beginning to school life, and going on to a study of older children between six and eleven years old, Moore found that boys who were the only child at home often continued to experience difficulty in adjusting, being generally reluctant to go to school at all, and having difficulties with teachers, work, and social occasions such as attending school dinners or mixing with others in the playground.

There are all sorts of reasons for anxiety at school, but is it always a bad thing? After all, a child may be anxious to do well, and work all the better. There may be some truth in this: the overanxious child may try hard in situations he feels he can cope with. But in novel situations, or at times when his anxiety becomes too much for him, his performance will almost certainly suffer. Jerome Bruner (1966) has suggested that children's attitudes to learning can be divided into two broad categories: 'coping' and 'defending'. A confident, coping child, may welcome new situations and the challenge they bring; the insecure child, with little belief in his own abilities, may shun anything he feels puts him to the test. In this sense, the 'defending' child brings his own attitudes into every aspect of his work: his first question may be not, 'Is this interesting?' but 'Can I do it?' Strategies he may adopt to defend himself against possible failure can include forever setting himself easy, unadventurous goals, or else drifting into a fantasy world where he feels safer than in the give-and-take of a classroom.

A teacher can do little about some of the factors that can produce a child of this type. There may be parents at home who have put too much stress on the child's need to succeed, making him over-fearful of failure (teachers as parents may occasionally be guilty of this!). Or else there may be children who have never been made to feel worth anything at all, with little opportunity in their lives ever to disprove this lowly assessment. But although the teacher cannot alter history, and educational failure can become something of a pattern in many families, she can do something about the classroom atmosphere, which in itself may help relax some of her more nervous pupils. Just as children tend to identify more with their parents if they are perceived as warm, supportive figures, the teacher's own positive enthusiasm and friendly attitude towards the class seems to elicit a greater response from individual children than any other single factor. This is not to say that a teacher *only* has to be friendly and affectionate in order to succeed: obviously other skills and attitudes are important too. But in an atmosphere where everyone is more or less accepted, and even the most prickly comes to feel less defensive, a teacher may still be able to achieve more than someone in the next classroom who has read all the books, gone to all the courses, but still does not really like children – and shows it. Once a child with an already existing bad self-image feels that this is being reinforced by the attitude of the teacher towards him, then future cooperation between them becomes less likely, with the pupil either withdrawing into himself, or else acting out the part of the bad child to the disruption of everyone else. Of course there are some children who are so disturbed that, however patient and understanding a long-suffering teacher may be, the child himself is too confirmed in his present maladjustment to be able to change without specialist attention. This would then be a case for the educational psychologist, but in less serious cases the teacher can certainly try to make an otherwise nervous child feel more at home within the classroom.

The role any teacher has to follow at this age is of course a complex one. If she identifies herself too closely with her pupils, almost becoming one of the girls in the process, she will be betraying her role as initiator of young people into adult ways of behaviour. If, on the other hand, she tries to keep everything in her classroom under her constant control, and always in her own image, she may finally push her class into opposition. At this age, the class is just as likely to side with an individual pupil as with a teacher if the two are in conflict, unlike younger children who may quite cheerfully betray classmates if this is going to get them any advantage with the authorities. The answer, as always, may lie in some middle way, where the teacher is firm enough to be looked upon as a competent guide to the adult world whilst also remaining close enough to the child to sympathize with some of his immature attitudes and values. Of course there will still be times when a child may wish to challenge any teacher who represents for him some of the demands of adult society, but the same pupil may also wish to identify himself *with* these demands at other moments. A certain amount of criticism and testing out may even be a necessary activity for the child, simply to discover whether adult figures really mean and believe in what they say. But a teacher can try putting some of this new-found critical ability to her own use, asking pupils to criticize their own or each other's work, or suggest new approaches to learning on their own initiative. The growing ability of a child at this stage to start standing outside himself and his immediate surroundings should not be wasted; it can be one of his most valuable assets.

I have concentrated so far on whether the pupils feel right in the classroom, and are not preoccupied with thoughts or feelings that get in the way of learning. So before moving on to consider more purely academic problems and approaches at this period, it is still worth a teacher's while to be sensitive to other ways in which any pupil may be diverted from classroom activities. Not that the teacher is often in such a God-like position that she can eradicate most difficulties at source, but even so, understanding and support at this stage, or in psychological jargon, accurate empathy with a particular problem, can still be enormously important – something a child may remember with gratitude long after a teacher has forgotten all about it.

In this sense, it is always valuable for a teacher to be on the look-out for pupils going through the sort of stress that can be so counterproductive for concentration in the classroom. Bright, athletic children, may be no problem at all – there may always be a queue anxious to sit next to them or otherwise bask in their favour. But what about the over-aggressive child, who puts other children's backs up by always insisting on getting his own way; or the depressed, withdrawn pupil, who will do his best to fade into the background, both with the teacher and with other children? Children who rule themselves out of the peer group can suffer considerably in the process. If they are very bright, they can sometimes put all their emotional investment in academic performance, preferring the library to the playground, and adults to other children – 'the teacher's pet' – forever anxious to take on more work, who do not always find much favour with their peers. But on the whole, bright children do make friends, their very intelligence attracting some of the others around them. More likely, the friendless child may be neither very bright nor attractive; his school attendance may be sporadic and his health record poor. Lack of peer group support may only increase his dislike of school and bad self-perception. If he has any friends at all, it may be children rather like himself – the type of relationship where individuals are thrown together because they cannot find anyone better, sometimes echoed later in some of those semi-delinquent gangs where members gather for the emotional support no one there is actually able to give, all sharing in the same immaturity. There are no easy answers for such children, but at least if the teacher is *aware* of what they are missing from their own contemporaries, there is always the chance for some *ad hoc* arrangement during the day that might begin to open up someone otherwise closed in upon himself.

As well as these more general patterns, the teacher – notwithstanding all her other responsibilities and duties – should be aware of changes in the child's family background that may explain some changes in the child himself. An illness at home, bereavement, unemployment, worsening parental relations, can all affect a child quite severely. If his own behaviour and personality suffer as a result, understanding the reason *why* at least helps a teacher to place this change in some sort of pattern, and possibly modify her own attitudes towards it. No one can remain endlessly patient, of course, whatever the causes of bad behaviour may be. But losing temper with a confused, hurt child may not be as bad for him as the feeling that he may be losing something more valuable as well – the teacher's ultimate sympathy. And here, understanding the child's total situation can help the teacher feel this sympathy, at least for some of the time!

Lastly, the child's actual physical development can sometimes be a useful indicator to the teacher at certain times. At the beginning of puberty, for example, some boys can go through a rounding of hips and thighs, with slight development of breasts. This can be rather embarrassing for him on occasions, and lead to an excess of modesty that perhaps should be respected – the fat increments usually disappear by the end of adolescence, anyway. Rather in the same way, early-maturing girls are often teased by their group as being 'fat' or 'clumsy'; later on, this position may be reversed, with the late-maturing girl now feeling left out and generally at odds with her contemporaries and herself. The late-maturing boy falls rather outside this age group, but even so a small, underdeveloped boy can become acutely anxious about his apparent lack of masculinity at an early stage, as compared with others. In some cases this self-consciousness can lead to irritating, undesirable compensatory activity, such as becoming the form fool, or going into more aggressive, antisocial acts as a way of proving himself. Again, the teacher cannot make a child grow, but a little understanding can still go a long way. Lessons on sex education as such, which should touch on the whole area of physical development, may be a help, but will never be the complete answer. It is astonishing how children will cling on to some irrational fears and anxieties about themselves, however reasonable they may appear on the surface, and however sensibly they are approached from outside. Emotional conflict may have to be worked through emotionally, rather than intellectually; to manage this, a child may have to feel that he is in an atmosphere where he is accepted for himself, and where he is to a certain extent safe to act out some of these tensions.

Let us say, though, that the teacher has got something of this atmosphere; her pupils are ordinary, bright children without a surfeit of additional social problems. How does she best set about releasing potential from some of these pupils, and building it up in others? Remember, at this stage the pupil can really start getting interested in things that do not relate directly to his personal experience; he may be more critically engaged in his learning now, more curious in some fields, and better able to formulate general ideas. How much active, discovery learning should there be, in contrast to the more passive learning via textbook and verbal instruction? How much guidance and assistance should the teacher offer, as opposed to letting the child learn from his own successes and failures?

Both methods have their adherents, of course, and each teacher (and headteacher!) will have her own preferences, perhaps partly based on what she is best at teaching anyway, theory or not. But if there is a golden rule in all this, it may be to try to adapt your curriculum, so far as you can, to the needs of the individual child. Some children, for example, are good at rote learning, but may have far more difficulty in tackling material requiring insight and understanding. This may or may not be due to an unstimulating home background, but in all events it would seem misguided to give such children a diet of discovery methods if such an approach simply makes them feel more inadequate. All learning is based on a mixture of habit and insight, rote memory and discovery; obviously children may be stronger in one area than another, and the teacher should act accordingly, whilst still being careful, of course, that she is not being too premature in assuming that some pupils can *never* benefit from a particular, perhaps less directed approach.

For all children at this stage, however, there is bound to be something of a mix in the approach to their learning. When children are faced by new subject-matter, it may be natural for them to tackle it initially in a concrete, intuitive way; more abstract approaches may follow later, when they are more familiar with the material. In the case of science, for example, practical experiments, techniques of observation or the opportunity to make apparatus, models or charts at an early stage, may well motivate the child and give him a good practical grounding for more theoretical work later on. In mathematics, a similar case is made for beginning with the practical. This is not to say that children *can't* learn in a more systematic, textbook way at this age – generations of traditional educational methods have disproved that. Rather, one might ask whether it is always desirable for them to do so, if the cost is an alienation from interest in learning for its own sake towards passive adherence to something a child can manage perfectly well, but which simply may not mean very much.

In other fields, the teacher again has the task of weaning the child away from the personal and familiar into more generalized areas. In geography, a pupil may start getting interested in areas beyond his own town or country, once the limit of his geographical comprehension. In history, he will become better able to extend his sense of time beyond the life span of his immediate family; the idea that, say, King Canute and Charles I could have lived at different times from each other, and yet not been alive when grandfather was young may now become more comprehensible. But even more exciting, as he gets older, will be the extension of his ability to make value judgments, to start entering into controversies, or seeing things as others might have seen them, both in the past and the immediate present. In the area of moral judgment, for example, things may no longer seem so simple. Circumstances can now be seen as altering some cases, people may not always be what they seem. Some of this he will begin to understand through talking to others, or responding to books and stories that may now start exploring this sort of area. When he thinks he has got something nicely worked out, the teacher – or another adult – may be at hand to talk to, and perhaps make things just a little more complex. Adults should not be over-wary of doing this, providing it is done with understanding. Although a child may at a certain stage of development not be expected to fully understand certain vocabulary and ideas in advance of his present level, he will always be interested in the area that lies just ahead of his comprehension, and the odd, challenging remark may be much more stimulating at times than a mere confirmation of what he already knows.

Within the arts, there is an ever-increasing ability towards the motor skills necessary for playing a musical instrument. Handwriting should be improving, too, and overall there will be less of a gap between a child's imagination and what he can express of it on paper. With painting, draughtsmanship will become more realistic, taking into account now some of the rules of perspective, and with human figures no longer shown in a stereotyped manner, but depicted with true variety, both in shape and colour, and with respect to age, sex, status and so on. Colours will be more realistic, too, without that flamboyant exaggeration of a younger age.

This may also be the time when there is more interest in team games – another indication of the child's growing socialization. The younger the child, the more likely he is to withdraw from organized games in favour of his own individual interests. If he starts to play at all, it may only be because an adult has initiated the game, and is now busy supervising it. By ten or eleven, however, children are more interested in team games, and loyal, sometimes to a highly emotional pitch, to whichever side they are on. The team may be carefully chosen, everyone anxious to advise the captain on his choice, and even if it goes on to lose, its members will probably not desert it. This concept of social responsibility and the ability to subsume an individual role in a group enterprise, may be quite beyond a younger child, who may wish to be a goalkeeper but score goals at the same time, and even then wander off halfway if he thinks of something better to do.

And yet, there will also be children who never like team games of any sort, possibly because their motor development is rather behind the others, or for many other reasons that can always apply when it comes to one child being different to another in anything. On some occasions, he may have to learn to sink these differences; at other times he should be encouraged to preserve them, as the individual he must eventually learn to be. This whole balance, between the child as private and public person, and the ways in which he sets about putting both worlds into some sort of coherent order, is perhaps the key to the middle years of childhood. It is a time when great demands can be made on adult patience and understanding, but it is also a giving age at the same time, where the child produces new ideas, new skills and new models of behaviour. If he gets through this period successfully, a child has a good base for his adolescent development. Most serious adolescent troubles are simply intensifications of difficulties that have already become apparent during earlier years. If a child is having difficulty at this age, he may need quite a lot of help and support; an investment at the time which may prove extremely valuable for his whole future.

References

BRUNER, J. S. (1966) *Toward a Theory of Instruction* Oxford University Press

DEARBORN, W. F. and ROTHNEY, J. W. M. (1941) *Predicting the Child's Development* Cambridge Sci-Art Publishers

HAVIGHURST, R. J. (1952) *Developmental Tasks and Education* New York: Longmans Green

MOORE, T. (1966) 'Difficulties of the Ordinary Child in Adjusting to Primary School' *Journal of Child Psychology and Psychiatry* 7

PIAGET, J. (1952) *The Child's Concept of Number* Routledge and Kegan Paul
PIAGET, J. (1956) *The Child's Conception of Space* Routledge and Kegan Paul
REYNOLDS, M. M. (1939) *Children from Seed to Saplings* New York: McGraw Hill
STRANG, R. (1959) *An Introduction to Child's Study* New York: Macmillan
SULLIVAN, H. S. (1953) *Concepts of Modern Psychiatry* New York: Norton

Useful further reading
BEARD, R. M. (1969) *An Outline of Piaget's Developmental Psychology* Routledge and Kegan Paul
BRUNER, J. S. (1961) *The Process of Education* Oxford University Press
BRUNER, J. S. (1966) *Studies in Cognitive Growth* New York: John Wiley
HADFIELD, J. A. (1962) *Childhood and Adolescence* Penguin
ISAACS, N. (1961) *The Growth of Understanding in the Young Child* Ward Lock Educational
KOHEN-RAZ, R. (1971) *The Child 9–13* Aldine-Atherton
KELLMER-PRINGLE, M. (1974) *The Needs of Children* Hutchinson
WOOD, M. (1973) *Children: The Development of Personality and Behaviour* Harrap
WRIGHT, D. (1971) *The Psychology of Moral Behaviour* Penguin

4.3   Sociology and the middle years: an essay in transition

Terry Sexton

When first invited to write this essay, I found myself with a problem which had a familiar ring. For several years I have been interested in a consistent, though minor, fashion in the sociology relevant to the lives of those young people which our society calls 'adolescent'. Now 'adolescence' is a category which most people would appear to wish to define in terms of age, in the way that its close synonym 'teenage' is quite clearly defined. But when I came to examine the problem more closely, there seemed to be no simple way of deciding at what age 'adolescence' began and at what age it ended: 'adolescence' was something that happened to most people somewhere between the ages of eleven and twenty-five years. So, when first investigating the middle school, I found myself with the perplexity so delightfully epitomized by the Department of Education and Science definition (1974):

> ... [middle schools] cater for older junior and younger senior pupils. The age ranges of these schools are 8 to 12, 9 to 13 and 10 to 13. Those for pupils aged 8 to 12 are deemed primary by Order of the Secretary of State for Education and Science, those for ages 10 to 13 are deemed secondary, while those for ages 9 to 13 may be deemed either primary or secondary according to the choice of the local education authority.

Fortunately, though perhaps only apparently so, this difficulty was resolved by the injunction from the editors that I should write about the sociology of the middle years, which were understood to be eight to thirteen years of age.

Now I doubt that this resolution is purely fortuitous, in that eight and thirteen encompass all of the age definitions referred to above. Moreover, it emphasizes the need to question the assumption that the right way to educate children in their middle years is to provide middle schools rather than, say, to provide proper and improved continuity and reciprocity between primary and secondary schools. But it does not complete the resolution of the dilemma which I face. On the whole sociology has not paid much attention to 'age', probably because it has developed in societies like our own where age is not an important determinant of relative social position amongst adults. Certainly there has been no apparent need to develop 'sociologies' specific to carefully defined age spans, and such as there are which concern themselves with age grades like 'childhood', 'youth' or 'old age', are noticeable more for their limited appeal than for their contribution to the central debates of sociology. It is only in the sociology of education that both a central concern of sociologists and an age-related status (that of child/pupil) have come together, and it is noticeable here what little part the youth or child status of the recipients of most educational processes have played in the sociological analysis of these processes. So there is no 'sociology specific to the middle years', and there may never be. (I fear that, as most abstruse 'sociologies' develop we may all be in danger of concentrating more and more of our efforts on such intrinsically important issues as 'the sociology of red-headed, left-legged men' thus moving away from the central issues of what holds social groups together or tears them apart.)

Consequently, I do not propose in this essay to attempt a sociology of the middle years. Rather, I shall attempt, in a rapid survey, to cover those aspects of sociology, in particular of the sociology of education, which are likely to be of interest and, hopefully, helpful to those concerned with the education of children in their middle years. After an examination of some aspects of 'age' in our society, I shall examine, in the middle sections of this essay, various features of the educational system: the social functions of education; the schools; and the processes that go on in the classroom, from a variety of sociological perspectives. Such a variety of perspectives is one of the advantages – and difficulties – of the developing nature of sociology. It emphasizes also the transitional nature of this exercise; 'transition' will serve as a focus for the concluding section.

The place of age in contemporary society
It has been asserted above that 'age' is not an important determinant of *adult* social position in our society. By this is meant the fact that, once adulthood has been achieved, his age plays only a very small part in determining the esteem in which a person is held and perhaps even less in defining the social role he should undertake. Thus for the adult male, his occupation is a major component of his social position, and his current occupation is determined more by his training, ability and previous experience than by his age *per se*. It is quite possible for a man to become a primary school headteacher at any point after the age of twenty-five years, and primary school heads will be found in all age groups between

twenty-five and sixty-five. More importantly, the reaching of a particular age is never used as a formal requirement for a particular post as headteacher. Of course, experience is age-related, but even in this respect it is important to emphasize that experience is dependent more upon the context in which recent years have been spent than on the sum total of years spent.

But age, or lack of it, is an important criterion in determining the status of a child; both in the more general sense that all young persons, certainly in the years before puberty, are perceived as children and in the more specific sense that, given the manner of entry by year-groups into our school system, differences in the year of birth create major social boundaries between groups of children. We can all doubtless remember how big and sophisticated those children a year above us seemed in the middle years of our own schooling, especially in comparison with the tiny and naïve 'kids' of the year below. It is quite clear that this importance of age in childhood is not simply a manifestation of our society, or of its perverse adult members, but is more due to the intimate relationship which exists between a child's age and the level of his development, both physical and psychological. The importance of ages and stages of development cannot be ignored, as is shown by my colleague, Nick Tucker, in his contribution to this volume. But it is also clear that, firstly, the relationship between chronological age and stage of development is by no means perfect, as witnessed by the development and usage of such concepts as 'reading age'; and that, secondly and perhaps as a partial consequence of this kind of mismatch, shared expectations, based on age, on the part of adults and others, of what constitutes relevant behaviour are an important factor affecting the behaviour of the child. More importantly, these expectations make a major distinction between what is the proper behaviour of a 'child' and that of an 'adult'.

The argument so far has suggested that, in our society, there are major differences in the expectations we have of the 'child' and of the 'adult' and that age seems a more important factor in determining our view of the child than of the adult. In an extremely cogent and concise article 'Continuities and Discontinuities in Cultural Conditioning', Ruth Benedict (1965) has argued that the extent to which societies, through shared patterns of expectation, emphasize the differences between 'child' and 'adult' is a major factor in determining the difficulties which a person experiences in changing from the status of 'child' to that of 'adult'; difficulties which are experienced during that period of life which we call adolescence.

One example of the distinction to which she is referring can be derived from our own argument. We have argued that age is an important component of the definition of 'child', i.e., that one of the things that clearly defines a person as a child is the relatively short number of years that he or she has lived. Moreover, it is an important component of the way in which we distinguish between different children, in terms of expected behaviour; we expect very different behaviour from young children of, say, five years as compared with older children of twelve years. The same cannot be said in regard to adults: we do not use their ages either as an important overall determinant of our expectations of their behaviour or as a way of distinguishing the differences in behaviour which we expect from adults. Many of us have faced, with some surprise, the sudden recognition, on taking up our first appointments, of the need to treat as colleagues and equals persons old enough to be our parents. Thus at some point the individual, as he moves from child to adult status, will have to learn how to behave in a world where age is no longer a major factor in determining the expectations that we may have of others. (This would not be true in other cultures, where age grading may continue throughout life as an important determinant of social position: see Eisenstadt (1956).) The need for this change of perspective in regard to age is a good example of one of the discontinuities of cultural conditioning to which Benedict is referring. There is no injunction, used by one adult to another, which relies as heavily on age-based expectations for its effect as, 'Now, fourth year, stop behaving like second years!'

Depending upon the age at which one assumes adolescence starts, or perhaps more subtly noting the difficulty of pinning the start of adolescence to any one specific age, it is clear that the concept is of some relevance to those concerned with the middle years of schooling. Either, if we assume that adolescence commences with puberty, a significant proportion of young people will have entered into adolescence before completing the chronologically middle years, or adolescence is the stage of development which immediately faces them on the completion of those years. In the former case, teachers will have to consider how to deal with early adolescents. In both cases, those teachers concerned with the middle years of schooling will have to consider how to prepare children for the next, adolescent, phase of their development. Thus it is important that we consider the transition that the individual will have to undertake in moving from childhood through 'adolescence' to 'adulthood'; from one social status to another. The remainder of this section is derived from the work of Eisenstadt (1956) though the argument presented is neither completely parallel to nor as complex as Eisenstadt's.

Briefly, Eisenstadt, in apparent agreement with Benedict, suggests that there are special difficulties to be experienced in adolescence in social contexts where there is a major distinction drawn between the expectations of behaviour that are held by, and of, children and those that are held by, and of, adults. He analyses this distinction in terms of the different bases on which expectations of behaviour are built and points to three such bases as being of especial importance in understanding adolescence in industrial societies. These bases can be viewed as the responses to three different questions concerning relationships between persons. The problem of transition occurs when a person moves from a context where the questions are answered in one kind of way to a context where they are answered in a different kind of way. As will be seen when the three questions are considered below, in the family – the major socializing experience for most children in our society – the questions are answered in one way, but in our wider society they are answered in another.

The first question concerns the evaluation of individuals in regard to the recognition of social position, or more briefly, 'Who (or what) are you?' Within the family, the child is born into his social position, he learns that there is nothing he can do with regard to this, the position is ascribed; there is no way in which a son can change places with his father. On the other hand, in the wider society in which we live, social position is based, at least ideologically and in fact to a large extent, on criteria of performance and achievement. Consequently, the individual on transferring from a childish to an adult status is faced with a need to learn new answers to this question. We have already seen how 'age', an ascriptive feature in which we can make no changes through action, plays a much greater part in the lives of children than in those of adults. Persons, called children, of a certain age are required to attend school, irrespective of their own wishes or achievements; older persons may choose whether to attend 'school' and their ability to do so is often dependent, to some extent, on their achievement.

The second question concerns the way in which an individual relates to others: does he relate to the other because of a particular bond which relates him to the other person alone? or do they both relate because of their membership of more universal categories? The first case would be most clearly exemplified within the family in the relationship that exists between parent and child which is unique, or at least limited to a very small number of persons and is, in any case, dependent upon the particular bond which our society recognizes as inherent in the parent-child relationship. A clear example of the second case exists in the relationship between patient and doctor. All persons who fit within the category 'patient' may expect that any 'doctor' will treat them; similarly a doctor is required to accept any sick person as a patient. The relationship between *a* patient and *a* doctor is defined, not on the grounds of any particular relationship that exists between them but because of their membership of these categories. So, too, as he moves up through the school, the child exchanges the more particularistic relationship that he has with *his* infant teacher for the more universalistic relationship that he has with subject teachers in the secondary school.

The third question concerns the extent of the relationship which one person within it may expect to have with the other. Is the relationship very diffuse, covering a wide range of different activities? or is it specific and limited to one kind of activity? Thus in the first case, as typified by the mother-child relationship, the child – especially the young child – has a vast range of activities which it is expected his mother will undertake with and for him: shoelace tying; teaching a wide range of skills; feeding; loving, etc. The list is endless and the relationship thus limitless. But in the second case, when for example, we relate to a shopkeeper, the relationship is much more specifically limited to an economic transaction; as long as he sells and I buy we are likely to enjoy a satisfactory relationship. Again, though teaching in itself involves a more diffuse relationship when compared with shopkeeping, it is apparent that the nature of the relationship between teacher and pupil becomes more specific as the child progresses through the school system. The infant teacher may be seen as a mother-substitute in the diffusion of services *she* is required to provide, in a way that the secondary science teacher is never viewed.

Having thus identified, albeit sketchily, the sorts of transitions that may need to be made, it is now necessary to consider how the transition is to be effected. Eisenstadt argues forcefully that the peer group, i.e. a group of persons of similar age and sex, is the main vehicle for the necessary relearning. It is true that membership of such a group is dependent upon the ascribed features of age and sex; but, once they are in the group, members are equal and share their common ascriptive features. This has two effects: firstly, it is an introduction to membership of a universalistic category because the members relate together because of their member-ship of that age-sex category. Secondly, because of their equality in ascriptive terms, the basis for allocation of position in the group must come to depend upon achievement rather than ascription. However, the peer group is still relatively diffuse in the pattern of its relations: experience of more specific relationships will, in Eisenstadt's opinion, be delayed until late adolescence and the breakdown of peer group relations, which is beyond our ken in this essay.

Now it may be argued that what has been offered so far is mostly conjecture, having never been empirically tested in Great Britain, though Eisenstadt's arguments, in their complexity, are supported by a large amount of anthropological evidence from a vast number of cultures. Yet it may be claimed that the thesis presented measures up to the first test of theory, in that it may begin to help us make sense of a pheneomenon – the social transitions inherent in adolescence, not previously amenable to comprehension.

Obviously there are many gaps in the reasoning and two of these should be reported here. Firstly, the thesis presented is more descriptive than analytic; it concentrates more on how things work than on why they work. Further development in this direction must await more detailed empirical work and the development of theory consequent upon it. Secondly, it must be apparent that schools, as such, are concerned with the transitions referred to above, independently of the existence of peer groups. They are very much concerned with the assessment of their pupils' social position, within the institution and in the educational system in general, in terms of achievement rather than ascription – or what are exams, tests and marks for? Increasingly, as school life progresses, pupils are introduced to universalistic notions, both in forms of knowledge and in terms of their own and other people's memberships of universalistic categories. It must be very difficult for pupils to relate in a particularistic way to one teacher amongst the many they encounter as they move through the secondary school. Even more difficult must this be for teachers, many of whom in comprehensive schools seem to be dealing with two hundred or more pupils a week. In any case, and certainly in the later stages of the pupil's career, one might argue that it is their membership of universal categories that bring 'teacher' and 'pupil' together. Finally, the gradual transfer from the relatively diffuse relationship which the younger pupil enjoys with his infant teacher to the highly specific relationship which older pupils have, say with an advanced level chemistry teacher, and the problematic debate about the role of the specialist teacher in the middle school which is related to this, are both evidence of the way in which the schools themselves provide a vehicle for the introduction of the increasingly specific nature of relationships to their pupils.

This section can now be summarized with some additional comment that may prove of value to those concerned with the middle years of schooling. It began with an attempt to show how age, as a criterion in the assignation of social position, is more important in the lives of children than it is in the lives of adults. In the examination of the transition towards adulthood, two aspects of the process of growing-up were emphasized: those aspects to be found in the processes of physical and psychological development which may be seen as intrinsically, though not perfectly, age-related; and that to be found in the changes of status which may involve, particularly in societies like our own, a considerable need for the learning of new answers to basic questions. These changes in status, though notionally age-related, are much less perfectly so and there seems to be no intrinsic reason why they should be tied to specific ages in any way.

The relearning involved concerns three areas: learning to assess persons for social position in terms of performance rather than ascribed attributes; learning to cope with social relationships based on one's own, and others', membership of universal categories rather than highly particularized bonds; and learning to relate to persons in terms of specific activities rather than in terms of a diffuse range of activities. It was suggested that the schools already play a major part in this process of social learning, though perhaps they are not conscious of it, but it was also suggested, following Eisenstadt, that the peer group too may play a major part. Whatever the relative effect of the peer group as compared with the school and the family, it is quite clearly a major influence on the lives of its members.

Two conclusions would appear to stem from this analysis, of relevance to those concerned with the middle years of schooling. Firstly, whether adolescence is seen as starting during the middle years, or as immediately following them, teachers concerned with those middle years must be ready to help children prepare for the transitions inherent in adolescence. This means, according to this analysis, that they will have to take account both of the social-education function of the school and, more practically, of the ways in which this function is to be undertaken.

Secondly, it appears that, in undertaking this task, the school could have more of an ally than a competitor in the adolescent, or pre-adolescent, peer group. In that this argument supports some concept of 'group work' in the middle years, it clearly requires that young people work *with* others in groups. Their learning will be concerned with the processes of working *together with* their peers in groups and not, primarily, with any tasks, academic or otherwise, which such groups might undertake. Quite clearly, it will not be enough to ensure that individuals do their own work but in a small-group rather than a whole-class context. Thus one of the functions of the middle years may well be to initiate the notion of 'working together'.

The social functions of education

Having covered, more than in passing, aspects of social education in the last section, it is not the intention to rehearse similar arguments in this section except, perhaps, to say that the preceding analysis is a beginning rather than an ending in terms of defining the role of schools in preparing young people for social life. Nor, it is hoped, is it necessary to rehearse the arguments which have been powerfully developed by sociologists in the last twenty years to show to what extent, apart from its basic skill- and academic-training function, the school system has also operated as a selection mechanism for the allocation of individuals to their future occupational and adult statuses. There can be no reason to take exception to this analysis since, if it is argued that one of the social functions of education is to prepare people for future adult status, then it must follow that they obtain their future occupational status on the basis, in the greater part, of their overt performance within the educational system.

Two criticisms of this approach must, however, be countered. Firstly, it may be argued that such a narrow view of education, from the perspective of society rather than any other, distorts in some way the true educational function of the system – to foster learning or to develop the individual, or whatever. It must be accepted that this is true but unavoidable. Since education operates within a social context and is a social process, it is impossible to see, given their pervasive nature, how it could avoid social influences and, more importantly, how it can avoid social interpretations being made of its activities. Basically, it is the way in which, for example, educational qualifications are used by employers and even institutions of higher education that distorts the work of the schools; such distortions are not the result of the analysis which demonstrates that they occur.

Two important points must however be made in regard to the selection function which schools perform. The first concerns the ability of the school system to affect the outcomes of the process of selection, rather than simply to carry out that process. It has become apparent that the dream, that many people saw enshrined in the 1944 Education Act, of equality of educational opportunity for all – and the insistence by an only slightly lesser number of interpreting this to mean that 'education' somehow would make us all equal adds to the problem – has been extremely difficult, if not impossible, to realize in practice. Every major report on education since the 1950s has given added evidence to show that a child's social background is an influence of major importance on his ability to do well at school. None has suggested that there has been any major improvement in the relative chance of success for children from the backgrounds most heavily correlated with failure to achieve in the educational system, in spite of a reasonably long awareness of the problem and some effort, perhaps more evident in America than in Britain, to provide a limited amount of extra resources for these children. 'Education', as Bernstein wrote in the title of one of his articles, 'cannot compensate for society'. This aphorism is important for two reasons: it rightly sums up the reality that education on its own cannot hope to bring about major changes in the access of different groups to power and resources; more importantly, however, it is perhaps indicative of the attitudes of teachers. Having learned that the lower-class child did not appear to do well in school, and that this lack of success appeared to relate to his background, teachers found a reasonable explanation of the performance of such children in that background, and no longer expected children from these backgrounds to do well. A body of evidence is beginning to develop which suggests, unexceptionably, that teachers' expectations are an important determinant of a pupil's performance but, more importantly, that it is through these expectations that the child's background has its apparently determining effect.

The second point is concerned with the nature of the selection process. Turner in a seminal article (1961) described two different ways in which education systems might function to enable children to change, or at least establish, their social status. In one, of which he saw the English system as an example and which he called 'sponsored mobility', children are selected at an early age for promotion to academic elite status and then given separate education seen as relevant to their predicted ability. In the other, of which he saw the American system as an example and which he called 'contest mobility', children of all levels of ability are subject to the requirement of attempting the same standards throughout their whole educational careers. Using the sporting analogy first developed by Turner, under sponsored mobility, children are first divided, perhaps even before being able to 'run', into 'fast runners' and 'slow runners' and each group is given 'training' relevant to their predicted speed. Under 'contest mobility' all children are runners and may participate in every event, though only a few will win prizes. Thus Turner would argue that, under sponsored mobility, children were allocated early in life to a particular track where there was a particular expectation of certain achievement, while under contest mobility they could be continually subjected to the rigours of competition with their fellows.

If these models bear some relation to reality, it would seem not impossible to suggest that, in general terms, English education has moved away from the sponsored mobility model towards the contest mobility model in recent years. Such trends as the abolition of the 11-plus; the introduction of comprehensive schools; mixed-ability teaching; and the notion of one form of public examination for all at age sixteen bear witness to this. Indeed it can be argued that the introduction of middle schools which are intended to circumvent the need for selection at 11-plus is a result of this trend and that, by taking all pupils from a particular area and teaching them on a nonselective basis, such schools give added impetus to the trend.

What are the consequences of this brief discussion of the social functions of education for those concerned with the middle years of schooling? The general point raised by this section, and by this whole essay, re-emphasizes the fact that schools carry out their activities within a social context: moreover this is a context from which they cannot remain aloof or immune. Teachers may reject the idea that the child's background and future in the wider society outside the school affect, and are affected by, what happens to him in school; unfortunately they cannot as easily ignore the consequences of that rejection.

The more specific point relates to changes in attitudes towards access to educational opportunity in our society, as they become apparent through changes in the structure of schools. If the inferences drawn from our discussion of the Turner models are correct, then the increasing development of comprehensive education, of which it is suggested middle schools are a part, may reduce the height but increase the number of the educational hurdles which *all* children are required to leap. The consequences of this are not clear, but it is probable that more children will be faced, for more of their school careers, with the need to attempt the 'race' and with the consequences of not 'winning a prize'. Thus, for example, it is not clear that anybody has yet worked out the consequences of the transition, which has been taking place gradually in English education over the last few years, from a situation in which a relatively small number of pupils, in separate institutions, took public examinations to the situation, which some envisage as occurring fairly soon, in which all pupils take the same set of public examinations at sixteen years of age. Those concerned with the middle years must consider the question of how to help those children who are unlikely to do well, both in their middle years and in prospect, to come to terms with that lack of success when it is likely to be more constantly reaffirmed than has been the case in the past.

The schools

Schools are social structures – sets of people in continuing relationships with one another. Moreover, they are also *organizations*: the sets of continuing relationships are not fortuitous in the sense that the relationships which may exist between people living in the same neighbourhood may be said to be fortuitous, but intentional – they are social structures created by men in order to bring about certain ends or to achieve certain goals. The two areas overlap since organizations are social structures; many of the relationships that develop within organizations may be seen as fortuitous, at least to the extent that their development is neither intentional nor necessary for the efficient functioning of the organization. These latter aspects have often been identified as the informal aspects of an organization as opposed to the intentional, established and publicly recognized or formal aspects. Much of the sociologists' interest in organizations has been concerned to examine the inter-relations between the informal and formal aspects of an organization and, especially, to examine the ways in which the former may impinge on the latter.

An oversimplified example may be helpful here. It has been no part of the formal organization of an English school to take account of, or to foster, patterns of friendship amongst school pupils and the peer groups that develop as a result of these patterns. Yet it is clear from the work of writers like Lacey (1970) that these groups may have an important effect on the attitudes of their members to school and its activities and consequently upon their academic work. Moreover the arguments developed in the first section of this essay suggest that the learning which goes on in such groups is a critical part of the socialization of the child in the middle years and subsequently. The alternatives here are clear. *Either* schools can continue to act as if such groups do not exist, or at least as if they were part of the constraining environment in which a school has to operate. Experience suggests that such a choice will mean that these groups and sets of relationships will only be taken into account when they create problems for the school, by which time it is usually too late. *Or* the school can take proper account of these groups, their effects and their importance in its formal organization and the consequent allocation of resources. Of course it will be argued that this is yet another burden being imposed upon the poor teacher and that the resources cannot be stretched that far, especially in times of economic scarcity and given the greater importance of academic objectives, etc. Unfortunately the problem is not some sociological invention. However, the work of youth organizations in this country; of schools in Russia, for example as reported in Bronfenbrenner's *Two Worlds of Childhood* (1974); or even of experimental schools, can be taken to demonstrate ways in which work with peer groups and friendship relations amongst pupils can be used to the advantage of the school and its pupils. (It is perhaps interesting to note here that boarding schools would probably reject the initial assumption of this argument; that peer groups have no place in the formal organization of the school, for what else are houses and dormitories but places in which such relationships are fostered? However, one might ask whether it is always the case that sufficient adult intervention of an informed type is involved in the processes of peer group relations in a boarding school.) The object of this example is not, however, to point especially to a specific problem – that of the schools awareness and utilization of its pupils' peer group relations – but to provide a simple demonstration of the ways in which aspects of the school's informal social structure and of its formal organization mix and affect one another. Many more examples could be provided, and it would seem too facile, and truistic, simply to respond to such dilemmas by suggesting that it is all a question of good management.

Another example of an issue to which sociologists can direct attention concerns the concept of 'role-conflict'. By 'role' is meant that set of expectations which we have about the behaviour of those occupying particular social positions; it is straightforwardly obvious that the expectations of the individual occupying such a position may differ from the expectations of those people who relate to him when he occupies that position, and some form of conflict may then occur. The individual may find himself in a situation in which the expectations of the others with whom he relates not only may conflict with his own expectations, but may also conflict amongst themselves and be incompatible.

The role of 'teacher' seems to be one in which such conflicts are especially to be found: most teachers are aware of and report on the problems that they face because of the differing expectations that headteachers, school colleagues, pupils and parents, for example, have of them. Much of this stems from a lack of clarity about the teacher's role which is in itself a product of the relative diffuseness of the role; it is one in which a wide range of activities may, or may not be, a proper part. Undoubtedly, the four walls and closed door of the traditional classroom provide more than a physical defence for the teacher against the anxiety which such conflict can engender; particularly when, as seems often to be the case, the teacher appears to believe that it is her failing as an individual which produces the problem rather than a fault inherent in the social process of the situation. Two simple questions may be raised here which those concerned with the middle years of schooling may have to consider. Firstly, given the various pressures towards open-plan schools, to what extent do such schools, at least initially, exacerbate such conflicts by bringing teachers out into the open? Secondly, given that middle schools are likely, for some time to come at least, to recruit from teachers whose previous experience has been either primary or secondary, to what extent are there differences in the expectations which primary and secondary teachers have of the role of 'teacher'? Such differences must either be resolved in the middle school or they may tear it apart.

One final point in relation to schools: the impetus inherent in the current concerns with the middle years of schooling seems most likely to be exhausted in the development of middle schools similar to other maintained schools save for the age range of their pupils and the consequent curricula. The minor aspect of this point, in relation to their 'middleness' though perhaps of greater importance in considering schools in general, suggests that the opportunity might be taken, in a controlled and limited way, to experiment with other structures for the school than the traditional headteacher/assistant teacher/class-based model; the development of teams of teachers working cooperatively to provide the educational experiences for a whole 'year' of middle school pupils is already an interesting indicator of possible developments in this direction.

The major aspect of this point asks: why middle schools at all? Obviously, the development of new schools is necessary in some contexts and should not be automatically ruled out. But an interesting opportunity is provided to arrange a curriculum which overlaps the primary and secondary sectors and which might give rise to some interesting methods of dealing with the problems of the child's transition from the primary school to the secondary school. The exciting prospect can be envisaged not only of having a curriculum which covered, say, the last two or three years of the primary school and the first two or three years of the secondary school, but also of making institutional arrangements fit in with such a curriculum. Thus it would not seem impossible to devise a simple scheme for an ongoing exchange of staff between primary and secondary schools, specifically concerned with the teaching of the middle years curriculum. The alternative, which one fears, is that of the individual child being faced with the prospect of moving from one school to a school which knows little or nothing about his previous school experience, at the age of eight or nine, and then facing the problem of a similar transition at the age of twelve or thirteen.

The classroom

It seems unlikely that anybody would deny that the most important goal of an educational system is that children should learn; such a statement is so basic to our view of what constitutes education that to restate it appears trite if not tautological. More importantly, it would appear that many people would argue that teaching is a necessary, if not sufficient, prerequisite for children's learning to take place. The context in which such teaching and learning come together is known as the classroom, or one of its close synonyms. It is clear that many interesting points could be raised by the further development of this analysis: one further question illustrates its potential: to whom is the classroom more important as a base for these teaching/learning activities – teacher or pupil? To attempt to provide a reasoned answer to this question, based on evidence, should provide a host of insights into the ways in which schools work.

It is interesting therefore to reflect, and may be a measure of the power of the 'taken-for-granted' nature of assumptions like those referred to in the preceding paragraph, that it is only in recent years that sociologists have turned their attention to the classroom and the processes that go on within it. A useful introduction to the work in this area, more detailed than can be provided here, can be found in Raggett and Clarkson (1974). However, it may be useful to rehearse briefly some of the arguments here, perhaps in the light of some recent developments. Two areas have emerged as important: the nature of the relationships that exist between teacher and pupil in the classroom context, with particular regard to the expectations that each party brings into the situation; and the nature and structure of that which is to be offered as 'knowledge' to be learned in that situation.

Much of relevance to the consideration of teacher-pupil relationships has already been alluded to in this essay. It is clear that much of a pupil's achievement is dependent upon the expectations that his teacher has of him; as clear now to the theorist as it has perhaps always been to the good teacher. Much work remains to be done on the exact ways in which the teacher's expectations affect the child's performance, since it is clear that over-demanding expectations may be as crippling for some children as the expectation of 'below-average' performance may be for others.

Keddie (1972) and Nash (1973) produce many examples of the complex ways in which teacher expectations may affect children's behaviour and performance. One brief example from Keddie may suffice to illustrate the difficulties involved. She examined the teaching of a humanities programme in a comprehensive school and shows how one aspect of the expectations on which the course was based was an assumption that pupils should be capable of 'working at your own speed'. She writes:

> It would seem inevitable that the principle of individual speeds should be incompatible with a course that moves in a structured way from topic to topic. The only leeway is for some pupils to work through more workcards than others.

The dilemma implicit in Keddie's analysis is found on a much wider scale. If it assumed, as seems to be the case, that different children, though all capable of reaching the same objective, will require different amounts of time to do so, then the notion of a course with a fixed amount of time for learning is bound to lead either to some children completing the work before time or to others not reaching the objective. A compromise, based on some notion of the mean amount of time required, is likely to bring about some measure of each of these potentially unsatisfactory outcomes. Lest it be assumed that this is yet another example of teachers being impaled on the horns of a dilemma, it should be pointed out that they are not alone in having this kind of expectation. Our educational system as a whole now appears to enshrine the expectation that all children can be given their basic education within the eleven years of compulsory attendance at school. The existence of this dilemma should not be used in a simple-minded way as an argument in favour of selection and streaming since these may hide, but they do not solve, the basic problem.

The second area of concern is with the nature and structure of that which is to be offered as 'knowledge' to be learned in the classroom situation. For many years, the sociology of knowledge, as such, has examined the relationship between types and forms of 'knowledge' and the social contexts in which they have been developed. A central tenet of such an approach is the assumption that what constitutes 'knowledge' is not something objectively given but is socially constructed: what is allowed to exist as 'knowledge' and the structure it is allowed to take is determined as much, if not more, by the social context in which that knowledge exists as by any intrinsic qualities of that knowledge itself. More recently, this approach has been applied to the content of learning; it is well exemplified in *Knowledge and Control* by Young (1972).

A simple example may help to make this clear. The shape of the earth, and its place in the universe, was a contentious issue for hundreds of years. It is now clear that the argument depended, not on any intrinsic 'rightness' or 'wrongness' of the various alternative views, nor even on appeals to evidence, but on the way in which changes in these views were not independent of, but vitally affected, the 'world-views' and consequently the prestige and power, of their various proponents and opponents. Returning to present-day earth: how many of our children *need* to know that the earth is round? Its flatness is a perfectly reasonable working assumption for the greater part of the lives of most of us. It is not until we take to the oceans, the air or space that the hypothesis collapses. If the argument is maintained that they need to know that the earth is round because it is, then it should perhaps be pointed out that it is not, it is oblate. The relevant question is, of course, who decides when and how children are introduced to concepts of 'roundness' and 'the state of being oblate' and for what purpose. If even further evidence of the way in which social factors determine what is accepted as knowledge, and the way in which it is to be offered to others, is required, then consider why 'oblate' was used

237

here, rather than 'like a spheroid flattened at the poles' or even 'orange-shaped'.

Perhaps teachers, at least those of a charitable disposition, will object that this is all too whimsical. It may be important therefore to conclude this section by pointing out that it has been largely concerned to stress the important effect that expectations which the various participants bring to the classroom have on what goes on in that classroom. These expectations are to be found at all levels but two have been stressed here; the expectations that teachers and pupils have of one another's behaviour and the expectations that each group has of knowledge – its content, structure and use. How many people have shared that great sense of loss, shame and treachery which I experienced when, on proceeding to A-level after successfully completing O-level, we were told that much of what we had learned, though presented as 'hard-fact' was wrong and we were now going to learn what was right.

Transition: a passing conclusion

Transition has served as something of a keynote in the writing of this essay. Perhaps most important is the way in which the concept of 'middleness' implies transition and itself emphasizes the transitional nature of schooling. Though we need to know much more about this transition, it seems inappropriate to attempt hard-and-fast conclusions, given the transitory state of our present knowledge of sociology in relation to the middle years of schooling. Consequently I propose neither to draw a series of conclusions nor to summarize more briefly the wide range of arguments already summarily presented above. Instead, I would like to finish by suggesting that those who have found the points presented stimulating or relevant should follow them up, in the hope that the study of the relevant books will enable us all to progress further through our transitional state.

All the works referred to in the text are relevant, at least to the area of the particular points to which they are related. In addition, I would like to draw more attention to some of them, and suggest other works which, although not referred to directly, have influenced what has been written. In connection with 'the place of age in contemporary society' and the consequences for social education stemming from its consideration, Davies and Gibson (1967) will be found helpful. It develops an argument, similar to the one presented here, more clearly and without recourse to unnecessary jargon and goes on to consider in some detail the implications for social education from an interesting non-school oriented viewpoint. One of the best texts covering the various points, together with much else, presented here under 'the social functions of education' is Banks (1971). For those interested in schools as organizations, Silverman (1965) is an invaluable guide. With regard to other aspects of schools, and also with regard to those points raised here under 'the classroom' Nash (1973) and

Lacey (1970) will be found most stimulating and readable. Similarly the various papers contained in Young (1972) and Eggleston (1974) which between them cover a wider field, and some of which are by no means as easily read, repay the effort of detailed attention.

References

BENEDICT, R. (1965) 'Continuities and discontinuities in cultural conditioning' in M. Mead and M. Wolfenstein *Childhood in Contemporary Cultures* Chicago: University of Chicago Press

BERNSTEIN, B. (1970) Education cannot compensate for society *New Society* 26 February

BRONFENBRENNER, U. (1974) *Two Worlds of Childhood, U.S. and U.S.S.R.* Penguin Education

DES (1974) *Statistics of Education 1973, v.1: Schools* HMSO

EISENSTADT, S. N. (1956) *From Generation to Generation* New York: Free Press of Glencoe

KEDDIE, N. (1972) 'Classroom Knowledge' in M.F.D. Young (Ed) *Knowledge and Control* Collier-Macmillan

LACEY, C. (1970) *Hightown Grammar: the School as a Social System* Manchester University Press

NASH, R. (1973) *Classrooms Observed* Routledge and Kegan Paul

RAGGETT, M. and CLARKSON, M. (1974) 'The Microcurriculum: interaction in the classroom' in M. Raggett and M. Clarkson (Eds) *The Middle Years Curriculum* Ward Lock Educational

TURNER, J. (1965) 'Modes of social ascent through education: sponsored and contest mobility' in A. H. Halsey (Ed) *Education, Economy and Society* Collier-Macmillan

YOUNG, M. F. D. (Ed) (1972) *Knowledge and Control: new directions in the sociology of education* Collier-Macmillan

Useful further reading

BANKS, O. (1971) *The Sociology of Education* Batsford

DAVIES, B. D. and GIBSON, A. (1967) *The Social Education of the Adolescent* University of London Press

EGGLESTON, S. J. (1974) *Contemporary Research in the Sociology of Education* Methuen

SILVERMAN, D. (1970) *The Theory of Organization* Heinemann

4.4   School-based evaluation

Michael Eraut

Evaluation and decision-making

Evaluation is still a dirty word. People prefer it that way. The mere mention of pupil evaluation conjures up images of the '11-plus', yet every day teachers make classroom decisions on the basis of what they think their pupils have learned. To discuss teacher evaluation is to evoke memories of payment by results, yet few would want promotions to be based on anything other than merit. Although evaluation is something we do all the time, we do not choose to talk about it. We reserve the term for when we wish to threaten someone else. If we want to change an institution we suggest evaluating it. If we wish to keep it the same, we insist that all possible changes should be evaluated. On our own terms, of course.

   In this chapter I want to look at ordinary evaluation, the kind of evaluation we already do in our schools, not the kind we threaten others with nor the kind we associate with esoteric research or Royal Commissions; and to think about the problems and opportunities it presents. People in schools are constantly making decisions. Pupils make decisions about what to attend to, who to talk to, what to do next. Teachers make decisions, both individually and collectively. Some are little decisions, semi-conscious, woven into the fabric of their teaching. Others are momentous, deliberate, and long-term. Heads often make formal decisions. The major ones determine policy and allocate resources, while the minor ones relate to specific incidents of apparently lesser significance. But even these can aggregate to create an implicit policy and to influence that all-pervading characteristic, the ethos of the school. Every decision involves some assessment of the situation, some consideration of alternatives, some basic sense of purpose or direction and some judgment. The process may be largely intuitive or openly rational. It may rely on the information already at hand or it may seek for more information. In either case it will involve evaluation. It has been said that the quality of a school depends on the quality of its decisions; and it is because we hope to improve that quality that we are concerned with evaluation.

Informal evaluation is perhaps best summed up by the maxim, 'Look before you leap'. It is a brief pause to 'take stock', to assemble the relevant information in one's mind, to analyse the evidence and to assess the situation. Obviously nothing will be gained from trying to examine short-term intuitive decisions too closely, both because they are relatively unimportant and because they can easily be distorted by over-rationalization. But it may well be worth reflecting on the general approach which underlies such decisions; because the cumulative effect may be at least as significant as more long-term decisions in determining what actually goes on.

More formal evaluation, on the other hand, implies rather more than just taking stock, as it usually involves some deliberate attempt to collect further evidence. Indeed, some authorities define evaluation as 'the collection and analysis of evidence to guide decision-making'. This assumes some kind of rational decision-making model, such as the one advocated by Stufflebeam (1971) and reproduced as Figure 1 below, in which the decision-maker formulates options, collects information, relates it to values and then finally decides.

Figure 1   Decision-making model (adapted from Stufflebeam, 1971)

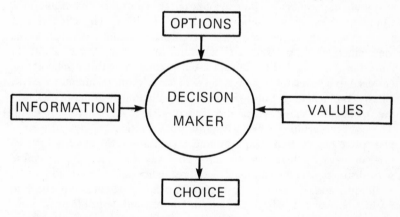

Of course the evidence collected is unlikely to be conclusive. One does not get conclusive evidence in education. But nevertheless it is likely to be helpful in reducing the general level of uncertainty. Some judgment will always be necessary in making educational decisions, and we hope that it will usually be informed judgment.

This still leaves us, however, with two very important questions. How much information do we need? And how much information can we afford to get? The former depends on the extent to which we believe further information can reduce the level of uncertainty and clarify the decision-making situation; and this will vary from case to case. But the latter is probably the more important question. It is not usually a matter of whether one needs more information but of whether we have the resources to get it. It seems reasonable to propose that the effort directed to any particular evaluation ought to be commensurate with the importance of the decisions that are likely to follow. But is it feasible? What are the pressures that prevent it? Though people are evaluating all the time, they rarely think of it in cost-benefit terms. The important question, 'How much effort should we devote to evaluation before we decide to act?' is usually not even asked. Nor do we consider at all carefully what information would be most useful. We make do with what we have in hand, and sometimes even ignore most of that. Our excuse, of course, is the pressure of time. Who has time to evaluate? Who even has time to take decisions? As I have suggested elsewhere, unavoidable decisions take precedence over avoidable decisions regardless of their respective importance. The pressure of day-to-day business postpones the policy review one also wanted to have. Discussing important issues always comes late on the agenda after the immediate business, when the meeting is nearly over and the feet are beginning to shuffle. It takes constant and deliberate effort to give time to important matters.

It is not my primary purpose to make out the case for more evaluation. I would rather leave it to others to judge the likely costs and benefits. Instead I want to create a new image. So often people think of evaluation as something remote, statistical, difficult and threatening. Some people do indeed evaluate in that kind of way. But evaluation within a school does not need to be a technical activity. There are relevant techniques, as with all aspects of teaching, but their function is only that of strengthening and improving what can often be quite adequately achieved without them. The most important characteristics of an evaluation are clear thinking, perceptive observation, empathy and consultation. So there is little to prevent many teachers from assuming an 'evaluator' role and performing with distinction. This chapter, therefore, deliberately avoids discussing techniques and concentrates instead on expanding a general approach to evaluation which I believe to be both feasible and desirable.

Before concluding this section, however, I would like to make one further point. Although we have defined and justified evaluation in terms of guiding decisions for the *future*, we have also used terms such as 'assessment of the situation' and 'policy review' which imply looking at the *past*. Evaluation is both prospective and retrospective, and this Janus-like characteristic has considerable influence on the way evaluations behave. (*Note:* The Roman God Janus had two heads so he could look behind him as well as in front of him; and the Romans saw the month of January which they named after him as being both the last month of the old year and the first month of the new year.)

The role of working parties

Though the approach to evaluation which I am advocating is applicable to all schools, my examples will be taken from the middle years. Moreover, I am assuming that the evaluations are likely to be undertaken by teachers, who have not had any special training in evaluation in the normal course of their duty. Hence my 'case studies' are of two kinds – those concerned with a single class, and those concerned with the whole school or a substantial part of it. For the single class I have assumed that the class teacher or a student-teacher is taking the role of evaluator; but in the latter case I have assumed that the evaluators are a group of teachers formally constituted as a working party. There are two main arguments in favour of this working-party approach – the need to pool ideas and experience, and the need for acceptance. The conclusions of an evaluation are more likely to be understood, adopted and welcomed if its authors are accepted as representative. These arguments will be amplified later, but first I wish to introduce a couple of examples to explore the role of working parties. In one the evaluation will be primarily prospective, i.e., linked with decision-making, and in the other it will be primarily retrospective, i.e., a policy review.

Let us suppose that a primary school wishes to make a more deliberate attempt to include science in its curriculum and appoints a teacher with special responsibility in that area. She goes to a conference where she discovers what a number of other local schools are doing and finds out about two potentially relevant Schools Council projects. Rather than attempt to impose her own ideas, she persuades her head to set up a working party to consider the various options. Though she is prepared to act as their technical adviser, there are educational issues involved in which every teacher should have a say. On a day when the school is closed for a local election, the working party visits two neighbouring schools whose science is highly commended but very different in kind; and two subgroups examine and report back on the two Schools Council projects. They then debate what kind of science programme is best suited for their own school, bearing in mind the limited scientific knowledge which most of them possess, the fit with the rest of the curriculum, and the availability of resources and facilities. In trying to anticipate the likely effects of the different options they are evaluating prospectively, but in observing what had happened in the schools they visited they were evaluating re-trospectively. They were probably also, at least implicitly, evaluating the previous science work in their own school. What were the factors that had constrained it and were they still important? Could any of the previous problems be avoided and overcome? Since, however, the evaluation arose from the need to make a decision about future work, the dominant emphasis was prospective; and there was considerably more discussion of goals and options for the future than of problems from the past.

Another example, in which the emphasis was more on retrospective evaluation, arose when an 8–12 middle school, following the publication of the Bullock Report (1975) and a little prodding from its managers, decided to review its language work. Were they giving it sufficient attention? Were any important aspects being neglected? Were they promoting language development right across the ability range? Were they satisfied with the standard of pupils' work? The head was concerned about continuity and anxious to get more professional discussion going in the school, so he set up a working party of five – the teacher with special responsibility for English and one other teacher from each year group. They met fortnightly for two terms, during which time they consulted their colleagues, looked at a quantity of pupils' work, visited two first schools and two other middle schools and invited comment from two visiting 'experts', an adviser and a college lecturer. Two staff meetings were devoted to discussing their report, some changes were agreed and the working party was asked to spend a further term working out more detailed proposals for presentation and discussion at a school closure day early in the autumn.

An interesting feature of the primarily retrospective review in the first two terms was that, although there was no specific decision in mind when the working party first met, their evaluation very soon began to acquire an implicit prospective function. They realized that some kind of change was likely and they knew that the information they collected was bound to influence subsequent policy. But there was little explicit discussion of options in spite of the outside comments and the visits to other schools. However, since no one can judge the worth of what *has* happened without at least implicitly considering what else *might have* happened, there were important hidden assumptions behind many of their arguments. Their work might have proceeded more smoothly and their extra term have been less necessary if these implicit assumptions about goals and options had been made explicit early on. It is usually better to bring implicit standards and values into the open, and to relate them to options that are being considered or rejected, than to operate on the basis of hidden standards. This brings us back to an earlier point – the need for an evaluation to gain acceptance. The efforts of a working party will be wasted if their report is rejected or, more likely still, ignored. Perhaps a major function of evaluation should be the fostering of discussion rather than the pre-emption of it. Even if a report is accepted, it is unlikely to be properly implemented unless all those concerned have debated its conclusions and participated in the subsequent decision-making. Moreover, hidden assumptions always engender mutual suspicion, and evaluation that is not intended to open up discussion often leads to hostility. Retrospective evaluation can easily turn into retributive evaluation; and this hinders self-evaluation and heightens resistance to change.

What then does an evaluation entail? If we return to the example of the

244

school which set up a working party to look at its science curriculum, we can usefully distinguish three tasks – the collection of evidence, the analysis of that evidence, and the formulation of recommendations for future action. But we cannot totally separate these tasks, for although they may be seen as successive phases in the working party's deliberations, they are by no means independent of one another. On the one hand the collection of evidence needs to be guided by some consideration of possible decision-making options: otherwise time and effort will be wasted. Yet on the other hand preconceived solutions can prejudice the whole evaluation process; and it is not unusual for a working party to negotiate its recommendations amongst its members without any apparent concern for evidence. There are, however, some possible safeguards that can be applied. Firstly, one can maintain a close liaison between the working party and its reference group in which the connections between their ideas of possible options and their plans for collecting and analysing evidence are openly discussed. For example, an early discussion of their plan of action might be followed later by an interim report which briefly assessed the existing situation and suggested two or three possible options for further investigation. Secondly, one can try to ensure that, even though the kinds of evidence being collected are related to preconceived expectations, the actual collecting procedure minimizes the possibility of bias – for example, an open interview which deliberately explores other perceptions, rather than a closed questionnaire. Then thirdly one can make occasional use of independent agents, particularly for suggesting additional options and disclosing hidden assumptions.

It is arguable to what extent the making of recommendations is part of an evaluation; and professional evaluators disagree on this point. But we do not need to concern ourselves with this issue so long as there is close communication, and overlapping membership between the evaluation group and the decision-making group; and we have already argued that in school-based evaluation this should always be the case. However, we shall concentrate our attention on the collection and analysis of evidence; because there is little to be said about translating properly analysed evidence into recommendations, other than that it is a matter of professional judgment; and that participation at this stage greatly affects the reception of that judgment.

The selection and organization of evidence

The first question that arises in any evaluation is that of what evidence one should seek to collect; and there is a considerable danger, from which professional evaluators are by no means exempt, that the problem will be conceived too narrowly. Hence, although the criteria for deciding what evidence to collect will depend on what is being evaluated, it is often useful to refer to a checklist or model to remind oneself of the range of possible evidence. I find the Data Organization Model of the American evaluator, Bob Stake (1967), particularly helpful because it not only indicates the range of evidence but also provides a framework for its organization and analysis. This model is presented in slightly modified form as Figure 2 below:

Figure 2   Matrix for Organizing Evaluation Data (adapted from Stake, 1967)

	Intentions	Obervations	Standards	Judgments
Conditions				
Activities				
Results				

The term *Conditions* applies to both antecedent conditions, i.e., to the situation prior to the activities being evaluated, and to contextual conditions, i.e., external influences on the activities. So when evaluating a set of workcards involving role-playing activities and a tape recorder, evidence about conditions might relate to such questions as:

How many could operate the tape recorder?
Were they used to working together?
Had they much previous experience of oral work with tape recorders?
Was the tape recorder available and working when needed?
Did it disrupt other classroom activities going on at the same time?

The teacher who designed the workcards will have had *Intentions* with regard to most of these issues, not all of which will have necessarily been corroborated by subsequent *Observation* of conditions at the time of use. Moreover these *Intentions* will be related to *Standards*. For example, one teacher may consider it essential that all pupils concerned can read the cards, another may consider it sufficient if one or two in each group can read them, a third may vary his standard according to age, ability range and previous experience of group work. Finally by relating the *Intentions* or the *Observations* to *Standards*, different people will make different *Judgments* as to whether the conditions were or were not appropriate for using those particular workcards.

Continuing with the same example, the teacher will also have planned that certain *Activities* should take place; and again his observations may not

246

entirely accord with his *Intentions*. The pupil group may not cooperate as hoped or a potentially stimulating idea may fail to capture their interest, or alternatively it may prove so successful that they continue the activity with improvised ideas of their own, even including other members of the class. Here particularly, different participants in the situation may vary in their views. Pupils also make *Judgments* about the *Activities* and their opinions vary widely, not only because of their differing *Standards* (some like one kind of activity more than another) but also because of their differing *Observations*. This question of differing sources of *Intentions*, *Observations*, *Standards* and *Judgments* is the third dimension of Stake's model, which we omitted from Figure 2 in order to keep the diagram simple.

Then thirdly we have the *Results* of the activity. As likely as not the workcards will not in themselves have any readily observable effects, except perhaps a product in the form of a tape recording. But they will be part of a language programme which has more definite goals, and possibly part of a social studies programme as well. Many people will *Observe* these results in some form or another and make *Judgments* according to their own personal *Standards*. Incidentally it is worth pointing out that partly because of differential access to information and partly because of the different perspective that comes from noninvolvement, participants in a situation, particularly in the middle years when exams are still relatively remote, will often give greater weight to *Activities* when making *Judgments*; whereas nonparticipants will tend to give greater weight to *Results*. Since the two are presumably connected this difference in perspective is not necessarily harmful. Indeed, it may merely be a reflection of the tension between avoiding an educationally counter-productive obsession with results and recognizing that we are all ultimately accountable for what we do.

Although the Stake model is usually associated with formal evaluation, the evaluation of the workcards which we have just been discussing was entirely informal. There were no *Intentions*, *Observations*, *Standards* or *Judgments* which might not have taken place naturally in the normal process of teaching. It could all have happened without anyone even mentioning the word 'evaluation'. The effect of adopting the perspective of Stake's model was not to introduce any new forms of evaluation but to clarify our understanding of evaluative activities that were already taking place. This clarification of natural evaluative processes is equally important when more formal evaluations are being planned. Because, unless the evidence gained from these more formal activities can be shown to mesh with natural informal evaluative processes, it is in considerable danger of being rejected. In Piagetian terms, people can more easily assimilate evidence to fit existing schemas than accommodate to a totally new analytic framework; and it is also, in my view, easier to recognize a variety of other people's schemas (we often know that others see things differently) than it is to reconcile oneself to an unfamiliar 'neutral' schema (do we really believe that neutrality is possible in education?). Hence the significance of the third dimension in Stake's model which takes into account as many different sources of opinion as one considers it appropriate to include.

Let us now consider an example of a rather more formal evaluation of a not untypical situation. A student teacher, about to embark on her second teaching practice, plans to teach and evaluate a short course in environmental studies for a class of ten year olds. It is agreed that the class will be taken out of school on two afternoons each week for half a term, the particular afternoons being chosen according to the weather; and that although the class will be kept within the same area, she will be responsible for the scientific aspects of the work (she is doing main subject science) while the regular class teacher is responsible for the geographical aspects. A third afternoon will be devoted to class work directly related to the field work; and it will also be possible to link the project with some of the language and number work which occupies most of the mornings. The school has not undertaken much previous work of this kind but is quite interested in the idea of doing 'environmental studies'. The student not only has to keep the usual teaching practice file but is required to write up a retrospective review of the project as part of her college assessment. Before submitting her final report, however, she has to present her work to a post-teaching-practice discussion group. In addition, it is suggested that she may wish to discuss it with her class teacher and possibly also with the head; and in the particular case we are discussing, the school's interest in the project has resulted in a request that her review should cover the project as a whole and not just her own personal activities.

The pattern she worked out for the first five weeks involved a different area or topic each week with the first afternoon out being devoted mainly to observation and collection; the second to consulting books in the classroom, discussing and planning; and the third to some form of minor investigation. Then the sixth week would be devoted to preparing a classroom display for the school's open day. Some observers may feel that five topics in five weeks is a little excessive; but it is nevertheless not unusual for either a student teacher or a school first embarking on environmental studies to be anxious that the children will not have enough to do. Moreover, since the school was particularly interested in what happened on 'field work' the classroom teacher agreed to make a short tape recording of his observations at the end of each afternoon out so as to give additional coverage.

The student's plan for documenting the course consisted of the following:

1   The original course proposal, arrived at in consultation with college tutors and with the school. This consisted of the pattern described

above, supplemented by a list of possible activities for each visit and a list of reference books.

2 A record of any plans for changing the proposal made during the course of implementation.

3 The brief tape recordings made by the classroom teacher.

4 A weekly diary of events completed by the student each week on the basis of notes made each day. The class teacher has agreed to glance through the daily notes and add comments where relevant in order 'to put the record straight for the school'. The diary will aim at complete cover of the afternoon work, but will only refer to those aspects of the morning work which have clearly been influenced by the project.

5 Interviews with pupils during the final week, aimed at finding out their perceptions of the course and getting further information about what they had learned.

6 A folder of pupil work.

7 A collection of comments made by parents, other teachers, other students, visiting college tutors, etc.

She collected all this evidence meticulously and then went off on vacation carrying two enormous folders.

Was this the end of the evaluation or was it the beginning? How was she to analyse all this evidence? By some remarkable coincidence her tutor was familiar with Stake's model and commended it to her. So she sorted out all her evidence into the twelve boxes of Figure 2 and prepared her presentation for the post-teaching-practice discussion group. By the time her thirty minutes was up, she had just finished describing the content of the third box; and the prospect of her preparing any document short enough or digestible enough for the teachers at the school to read was becoming progressively more remote. Her unfortunate tutors didn't have the chance to exercise that option, and hastily mumbled something about introducing a word limit for the following year. What went wrong?

Like many others before her our unfortunate student had thought that the collection and organization of evidence was sufficient and that no further analysis was necessary. As a result she failed 'to see the wood for the trees' and subjected her various audiences to information overload. No doubt she was a little timid of exercising her personal judgment as analysis implies drawing attention to particular features of the evidence and ignoring (or failing to notice) other features, thus exposing the evaluator to criticism and breaching her protective wall of data. Another reason why this approach to evaluation is quite popular is because it protects the evaluated as well as the evaluator. An indigestible evaluation report is good for everybody's conscience: duty is done and nothing is challenged.

The analysis of evidence

Stake's model immediately suggests two forms of analysis, one based on horizontal relationships between the boxes and the other based on vertical relationships. The horizontal links have been mentioned already in the context of explaining the model, so we shall discuss them first. Some of them (for example, comparisons of *Intents* and *Observations*) are based on empirical data, some (for example, relating *Standards* to *Judgments*) on judgmental data and some (for example, linking *Observations* with *Standards*) on a combination of both forms of evidence. Usually the empirical evidence is easier to handle than the judgmental evidence, because many standards are implicit and many judgments are conflicting. Though conflicts in *Intentions* and *Observations* are also common, they are usually not so difficult to characterize. But judgmental conflicts are often within people as well as between people; and it is not unusual for one set of criteria to be used in public debate while another set appear to determine private opinions. One strategy which evaluators can adopt to cope with the problems of handling judgmental data is the designation of 'ideal types' to represent different judgmental perspectives. For example 'Integrated Day Man' can be defined in terms of one set of standards and 'Separate Subject Man' in terms of another, even though no one involved may actually hold these extreme positions. Then relating *Intentions* and *Observations* to the *Standards* of 'ideal types' reveals the basic issues and illuminates the particular compromise positions which have been adopted. These ideal types can be constructed partly from the judgmental data and partly from the literature. Though it is important that the evaluators should include the perspectives of the relevant people involved there is no reason why they should not add one or two others. The purpose is to offer the evaluation audience the full range of arguments that might be deployed either for or against the activities under review; and to relate the arguments to different standards and values. The 'ideal type' strategy enables this to be done without putting any pressure on people being consulted to give final judgments rather than just offer views. When evaluation takes place within a school pressure for judgment would have the effect of encouraging the teachers concerned to reach premature conclusions about issues which are better left for later discussion – after rather than before the completion of the evaluators' report.

In order to illustrate some of these points about the analysis of horizontal relationships, let us return to the example of the environmental studies project. Firstly, there is the student's report about the effect of the project on the basic skills work in the mornings. Her own observations were the only record of the morning work, and she claimed that there had been a noticeable effect and that a significant amount of integration had been achieved. What she had done was to prepare some workcards each week which used examples from the environmental topic of the week to practise appropriate number skills. Two 'tables' of children had used these under her supervision on Thursday and Friday mornings. The class teacher, however, commented that she thought integration with the morning work would be extremely difficult; and, when questioned, disclosed that she had not regarded these workcards as anything more than useful practice to the student. They were elaborately prepared and specific not just to the topic but to the particular aspects of the topic that were pursued at the time. The chances of using them again were remote, she would never have time herself to prepare those sorts of cards and only two of the six tables had been involved. For her the student's claim would only have been substantiated if the work had been repeatable under normal conditions. The college tutor also challenged the student's claim but for quite a different reason. She regarded changing one kind of workcard for another as no change at all, and was obviously disappointed that there had been no attempt to get the children to write imaginatively about their field-trip experience. To summarize, the class teacher and the student had different *Standards* when considering *Conditions*; and the tutor and the student had different *Standards* when considering *Activities*.

A second instance of the limitations of the student's own perspective was disclosed by her reporting of the attitudes of other teachers in the school. She had been extremely skilful in engaging them in incidental conversation in the staffroom and in getting their 'off the record' comments on the project. But she tended to interpret it all in terms of personal support or criticism. Did they think she was a good teacher or not? What she failed to realize was how little they really knew about what she was doing, and how much they were making judgments on the basis of comparing their image of her project with their own personal views about environmental studies. One teacher was interested in local history and wondering whether it would ever be compatible with science and geography; another was concerned about pollution and looking for a moral emphasis; and a third who was interested in science was obviously disappointed when she heard that the children were studying a block of flats. Not only did the student miss the significance of these differing aims but she also failed to see the extent to which two of her own aims were in conflict. She was trying to develop knowledge about the environment and general inquiry skills (learning through the environment) at the same time; and though at times the two aims were mutually supporting they often came into conflict. For example, during the afternoon back in the classroom between the two 'field trips' there was always some doubt as to how much of the time should be spent following up the first visit (and hence in increasing knowledge about the environment) and how much in preparation for the second visit (developing inquiry skills).

An awareness of all these different views about environmental studies would have made her report much more useful to the school. If she had presented her project in the context of a range of possible aims and rationales, there would have been some chance of focusing the ensuing discussion on some of these wider issues and avoiding over-generalization from a single example (for example, assuming that environmental studies cannot include history). As it was, the discussion tended to focus on a single crude decision – 'We like it and we want to do more' versus 'We don't like it and think environmental studies is only a passing fad anyway' – rather than on wider policy issues such as, 'Are there any aims which might be better achieved if we did more work of this kind?' or 'What have we learnt from this project about how we might attempt environmental studies in the future?'

While the analysis of horizontal relationships in the Stake model tends to focus attention on issues of desirability, the analysis of vertical relationships focuses on feasibility. The assumption that a plan is feasible can be interpreted as saying, 'Given the expected *Conditions*, pursuing the *Intended Activities* will lead to the *Intended Results*'. Moreover assumptions of this kind are usually based on professional experience, possibly organized into what Argyris and Schon (1974) call 'a theory of action' but more probably just a cluster of 'contingencies'. These are minor assumptions of the general type, 'If I do A, then B will happen'; and most of our everyday actions are based on them even if they are rarely made explicit. As Stake (1969) comments:

> For as long as there has been schooling, curriculum planning has rested upon faith in certain contingencies. Day to day, every teacher arranges his presentation and the learning environment in a way that – according to his logic – leads to the attainment of his instructional goals. His contingencies, in the main, are logical, intuitive, supported by a history of satisfactions and endorsements. To various degrees teachers test out these contingencies. Even the master teacher and certainly less experienced teachers need to examine the logical and empirical bases for their 'believed-in' contingencies.

This disclosure and examination of contingency assumptions implies analysing the vertical relationships in the *Intentions* and *Observations* columns, but ignoring the *Standards* and *Judgments* columns. However, there are 'standard' contingency assumptions which can be detected in common practice or derived from theory, and many *Standards* and *Judgments* are based on them. So these also need to be brought into the analysis. Though here it is particularly important to remember the main purpose of the evaluation. We are concerned with questions of feasibility and explanation and with the constructive modification of our plans, not with instructional research.

Once more we shall take an example from the environmental studies project to illustrate some of the points which have been discussed.

The student had felt considerable concern over her observation that each week those pupils who had followed a more geographical line of inquiry had produced quantities of work, whereas the 'scientists' in her own care had very little to show. She felt that the work had gone well because the children talked a lot and became very enthusiastic about what they were doing. Sometimes it started rather slowly, but by the third afternoon interest was growing and a number of interesting inquiries were usually under way. The problem was that often these inquiries had to be cut off in midstream, and there was no time left to turn a few rough notes into something that could be displayed. As a result the 'Open Day' exhibition was dominated by the geographic work and very little science work was on show. She attributed this problem to her lack of experience, but still remained puzzled as to why her children who were obviously enthusiastic had not produced results.

In later discussions with her tutor a possible explanation evolved. The class teacher was always full of suggestions for geographical activities, and the children who attached themselves to her settled down early on with the result that by the end of the first afternoon they had completed a lot of work. This was tidied up back in the classroom on the second project afternoon, and then checked and added to on the third project afternoon when they had their final outing of the week. The student's own group, on the other hand, tended to 'muck around a bit' at first but usually got involved in something of interest before the afternoon was up. This led to consulting books back in the classroom and to a lot of heated discussion about what to do on the third afternoon. Their interest was still growing when the topic concluded at the end of the week, so for them the ending was premature. Some of their inquiries were quite original and could have continued for three or four weeks. The 'geographers', on the other hand, were ready to start the next topic. Their work had been largely confined to practising and consolidating mapping skills so they had not been engaged on any longer term inquiry. As the tutor pointed out, a topic a week was far too fast for genuine enquiry to develop; and by some people's standards the student's more fumbling approach could have been judged the more valuable.

The student had set up an unworkable series of contingencies because she was trying to pursue *Activities* – which were in accord with the inquiry approach, under *Conditions* which only allowed a basic-skills approach – and to obtain *Results* which could be judged by the same criteria as those of her class teacher, who clearly operated under a different set of assumptions. But how did this pattern of explanation evolve? The tutor also held certain beliefs about the role of the teacher in inquiry learning; and this led him to question the student further to see if his contingency assumptions were confirmed by what had happened. Looking for vertical relationships inevitably involves thinking up hypotheses and testing them against the evidence. Moreover, such hypotheses do not arise out of the data by some automatic process but require imagination, knowledge and experience.

Given these qualities, empirical data may be a fruitful starting-point; but so may be the education literature or the folklore of the profession. Group discussion can also be a profitable source of ideas; and several suggestions came out of the student's presentation to her peers. But by then it was too late as she had little time to follow them.

Although the use of Stake's model and the analysis of horizontal and vertical relationships has developed our understanding of the student's evidence, it has not contributed to the problem of information overload. However, it has prepared the ground for the final 'focusing stage' of our analysis by drawing attention to significant aspects of the data. For it is now that the evaluators have to choose a relatively small number of issues around which to focus their final report. If carefully chosen these issues will illuminate the situation under review and help people to understand it, while at the same time providing themes to which nearly all the most significant data can be attached. For example, the environmental studies project might have been reported back to the school under three main headings:

Aims   What different aims might we have for environmental studies? Who supports which aims and why?

Skills   What skills can be developed in the framework of environmental studies? What are the advantages and disadvantages of seeking to develop them in this way?

Inquiry   What do we mean by pupil inquiry? Do we want it? What conditions are necessary for it to grow? What is it likely to achieve?

Although the student's project will have provided only a small amount of the evidence needed, these questions will have to be answered if the school is to make an informed decision about environmental studies.

With a retrospective review themes like these are usually the most appropriate, though they will not always be quite so broad in scope. But in prospective evaluation, a focusing on options is also possible. Either one can prepare for decision-making by listing the advantages and limitations of each option, or one can adopt some kind of flow-chart approach in which options are progressively eliminated, perhaps starting with *Aims* as shown in Figure 3.

However, many educational issues cannot be analysed as neatly as this, so a flow-chart can become a dangerous oversimplification. I myself prefer to use a two-dimensional framework in which themes or options form one dimension and ideal types such as 'Integrated Day Man' form the other. The final analysis would then attempt to show how each theme or option would be judged by each individual type in terms of arguments both for and against the activities being evaluated. But perhaps even this is becoming too elaborate?

Figure 3   A flow-chart for selecting decision options

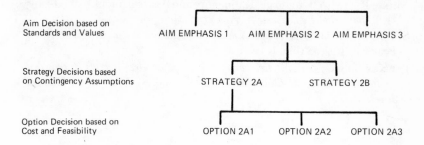

In conclusion I would like to state the five qualities which I think matter most in school-based evaluation:

Openness   The ability to pursue and be seen to pursue the truth rather than the proof.

Participation   The ability to make even the nonevaluators feel involved and responsible.

Divergence   The ability to consider a variety of viewpoints and to conceive of a variety of options.

Rationality   The ability to disclose and examine implicit standards, value judgments and contingency assumptions.

Perspective   The ability to focus attention on a few key issues and avoid being overwhelmed by information overload; and to know what kind of discussion is needed in each particular context.

References and further reading

ARGYRIS, C. and SCHON, D. (1974) *Theory into Practice: increasing professional effectiveness* San Francisco: Jossey-Bass

DES (1975) *A Language for Life* (Bullock Report) HMSO

ERAUT, M. R. (1970) 'The Role of Evaluation' in G. Taylor (Ed) (1970) *The Teacher as Manager* Councils and Education Press

ERAUT, M. R. (1972) 'In-service Education for Innovation' NCET Occasional Paper 4, Councils and Education Press

ERAUT, M. R., GOAD, L. and SMITH, G. (1975) 'The Analysis of Curriculum Materials', Occasional Paper 2, University of Sussex Education Area

HAMILTON, D. (1976) *Curriculum Evaluation* Open Books

STAKE, R. (1967) 'The Countenance of Educational Evaluation' *Teachers College Record* volume 68

STAKE, R. (1969) 'Language, Rationality and Assessment' in W. H. Beatty (Ed) *Improving Educational Assessment* Washington: ASCD

STUFFLEBEAM, D. *et al* (1971) *Educational Evaluation and Decision Making* Peacock, Itasca, Illinois

TAWNEY, D. (Ed) (1976) *Evaluation in Curriculum Development: Trends and Implications* (Schools Council Research Studies) Macmillan Education

The Contributors

Howard Ainsley has produced for publication a number of modular learning units on source materials and industrial archaeology. He is also the historical adviser to a television series. He is a Principal Lecturer in History in the Department of Humanities at Brighton Polytechnic.

Colin Alves is Director of the National Society Religious Education Development Centre at St Gabriel's College, Camberwell. He was previously on the staff of Brighton College of Education and before that at King Alfred's College, Winchester. He is Chairman of the Schools Council Religious Education Subject Committee and a committee member of the Religious Education Council. His other publications include *Religion and the Secondary School* (SCM Press, 1968) and articles and reviews on religious and moral education in *Learning for Living, Education,* etc.

Armin Beck is Professor of Inner City Studies at Northeastern Illinois University and Director of Community Laboratories at the University of Illinois at Chicago Circle, and has been the organizer of many training programmes for teachers of urban pupils. At the moment he is Centre Associate at Chicago's Centre for Programme Development in Equal Educational Opportunity and Director of Academic Programmes at the Chicago Campus of National College. Dr Beck has also been a consultant in urban education to the Open University and is co-author of 'The City as a Centre for Learning' (*Journal of Negro Education* Summer 1975) with Dr Krumbein.

Joan Bird is Head of the First School Division in the Faculty of Education Studies at Brighton Polytechnic. She has taught for many years in primary and secondary schools and in a school for the educationally subnormal. She has also been involved in teaching in prisons. Her qualifications include a

B.A. (Hons) degree, Certificate in Education and a Diploma in the Education of Maladjusted Children from the Institute of Education, University of London. During her years in the college she has maintained contact with a number of schools for problem children and has run courses on the subject.

Colin Brent researches into the economy and society of Sussex since 1500. He has prepared several archive teaching units and local history publications and has edited a bibliography of Sussex in the sixteenth and seventeenth centuries. He is a Senior Lecturer in History in the Department of Humanities at Brighton Polytechnic.

Malcolm Clarkson is Principal Lecturer in Education at Brighton Polytechnic. He studied at the Universities of Birmingham and London. He has taught in secondary schools in England and abroad and has developed a special interest in the curriculum.

Brenda Cohen studied philosophy at London University under A. J. Ayer and has since taught philosophy in universities in England, West Africa and the United States of America. At present Lecturer in Philosophy at the University of Surrey, she was for several years a Senior Lecturer in Education at Brighton College of Education, where she had contact especially with children and schools in the middle years range. Publications, in the field of philosophy and philosophy of education, include a book, *Educational Thought*, contributions to *The Teaching of Politics*, edited by D. Heater, and articles and reviews in *Mind*, *Proceedings of the Aristotelian Society*, *Philosophical Quarterly*, etc. She is married, with four children who are presently being educated at comprehensive and direct grant schools.

Frank Dain was trained at Saltley College, Birmingham, and Loughborough College. After six years in the Royal Air Force he taught at a secondary school and then spent the next five years lecturing in Wing Physical Education College. For the next twelve years he was an adviser to the Brighton and Somerset LEAs before returning to teacher training at Brighton Polytechnic, where he is in charge of Physical Education and Recreation.

Michael Eraut is Reader in Education and Director of Research for the Education Area at the University of Sussex, and has been widely involved in curriculum development and evaluation and in inservice evaluation, both in cooperation with schools and within the university itself. He was the founder convenor of the Sussex M.A. in Curriculum Development and Educational Technology, and has recently completed a three-year research project on the Analysis of Curriculum Materials.

Kate Fleming is Senior Lecturer in Drama at Brighton Polytechnic. She trained at the Rose Bruford College of Speech and Drama. After leaving college she spent some time in the professional theatre, prior to entering teaching. She has had some experience in all fields of education from infants to school leavers, and has been in teacher education for ten years. She is also a freelance broadcaster and writer.

Brian Gates is Head of the Religious Studies department at St Martin's College, Lancaster. He was previously on the staff at Goldsmiths' College. He is a member of the Shap Working Party on the teaching of world religions and a committee member of the Religious Education Council.

David Gray was born in Peterborough and educated at Stamford School and the University of Nottingham. He studied violin with Frederick Grinks, and has wide experience of working with students both in this country and overseas. After an early career in theatrical music, he held a series of posts teaching music in a wide variety of schools, later becoming Lecturer in music at Whitelands College of Education, London, and a Senior Lecturer in music at Brighton College of Education. He became Music Adviser for Brighton in 1969. In 1974 he conducted the Youth Symphony Orchestra of America on their European tour and he has also taken part in the L'Ete Musicale de Luxembourg. He has been Conductor of the Brighton Youth Orchestra since 1963. His compositions include music for the theatre, orchestral and chamber music, and two children's operas. In 1972 he was made an Honorary Associate of the Mount Royal Conservatory of Canada.

Seymour Jennings teaches at Brighton Polytechnic and is Principal Lecturer in Art Education. He received his full-time art education at Canterbury College of Art and at Brighton College of Art and Design. He is author of *Art in the Primary School* and has contributed various articles for publication. He has just finished reading for a research degree at the University of Sussex.

Eliezer Krumbein is Professor at the University of Illinois at Chicago Circle. He is a psychologist and works principally in the Department of Policy Studies. He also prepares counsellors, working through the University and the Chicago Transactional Analysis Institute. He is presently a Centre Associate in the National College of Education's Centre for Programme Development in Equal Educational Opportunity. As a consultant to several professional societies he has initiated programmes in continuing education for the professions.

Jan McKechnie trained at Bishop Otter College, Chichester, specializing in physical education and English, and then taught for two years at a secondary school which involved voluntary youth work at the weekends and in the evenings. Following this she was employed for two years as a youth tutor at a secondary school in Brighton, a job which involved both teaching and working with young people in a purpose-built youth wing. For four years she was assistant Warden/Instructor at Burwash Place Outdoor Centre which involved her in working on both field courses and outdoor pursuits with children from nine years to adulthood. She is a British Canoe Union Senior Instructor, both sea and inland, and holds the Mountain Leadership Certificate of the Mountain Leadership Training Board. She is at present preparing to go to the United States of America to take part in their outdoor programme.

John Miller is Senior Lecturer in Drama. He trained at Goldsmiths' College, London. Before going to Brighton College of Education he taught for fifteen years, both in primary and comprehensive schools, where most recently he was Head of Drama at Thomas Bennett School, Crawley. He now lectures at Brighton Polytechnic.

Michael Raggett is a Principal Lecturer in Education and Leader of the Research and Development Area in the Faculty of Education at Brighton Polytechnic. He has studied sociology and education at four universities and taught for many years in primary and secondary schools and at two colleges of education. He has also acted as consultant and tutor to the Faculty of Educational Studies at the Open University.

Terry Sexton has lectured in sociology and education at the University of Sussex since 1966. After a grammar school education he came to sociology from experience as a house painter and as a professional youth and community worker. His compulsive interest in education started with a concern for undergraduates and their learning and has gradually moved down the age scale.

Helen Stubbs is a Principal Lecturer in Physical Education at Brighton Polytechnic. She qualified as a nurse in New Zealand before coming to England and training at Coventry College of Education. She taught in three secondary schools before taking up her present position.

Nicholas Tucker is a Lecturer in Developmental Psychology at the University of Sussex. Before this, he was a teacher in London secondary schools before going on to qualify and practise as an educational psychologist in the east end of London. He has written books both for adults and children, and now writes fairly regularly for *New Society*, the *Times Educational Supplement* and numerous other publications. He is married and has three children.

Index